HIGH-PERFORMANCE
SUBARU
BUILDER'S GUIDE

JEFF ZURSCHMEIDE

CarTech®

S-A DESIGN

CarTech®

39966 Grand Avenue
North Branch, MN 55056
Telephone (651) 277-1200 • (800) 551-4754
Fax: (651) 277-1203
www.cartechbooks.com

Edited by: Josh Brown
Designed by: Connie Nordrum

ISBN 978-1-61325-134-8
Item No. SA141P

Printed in USA

Title Page:

This car has a complete bodywork kit by Revolution Motorsports, featuring Kakumei carbon fiber body panels. Look and you'll see widened fender flares, a front-end kit, hood, wing, and side skirts on this 2002 WRX. (Photo courtesy of Revolution Motorsports)

Back Cover, Top:

Chuck Hemmingson heads for the SCCA Touring 2 National Championship in a mostly stock 2006 WRX STI.

Back Cover, Bottom Left:

With a few basic modifications, the Subaru WRX engine can remain reliable while giving you quite a bit more power than the factory offered. (Photo Courtesy of Perrin Performance)

Back Cover, Bottom Right:

Rallycross is one of the most popular sporting uses of Subarus. You can Rallycross your street car with no changes and get the feel of rally without much risk or expense.

OVERSEAS DISTRIBUTION BY:

PGUK
63 Hatton Garden
London EC1N 8LE, England
Phone: 020 7061 1980 • Fax: 020 7242 3725

Renniks Publications Ltd.
3/37-39 Green Street
Banksmeadow, NSW 2109, Australia
Phone: 2 9695 7055 • Fax: 2 9695 7355

TABLE OF CONTENTS

Introduction 4
  A Brief History of Subaru............5
  Building Your Car Right 6

Chapter 1: Model/Buyer's Guide 9
  What is a VIN? 9
  Subaru VIN Code Reference.......10
  About The Engine Bay ID Plate.13
  Example VIN Decoding................14
  Choosing Your Subaru 15

Chapter 2: The Subaru Engine 19
  The Subaru Boxer Engine 20
  Subaru Engine Types....................27

Chapter 3: The Induction System 32
  How the Engine Does its Work ..32
  Getting Air Into Your Engine 33
  Getting Fuel into Your Engine....36
  Controlling the Engine:
     ECU Upgrades....................37

Chapter 4: Turbochargers and Related
  Components....................................42
  About Turbochargers....................42
  Some Example Turbochargers 47
  Intercoolers and Other
     Turbo-Related Parts...............49
  Intake Manifolds 51

Chapter 5: Exhaust Components.......53
  Catalytic Converters 53
  Exhaust Headers 55
  Up and Down Pipes.....................55
  Cat-Back Exhaust Systems..........58

Chapter 6: Clutch, Transmission and
  Drivetrain 59
  Manual Transmissions..................60
  Automatic Transmissions 66
  Differentials 67
  Final Drive Gears 70
  Front and Rear Axle Upgrades....71

Chapter 7: Suspension & Steering......72
  Sway Bars....................................76
  Strut Bars and Braces 77
  Bushings and Control Arms........79
  Steering Rack Upgrades...............82
  Shock Absorbers and Struts........82
  Suspension Upgrades 83
  Alignment and Corner Weights ..86

Chapter 8: Brakes 87
  Upgrading Your Brakes.................89
  Brake Hydraulics.........................89
  Brake Pads 90
  Calipers 91
  Rotors...92
  Big Brake Kits 93

Chapter 9: Wheels and Tires 95
  The Physics Of Wheels................95
  Selecting Wheels 96
  Selecting Tires.............................100

Chapter 10: Body and Interior 103
  Aerodynamic Devices.................103
  Body Kit Basics...........................107
  Chassis Stiffeners 110
  Lights..111

Gauges and Indicators 111
Steering Wheels & Shift Knobs.112
Safety Equipment 113

Chapter 11: Getting Exotic...............115
  JDM Parts...................................115
  Exotic Turbochargers.................116
  Intercooler Sprayers 120
  Water/Alcohol Injection.............121
  Nitrous Oxide.............................122
  Exotic Engine: H6 Turbo/6MT.122
  Exotic Transmissions..................123
  The Bottom Line on Exotics 123

Chapter 12: Subarus in
  Competition 124
  Autocross....................................124
  Track Day 126
  Time Attack................................126
  Hill Climb 128
  Drag Racing................................128
  Amateur/Club Racing 129
  Pro Racing 130
  Drifting.......................................132
  Rallycross....................................133
  Stage Rally 134
  TSD Rally 139
  Car Show Competition 140

Appendix A 141
  Websites, Clubs, Books, Resources

Appendix B 142
  Engine Tables

INTRODUCTION

Some automotive books are the product of one expert pouring out the vast library of information in his head. Usually that expert is someone who has spent years working on a particular kind of car, and has seen it all. That's not this book.

I believe a variety of opinions and experiences make a better guide. I'm a journalist by profession, writing for *Subiesport Magazine* and other outlets. Through *Subiesport,* I've talked with folks who know Subarus down to the last nut and bolt. This book is the result of extensive consultation with a great many of those subject-matter experts. The experts I interviewed are quoted in this book and the project would have been impossible without them. Most of them sell, install, and maintain the products they talk about, and their names and contact information are collected in an appendix at the back of the book.

This book is designed to give you some background information as you consider various performance modifications and products available for your car. This is not a repair or maintenance manual. If that's what you need, I recommend you get an official Subaru factory shop manual for your car. Also, most aftermarket parts come with installation instructions, and you should follow those.

This book covers the Impreza and Legacy models and their derivatives

A well-kept, well-developed Subaru can be a source of personal accomplishment and pride. (Photo courtesy of Sacha Potter)

(Outback and Forester) back to the beginnings of the two product lines. We do not attempt to cover other models in any detail, though some products and parts listed in this book may be suitable for those models.

Information regarding those models is provided where convenient, for comparison purposes only.

This book also contains snapshot overviews of a variety of successful custom Subarus, built for a wide range of

The 1991–1994 Legacy Turbo is still prized among Subaru enthusiasts for its strong engine and good design.

Subaru dominates the sport of rally in North America, with a tremendous following of amateur rallyists and rallycrossers, and the pros at Subaru Rally Team USA.

purposes. These show how all aspects of the car come together to enhance performance for a particular purpose, and to provide a model for you to consider as you plan and build your own ride.

In general I avoid endorsing any particular brand of parts or any particular setup for a car. If your favorite manufacturer or product is not mentioned by name, it's only because it is impossible to mention everything available for Subarus. Also, I have not personally tested every kind of brake, every kind of shock, or every kind of turbo. In each area, I simply chose a few representative products to show what's widely available on the market. I have not included prices, because those change constantly.

This book would not have been possible without the cheerful assistance of Jeff Perrin and John Herring at Perrin Performance, Sean Sexton, Marc Lein, Garner Thomas, Kelly Gibner, and David Bush at Rallitek/IPD, Jeff Sponaugle, Mick Posner, Tim Bailey, Jarrad Bowen, Forrest Huntington and Dustin Harris at PDXTuning, Dan Hurwitz at www.fastwrx.com, Barrett Dash of All Wheels Driven, Paul Eklund of Primitive Racing, Travis Geny and Armin Ausejo of *Subiesport Magazine*, Robert Young at Forced Performance, Meng Vang of Nukabe Automotive/Cusco, Warland Wight of Revolution Motorsports, Quirt Crawford of Crawford Performance, Trey Cobb of COBB Tuning,

Lance Smith of Vermont Sports Car, Ali Afshar and Jamie Montesalvo of ESX Motorsports, Matt Iorio of Paladin Rally, Dan Rosenblum at Inner City Youth Racing, Andy Howe, Scott Fisher who lets me tear apart his WRX, Matt Tabor who lets me tear apart and co-drive his 2.5RS rally car, Erik Lyden for displaying proper style and attitude, Yuji Otsuki, Andy Lee, and Sacha Potter for amazing photographs. And of course the guy who got me started on Subarus: Ryan Douthit, publisher of *Subiesport Magazine*. And most of all my long-suffering wife Jill and my daughter Kate for putting up with lonely nights and long weekends while I've been working on this book.

A Brief History of Subaru

In 1917, Chikuhei Nakajima founded the Aircraft Research Laboratory for the Imperial Japanese Navy. This lab grew into the Nakajima Aircraft Company, which was among the leading Japanese aircraft manufacturers during World War II, along with Mitsubishi.

After the war, Nakajima, like many other Japanese industrialists, changed his focus and retooled his company to produce motorcycles, trucks, and automobiles to help rebuild Japan. The name of the company changed to Fuji Sangyo, and then to Fuji Heavy Industries in 1953.

In 1954, Fuji brought out its first passenger car, called the P-1. In 1955, the P-1 name was changed to the Subaru 1500. The car featured unibody construction, independent front suspension, and a solid rear axle.

In 1968, the company founded Subaru of America and began exporting cars to North America. By late 1971, the first of the cars that would define Subaru were seen on American roads. The 1972 introduction of Subaru's first 4WD station wagon in 1972 marked the beginning of all-wheel drive in general-purpose mass-produced passenger cars.

In 1977, Subaru introduced the Brat—a little pickup-like vehicle with AWD and the sense that you could take it anywhere. The Brat has become a favorite "old car" for Subaru enthusiasts today, and enjoys wide popularity in Rallycross competition.

By 1990, Subaru had introduced the Legacy line, and in partnership with Isuzu, began manufacturing cars in Indiana. In 1992, Subaru introduced the Impreza line, completing the modern brand lineup. The Legacy and Impreza lines have been extended and revamped in many ways since the early 1990s, but these products have been at the core of Subaru's success, and they are the cars we focus on throughout this book.

Along the way, Subaru came to dominate the sport of Rally in the 1990s and into the new century. The impressive string of victories in WRC

The hot rod Subaru world is not limited to Impreza sedans. This Forester is among the leaders at a track day competition.

It's a beautiful and fast car, and it would be a shame to have it land on you while you're working on it.

competition led the way for Subaru to become the brand of choice at every level of professional and amateur Rally, right down to every local Rallycross series. Subaru has supported this phenomenon at every opportunity, and that in turn has led to one of the best aftermarkets for performance parts of any manufacturer in the modern era.

Subaru has also made it easy for the builder and tuner by making so many of the parts for its cars interchangeable. Taking a cue from automakers such as GM or BMC before them, the Legacy and Impreza platforms each accept a common engine format, brake components, and so on. This provides the performance builder an essentially blank canvas on which to build a car perfectly suited to taste and application.

Building Your Car Right

Building up and personalizing your ride is a tradition that goes back to the very first vehicle. I have no doubt that some ancient Egyptian once looked at his neighbor's chariot and said, "You know, if I used lighter wood and narrower spokes, I bet my rig could go faster and turn better than his." The rest, as they say, is history.

But throughout history, we've learned a few things about going fast, staying in control, and the need to stop. We've also learned a few things about the dangers of fiddling with the design that the manufacturer decided was good. Stepping out of the safety zone and modifying your car means taking responsibility for the changes you make and the effect those changes have on performance, safety, and longevity.

There's an old saying in racing: "Speed, low cost, and longevity—pick any two." I've never seen that saying disproved, but a modern Subaru comes as close as any car ever built to picking up all three. Still, the stories of blown motors, broken transmissions and cooked brakes are all around us, and you have to understand that possibility before you start. When you exceed the power and the stress tolerance that the engineers designed into the car, you're going to break things from time to time. Only a chump tries to blame the manufacturer when his hot new engine breaks a CV joint.

You can take some tried and true steps to have fun and get a good outcome when modifying your car. Read them through and give them careful consideration before you start.

Step One: Play Safe

I'm only going to write this once. I knew a guy who died when the car he was working on fell on him. He had jack stands but didn't use them that day, probably because it was just a quick little job. His ten-year-old daughter was the one who found him. Get yourself a set of good jack stands and a good floor jack and use them every time.

Similarly, be smart when you're making changes to your car. Don't go out and drive hard on brand new parts or brand new work. Have other people check your work whenever possible. Even professionals make mistakes from time to time—they leave nuts untightened, forget to adjust new parts, and leave fluids unfilled. Any of these mistakes may happen to you, and if you do this long enough they may happen to you multiple times. At best these mistakes are embarrassing, and usually they are expensive; at worst they are dangerous or lethal. Be smart, play safe, and you'll have a good time.

Step Two: Learn About Your Car

You need to read and learn before you whip out your wrench or whip out your checkbook. The world is full of people who have spent a lot of money on their cars only to find that they've got a ride that is slower and uglier than when they started. The final tragedy is that they've cut up so much of the original car that they can't ever get it back to stock.

It pays to do your homework. Learn what's available for your car today and what fits on your particular model, because this book started getting stale the minute it went to the printer, and new products come out every day. Also, learn from what others have done before you. You can download a full shop manual for your year and model from Subaru for just a few dollars. Your local Subaru specialty shop has valuable information and expertise for you. Enthusiast publications such as *Subies-*

This is a bone-stock 2006 WRX—it's got three years of factory warranty ahead of it and it cost a few paychecks to buy. The smart owner is careful about mods for a while.

port Magazine (www.subiesport.com) help keep you up to date on new products and developments. Finally, Internet forums such as NASIOC (www.nasioc.com) are a great tool.

Step Three: Understand What You're Doing, and Why

Once you know what's available, sit down and go over what you want your car to do for you. If you're looking at competition, make sure you've got the current rules in front of you. The worst thing you can do is show up to race with some trick modification that just put you right into the "unlimited" class in an otherwise stock vehicle.

Do you want to design for supreme handling for autocross competition? Do you want to drag race or drift? Or do you just want to look great, sound hot, and hit some car shows this summer? When you know what you really want to do, you can start your plan to get there.

The Japanese have a concept they call "Jinba Ittai," which translates to "horse and rider are one." What that means is that your car should be built so that it functions smoothly and comfortably. If you overdo one aspect of a car and neglect another, you'll have problems. Ask anyone who ever built a really fast car, and never thought about his brakes! As you consider, plan, and build your car, think about balance and Jinba Ittai.

One of the most common mistakes people make when building a performance car is they try to make a car that's excellent for two or more very different purposes. Trust me, a stage rally car isn't going to be any good at an autocross, and a really pumped drag racing car makes a terrible daily driver. If you try to split the difference between two radical applications, you will end up with a car that isn't particularly good at anything. Get your vision and your budget together and build your car to do one thing really well, or build it to do everything pretty well.

When you know what you want to do and you understand the rules, you can usually come up with a comprehensive shopping list. That's where this book is designed to help you, by going over many common modifications people make and the major products on the market, with some pros and cons to help you make your choices.

Step Four: Define Goals and Objectives

You need to be realistic about what you can afford and what you plan to do with your car. Diving in and modifying your car always costs more than you expect. Double your estimate and it still costs more than you expected. So make an accurate budget and realize that Rome wasn't built in a day, and your car won't be done next weekend, or next month. That's why you see so many people driving around with unpainted body kits.

My suggestion is that you start with a notebook. I'm a computer-literate guy, and I still use a paper notebook for each project car I have. The notebook stays in the car and I use it to log changes I make and results that I notice. Some people prefer a spreadsheet or a blog—use whatever works for you. The point is to get into the habit of logging what you've done and the results you saw. The more you can get objective data (lap times, dyno sheets, and so on) the better your log will be.

For most people, the car they're modifying is also the car they drive to work every day. There's usually not a lot of downtime available in the car's schedule. And some people aren't handy with a wrench, so take this to heart: If you've never done serious

This is a nicely balanced Impreza 2.5RS from the late 1990s. A little customization—and nothing too radical—makes cars like this a joy to drive and care for over the years.

Make sure you have a clear goal in mind as you start to work on your car. An older Impreza like this one is a great choice for a hot rod that won't break your budget.

A nicely turned-out late model Legacy GT has performance and style potential to run with European sports sedans at twice the sticker price.

work on your car before, upgrading the brakes or adding a turbo to your daily work mobile is a bad way to start.

Take your shopping list and divide it up into functional areas: engine, transmission, suspension, steering, brakes, interior, and so on. This book is divided into chapters on that basis to help you. In each functional area, list the things you want to do and the price of each item you need. Don't forget labor costs, gaskets, and fluids. If you're doing the work yourself, account for the cost of tools you need to buy.

With a good shopping list in your hands, and a total budget that is probably surprising you, it's time to prioritize.

Most new builders start with cosmetics. This is only natural but I think it's backwards for a performance car. In general I like to improve stopping and handling before I put money into the engine, and I leave cosmetics for last. Who wants to scratch or dent an expensive paint job when a wrench slips?

With your itemized and prioritized list of mods, you should be able to make a budget and a schedule for work that fits your finances and your calendar. Don't sweat it too much if you get behind—everyone does. Right now the trick is to enjoy the journey as much as the destination.

Step Five: Have Fun and Don't Overextend Yourself

One key to a successful build is to make sure you reward yourself from time to time. There's nothing as satisfying in a project as being able to tell the difference when you've made a change. So schedule your mods to make sure that you get a noticeable goodie from time to time. Maybe that means putting in the racing seats before the urethane bushings, but that's okay if it keeps your interest in the project.

There's a trap out there that you have to keep in mind, because it can grab you and cause no end of pain. The trap springs when you get financially overextended in your car and then run into trouble. The world is full of cars for sale where the owner has $20,000 in receipts and is looking for $10,000 or best offer by next weekend because he has to pay the rent. Don't be that unhappy person if you can help it. It's worse if your car is half-done, because if you can sell it at all, it's probably worth less than when you started.

Unless you find a nice, cheap, low-miles all-original 427 Cobra in a barn somewhere and take it to a big-time auto auction, you're not going to make a profit building and then selling your car. You're not even going to get your cash expenditures back out of it,

so don't view this hobby as an investment. There's no reason to think that the person buying your car even thinks any of your mods are worth keeping. For your own protection, you should view this process as building yourself a unique car that you customized for your own tastes and no one else's.

Finding a group of like-minded people in your area will help keep your project going. The Internet is a nice tool for learning and discussion, but folks on the other side of the country can't help you pull an engine, or give you a ride to pick up your car from the mechanic. A local club is also a good way to get access to specialty tools. If one member has an engine hoist, then everyone has an engine hoist, and you can spend your budget on a tool that no one else has yet. Treat your club right, and you'll always have help when you need it.

The last thing to say about having fun and sticking with the project is that you should make sure that the car stays drivable, registered, and insured as much of the time as possible. Nothing kills enthusiasm for a project car as fast as spending money that just disappears under a tarp in the garage. Keep yourself behind the wheel to keep the rewards of your project coming back to you, and that will keep your enthusiasm going strong.

MODEL/BUYER'S GUIDE

The following is a brief guide to the models and model years discussed in the balance of this book. To make this as clear and simple as possible, we cover only those Impreza and Legacy models and derivatives commonly available in the United States from the rollout of each model to the present day.

The tables in this chapter are accurate enough to allow you to identify the vast majority of Imprezas and Legacies in the United States correctly. If your car is gray-market, JDM, European, Australian, or otherwise unique then you have an advantage at car shows, but you are at a marked disadvantage for confident parts-matching.

Numerous publicly accessible websites offer detailed standard and optional equipment lists by year, model, and trim level. For detailed information on what equipment was available with any given car, those sites are your best bet.

What is a VIN?

VIN stands for Vehicle Identification Number, and in earlier times this was no more than a serial number applied to each chassis at the factory. Each manufacturer had its own system, and these were generally not well documented. Rare or valuable models may be faked in many cases, and this is why there are so many controversies about "provenance" on antique and vintage cars. That's not a big problem with Subarus, but as you will see there's sometimes more to a car than meets the eye.

The WRX is perhaps the best-known Subaru product for performance. This 2004 model has been modified with lowering springs, wheels, tires, and several modifications you can't see with the hood closed.

The latest generation of the Legacy line—the 2005–2007 Legacy GT—sports a turbocharged 2.5-liter DOHC engine and your choice of transmissions, plus the intelligent SI Drive system.

In 1981, the world's auto manufacturers adopted a standard 17-position VIN coding scheme, but manufacturers can and do change the meaning of the various letters, numbers, and even code positions with each new model year. Therefore, there is no quick and easy method for decoding all possible VIN numbers on an otherwise unknown car. Several online VIN research services exist, and it's a good idea to use one if you have questions or suspicions about a car you're thinking of buying.

The basic post-1980 VIN coding scheme is shown in **Table 1**.

The first three digits of any VIN are the "World Manufacturer Index"—a three-digit code that uniquely identifies the company that made any car. For Subaru, the code is JF1 for Fuji Heavy Industries in Japan, and 4S3 or 4S4 for Subaru-Isuzu of America.

The rest of a standard VIN is broken down as shown in **Table 2**.

Table 1: Standard VIN Format

VIN Position	1	2	3	4	5	6	7	8	9	10	11	12	13	14	15	16	17
Major Divisions	WMI			Vehicle Descriptors						Vehicle ID Information							
Specific Divisions	Mfgr ID			Equipment Codes					Check Digit	Model Year	Factory Code	Serial Number					

Table 2: VIN Positions General Usage

Position	Purpose
4-8	Specifies the model and other descriptive information about a car.
9	A check number that is derived from the balance of the VIN to catch fakes.
10	Indicates the vehicle model year.
11	Indicates the factory where the vehicle was assembled.
12-17	The chassis serial number.

Table 3: Relevant Subaru VIN Positions

VIN Position	4	5	6	7	8	10	11
Indicates	Chassis	Body	Engine	Trim	Safety	Model Year	Factory & Transmission

Table 3 shows the basic breakdown of relevant Subaru VIN codes since 1981.

How To Find The VIN

The VIN on a modern Subaru is found in several locations. The most common place to find the VIN is on the driver's side dashboard where it meets the bottom of the windshield. The VIN is usually also present on a sticker on the driver's doorjamb, and also on the engine plate found on the driver's side strut tower. Subaru also stamps the VIN elsewhere on the chassis, but these locations are difficult to find. If a car is missing the three main VIN locations, it's probably stolen, or in some cases it has been irrevocably turned into a racing car and doesn't need VIN plates any more.

Subaru VIN Code Reference

Unless you have access to the Subaru factory records, you don't have a definitive key to all Subaru VIN codes. However, in general, the VIN positions most Subaru buyers care about are 4 through 8, 10, and 11. On a modern Subaru, these tell you the basic chassis type, body type, engine and drive wheels, transmission type, trim level, safety equipment, model year, and factory of origin. Tables 3 through 17 decipher the common VIN codes for North American Subaru Imprezas, Legacies, Outbacks, and Foresters. Other common codes are listed where relevant.

Chassis and Body Codes

Table 4: Subaru Chassis Codes

VIN Code	Chassis Type
A	Subaru X and XT (Alcyone line) and Brat
B	Legacy and Baja
C	SVX
G	Impreza
K	Justy
S	Forester
W	Tribeca

Table 4 shows the most common variants for VIN Position 4—Chassis type.

This VIN plate is from an early 2WD basic Impreza. Many of these cars have been upgraded over the years, so if someone claims to have a factory hot rod, the VIN plate will tell the truth.

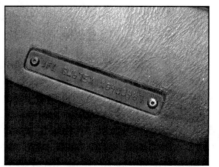

The easiest VIN to find is on the driver's side of the dashboard at the base of the window. Make sure this VIN matches the other two before you buy any used car.

You can also find a VIN number on the plate here at the rear base of the driver's door.

Table 5: Impreza Body Type Codes

VIN Code	Impreza Body Type
A-B	Not Used
C	Impreza 4D Sedan (1993-2001)
D	Impreza 4D Sedan (2002-2007)
E	Not Used
F	Impreza Wagon (1993-2001)
G	Impreza Wagon (2002-2007)
H-L	Not Used
M	Impreza 2D Coupe (1995-2001)
N-O	Not Used
P	Impreza Outback Sport Wagon?

Table 5 shows the most common variants for VIN Position 5–Body type on the Impreza line.

Table 6

Legacy Body Type Codes

VIN Code	Legacy Body Type
A-B	Not Used
C	Legacy 4D Sedan (1990-1994)
D	Legacy 4D Sedan (1995-1999)
E	Legacy 4D Sedan (2000-2004)
F	Legacy Wagon (1990-1994)
G	Legacy Outback Wagon (1995-1999)
J	Legacy AWD Wagon (1990-1994)
K	Legacy Wagon (1995-1999)
L	Legacy 4D Sedan (2005-2006)
M-S	Not Used
P	Legacy Wagon (2000-2006)
T	Legacy Baja

Table 6 shows the most common variants for VIN Position 5–Body type on the Legacy line.

Table 7

Other Subaru Body Type Codes

VIN Code	Body Type
C	GL 4D Sedan
D	Justy
F	Forester (1998-2002)
G	Forester (2003-2007)
M	DL/GL AWD Wagon
N	DL/GL 2WD Wagon
T	Brat
X	Alcyone SVX, X, and XT
X	Tribeca

Table 7 shows the most common variants for VIN Position 5–Body type on other Subaru lines.

Engine and Transmission Type Codes
VIN position 6 indicates the engine type. Note that not all part selections that vary by engine type are necessarily specified by the engine type code, but may vary according to the more detailed information found on the engine plate. For example, ancillary components such as exhaust systems and engine cooling parts are dependent on the engine configuration and chassis/body and sometimes trim level. The engine plate specifies these parts as well.

Table 8: Impreza Engine Type Statistics

VIN Code	Impreze Engine Type	Statistics
1	Not Used	
2	EJ18 1.8L 16V NA SOHC FWD (1993-1996)	110 bhp, 110 ft-lbs torque
	EJ205 2.0L 16V Turbo DOHC WRX (2002-2005)	227 bhp, 217 ft-lbs torque – "open deck"
3	Not Used	
4	EJ22 2.2L 16V NA SOHC (1995-1998)	135-137 bhp, 140 ft-lbs torque
	EJ22 2.2L 16V NA SOHC (1999-2001)	142 bhp, 149 ft-lbs torque – Phase 2
5	EJ18 1.8L 16V NA SOHC (1997)	115 bhp, 120 ft-lbs torque
6	EJ25 2.5L 16V NA DOHC (1998)	165 bhp, 162 ft-lbs torque – Phase 1 – "open deck"
	EJ25 2.5L 16V NA SOHC (1999-2005)	165 bhp, 166 ft-lbs torque – Phase 2 – "open deck"
	EJ25 2.5l 16V NA SOHC (2006)	173 bhp, 166 ft-lbs torque – IAVS – "open deck"
7	EJ257 2.5L 16V Turbo DOHC STI (2004-2005)	300 bhp, 300 ft-lbs torque – "semi-closed deck" - AVCS
	EJ255 2.5L 16V Turbo DOHC WRX (2006)	230 bhp, 235 ft-lbs torque – "semi-closed deck" IAVS
8-0	Not Used	
E/F	EJ207 2.0L 16V Turbo DOHC JDM STI	280 bhp, 260 ft-lbs torque – Not sold in North America

Table 8 shows the most common variants for VIN Position 6–Engine type on the Impreza line.

Table 9: Legacy Type Codes

VIN Code	Legacy Engine Type	Statistics
1	Not Used	
2	Not Used	
3	EJ22 2.2L 16V SOHC FWD (1990-1996)	130 bhp, 137 ft-lbs torque
4	EJ22 2.2L 16V SOHC AWD (1990-1994)	130 bhp, 137 ft-lbs torque
	EJ22 2.2L 16V SOHC AWD (1995-1996)	135 bhp, 149 ft-lbs torque
	EJ22 2.2L 16V SOHC AWD (1997-1998)	137 bhp, 145 ft-lbs torque
	EJ22 2.2L 16V SOHC AWD (1999)	142 bhp, 149 ft-lbs torque – Phase 2
6	EJ22 2.2L 16V SOHC (1991-1994)	160 bhp, 181 ft-lbs torque Legacy Turbo closed deck engine
	EJ25 2.5L 16V SOHC (1996)	155 bhp, 140 ft-lbs torque
	EJ25 2.5L 16V DOHC (1997-1999)	165 bhp, 162 ft-lbs torque
	EJ251 2.5L 16V NA SOHC (1999-2004)	165 bhp, 166 ft-lbs torque – Phase 2
	EJ251 2.5L 16V NA SOHC (2005)	168 bhp, 166 ft-lbs torque
	EJ251 2.5L 16V NA SOHC (2006-2007)	175 bhp, 169 ft-lbs torque
AVCS	EJ255 2.5L 16V Turbo DOHC (2005-2007 Legacy GT)	250 bhp, 250 ft-lbs torque – semi-closed deck -
7	Not Used	
8	EZ30 3.0L 24V NA DOHC (2003-2006)	220 bhp, 213 ft-lbs torque – open deck
9-0	Not Used	

Table 9 shows the most common variants for VIN Position 6–Engine type on the Legacy line.

Table 10

Other Subaru Engine Type Codes

VIN Code	Other Subaru Engine Type
1	Not Used
2	
3	3.3L NA ?OHC 6 Cylinder - SVX
4	
5	1.8L NA SOHC 4 Cylinder - Brat
6	
7	
8	Inline 3 Cylinder - Justy
9	
0	

Table 10 shows the most common variants for VIN Position 6—Engine type on other Subaru lines:

VIN position 11 is unusual in that it specifies both the factory of origin and the transmission type for all vehicles. Subarus offered for sale in North America are assembled either in Japan or in Indiana, with a selection of transmission types at each factory.

Table 11

Factory and Transmission Type Codes

VIN Code	Transmission Type and Factory
C	FWD 4EAT – FHI in Japan
G	AWD MT5 5/R – FHI in Japan
H	AWD 4EAT – FHI in Japan
L	AWD MT6 6/R – FHI in Japan
4	AWD 5EAT Sport Shift – SIA in Indiana
5	AWD 4EAT Sport Shift – SIA in Indiana
6	AWD MT5 5/R – SIA in Indiana
7	AWD 4EAT – SIA in Indiana
8	AWD 4EAT – SIA in Indiana (Postal Vehicle)
-	AWD MT6 – SIA in Indiana (STI)

Table 11 shows the most common variants for VIN Position 11—Factory and Transmission type on all Subaru lines:

Trim Level, Safety Equipment, and Model Year Codes

Table 12

Impreza Trim Level Codes

VIN Code	Impreza Trim Level
1	Base Model (1993-1995)
2	Brighton (1996-1997)
3	L (1993-2001)
4	L+, LS (1993-1994)
5	LX (1995-1996) TS (2002-2004)
6	
7	RS (1998-2006)
8	Outback Sport (1995-2006)
9	WRX (2002-2006)
0	WRX STI (2004-2006)

Table 12 shows the most common variants for VIN Position 7—Trim level on the Impreza line

Table 13: Legacy Trim

VIN Code	Legacy Trim Level
1	2.5i Base Model (2005-2006) Baja (2003-2006),
2 (2000)	Legacy Base Model (1995-2000) 35th Anniversary Special Edition (2004) 2.5i Limited (2005-2006) 2.5i Base Model (2006) Baja Limited and Sport (2003-2006)
3	Legacy L, L+, LS (1990-2004) Baja Turbo (2004-2006)
4	GT (1996-2004)
5	Legacy LS Special (1990) LS (1991) GT (1996-2004)
6	LSi (1998-1999)
7	Turbo (1991-1994) GT (1996-1999) GT Limited (2005-2006)
8	Limited Sedan & Wagon (2000) GT (2005-2006)
9	RHD US Spec Postal Vehicle (1995-1999)
0	Not Used

Table 13 shows the most common variants for VIN Position 7—Trim level on the Legacy line.

Table 14

Legacy Outback Trim Level Codes

VIN Code	Legacy Outback Trim Level
1	H6 35th Anniversary Wagon (2004) Outback 2.5i & SE (2005-2006)
2	Outback 2.5i Limited (2005-2006)
3	Legacy L Outback Trim (1995)
4	Outback 3.0R H6 Sedan (2005-2006)
5	Outback 3.0R H6 VDC Wagon (2005-2006)
6	Outback Wagon (2000-2002) Outback 3.0R H6 LL Bean (2005-2006)
7	Outback Weather Pkg (1998-2002) Outback Wagon (2003-2004) Outback XT Limited (2005-2006)
8	Outback Wagon (1996-1999) Outback Limited(2000-2004) Outback 2.5 XT (2005-2006)
9	Outback H6 VDC Limited (2001-2004)
0	Outback H6 LL Bean Edition (2001-2004)

Table 14 shows some variants for VIN Position 7—Trim level on the very complex Legacy Outback line.

Table 15

Other Subaru Trim Level Codes

VIN Code	Trim Level
1	Forester Forester 2.5i
2	Forester 2.5i Limited DL
3	Forester X Forester L GL Brat
4	SVX Alcyone XT
5	Forester XS Forester Premium SVX LSi
6	
7	Forester XS Moonroof Forester LL Bean
8	Forester 2.5 XT
9	Forester XT Limited
0	

Table 15 shows some common variants for VIN Position 7—Trim level on the other Subaru lines.

Table 16

Subaru Safety Equipment Codes

VIN Code	Trim Level
2	Passive restraint seatbelts with no Air Bags
4	Seatbelts with Dual Air Bags
5	Seatbelts with Dual Air Bags
6	Seatbelts with Dual and Side Air Bags

Table 16 shows the most common variants for VIN Position 8—Safety equipment on all modern Subaru lines.

About The Engine Bay ID Plate

In addition to the VIN codes, a plate is found in the engine bay on the driver's side strut tower that provides additional and different codes that more completely describe the engine, transmission, option codes, trim levels, original paint color, and other information about this particular vehicle. Tables 18 and 19 identify some of these codes for 2002–2006 Impreza WRX and 2005–2006 Legacy GT variants.

Here is the plate from a late-model Legacy GT. It's found on the strut tower on all years and models.

Table 19: 2005-2006 USDM Legacy GT Engine and ECU Codes

MY	Start	Model Description	Engine Code	ECU
05	11/3/03	Legacy 2.5 GT (mt)	EJ255BTAUB	22611AA17A/B/C
05	11/3/03	Legacy 2.5 GT (at)	EJ255BLAUB	22611AA18A/B/C
05	11/3/03	Legacy Outback (mt)	EJ255BLAUB	22611AJ65A/B/C
05	11/3/03	Legacy Outback (at)	EJ255BLAUB	22611AJ66A/B/C

Table 17

Subaru Model Year Codes

VIN Code	Model Year
L	1990
M	1991
N	1992
P	1993
R	1994
S	1995
T	1996
V	1997
W	1998
X	1999
Y	2000
1	2001
2	2002
3	2003
4	2004
5	2005
6	2006
7	2007
8	2008

Table 17 shows the codes for VIN Position 10—Model year on all Subaru lines.

Table 18

2002-2006 USDM Impreza Model, Engine & ECU Codes

MY	Start	Model Description	Model Code	Engine Code	ECU Code
02	3/1/01	Sedan WRX (mt)	GDAAY8D	EJ205AW3B9/BB	22611AF421/422/423/424/425
02	3/1/01	Sedan WRX (at)	GDAAY8P	EJ205AX3B9/BB	22611AF411/412/413/414
02	3/1/01	Sport wagon WRX (mt)	GGAAY8D	EJ205AW3B9/BB	22611AF421/422/423/424/425
02	3/1/01	Sport wagon WRX (at)	GGAAY8P	EJ205AX3B9/BB	22611AF411/412/413/414
03	3/1/02	Sedan WRX (mt)	GDABY8D	EJ205BW4BB	22611AJ030/031/032
03	3/1/02	Sedan WRX (at)	GDABY8P	EJ205BX4BB	22611AJ040/041
03	3/1/02	Sport wagon WRX (mt)	GGABY8D	EJ205BW4BB	22611AJ030/031/032
03	3/1/02	Sport wagon WRX (at)	GGABY8P	EJ205BX4BB	22611AJ040/041
04	3/1/03	Sedan WRX (mt)	GDACY8D	EJ205BW6BB	22611AH791/792/793
04	3/1/03	Sedan WRX (at)	GDACY8P	EJ205BX5BB	22611AH801/802/803
04	3/1/03	Sport wagon WRX (mt)	GGACY8D	EJ205AW5BB	22611AH791/792/793
04	3/1/03	Sport wagon WRX (at)	GGACY8P	EJ205AW5BB	22611AH801/802/803
04	3/1/03	Sedan WRX STI	GDFCYEH	EJ257BW5CB	22611AJ240/241/242/243
05	3/1/04	Sedan WRX (mt)	GDADY8D	EJ205BW7BB	22611AJ890
05	3/1/04	Sedan WRX (at)	GDADY8P	EJ205BX7BB	22611AJ900
05	3/1/04	Sport wagon WRX (mt)	GGADY8D	EJ205BW7BB	22611AJ890
05	3/1/04	Sport wagon WRX (at)	GGADY8P	EJ205BX7BB	22611AJ900
05	3/1/04	Sedan WRX STI	GDFDYEH	EJ257BW7CH	22611AJ930
06	3/1/04	Sedan WRX (mt)	GDAEY8D	EJ255BE8JB	22611AL350
06	3/1/04	Sedan WRX (at)	GDAEY8P	EJ255BP8JB	22611AL360
06	3/1/04	Sport wagon WRX (mt)	GGADY8D	EJ255BE8JB	22611AL350
06	3/1/04	Sport wagon WRX (at)	GGADY8P	EJ255BP8JB	22611AL360
06	3/1/04	Sedan WRX STI	GDFDYEH	EJ257BW8CH	22611AL370

Table 18 is a best estimate of the standard codes used on USDM Impreza WRX-series automobiles from 2002 to 2006. This is a compiled list, not certified by Subaru, so discrepancies with actual cars may be noted. The terms "mt" and "at" stand for Manual Transmission and Automatic Transmission.

Example VIN Decoding

The following are a couple of interesting VIN cases. Often, a heavily modified car varies substantially from what the VIN specifies as factory-installed equipment. Therefore, if someone claims to have a real JDM GC8 STI, check the VIN against the tables provided in this chapter.

Example 1: Is This a JDM STI or Not?

Here's the text from an interesting car that was listed for sale on the Internet. What do you think? (The serial number has been omitted for privacy.)

VIN Number: JF1GC2443PKXXXXXX
Engine: 1.8-liter gasoline
Transmission: Manual
Standard Equipment: Air Conditioning, AWD, L, 4-Cylinder 1.8 Liter
Optional Equipment: Sunroof

Here's what the seller had to say:

Up for auction is a 1993 GC8 that was completely built from a 1998 JDM Ver 5 STI that was imported from Japan. It has the 2.0 turbo that has aprox. 317 hp that runs on pump gas and has the DCCD trans along with a 4:44 rear diff. Aprox. 10,000 KM ago the motor was completely gone through by a Subaru tech to make this car completely reliable and I would not be afraid to make a cross-country road trip in it. The car also has all the body panels from the Ver 5 including the aluminum hood and roof scoop. It has the JDM 4 pot/2 pot brake combo, Ohlins coilovers with cusco adj top plates front & rear along with strut braces.

There's no reason to doubt that the car has all the good stuff the seller listed, but let's take a look at that VIN:

- JF1 indicates a Japanese-built car.
- GC specifies an Impreza 4-door Sedan from 1993 to 2001
- 2 in the sixth position tells us that this car left the factory with a 1.8-liter engine.
- 4 in the seventh position indicates

the LS trim level on a 1993 Impreza.
- 4 in the eighth position indicates that the car came with manual seatbelts and dual airbags.
- 3 in the ninth position is the checksum number.
- P in the 10th position indicates that this is indeed a 1993 model year car.
- K in the 11th position indicates the car was assembled at the Gunma factory with a 4EAT automatic FWD transmission.

First, there's no cause to suspect fraud here, because the seller told all potential buyers that he installed the go-fast parts from a 1998 JDM car. But now you know for sure that according to Subaru, this is a pretty basic automatic transmission FWD 1.8-liter Impreza LS. And that's good information to have before you buy.

Example 2: What Have We Here?

Here's another Internet listing. Again, the owner gets points for honesty, but let's take a look at what he's offering:

VIN: JF1GM6754XGXXXXXX
Body Style: Coupe
Doors: 2
Engine: DOHC
Transmission: 5 Speed Manual
Fuel type: Gasoline
Wheel Drive: All Wheel Drive
# of Cylinders: 4 cyl
Color: Silver
Mileage: 91,000 miles
HP: 220 hp
Torque: 220lb/ft

Here's the owner's description of the car:

This car has been supercharged and has fuel management. I believe the previous owner hardened the tranny and put bigger gears in it. It has a Rick Rimmer kit that I have modified, and now it seems to work much better than it did before. I changed the size of the supercharger and idler pully and also added another pulley to take up some

of the slack it creates when you floor it. It does have a 2 pillar gauge cluster with boost pressure and air/fuel level. It has 17" Konig wheels that have been scraped, but it is only cosmetic. I got into a MINOR car accident that caused the hood to crumple. Body and frame are still as straight as from the factory. I replaced the hood with a carbon fiber hood. I also replaced the grill with a V5 STI grill and the headlights are APC projection headlights which have cracked. It also has a 6-disc in-dash CD player and I just got BRAND NEW tires - only 2 days of use!!! If interested it runs 15.01 in 1/4 mile with a full tank of gas. Car's body is in GREAT condition. Car is worth 11,500. But I'm selling it for cheaper due to mechanical problems. Something mechanical is wrong with the engine but should be able to be fixed for under 1k.

For the sake of the exercise, let's ignore the fact that this car has been fitted with a supercharger that makes less power and runs slower 1/4-mile times than a stock WRX. First, let's break that VIN down and see what we've got:

- JF1 indicates a Japanese-built car.
- GM indicates that this is a 2-door coupe
- 6 in the sixth position specifies a 2.5 liter engine from the factory
- 7 in the seventh position indicates the RS trim level on an Impreza
- 5 in the eighth position indicates that the car came with manual seatbelts and dual airbags.
- 4 in the ninth position is the checksum number.
- X in the 10th position indicates that this is a 1999 model year car—something the seller failed to list!
- G in the 11th position indicates the car was assembled at the Gunma factory with a 5-speed manual AWD transmission.

We still don't know for sure what engine is currently living in this car, but if we assume that it's a 1999 2.5RS, we know it's a Phase 2 SOHC motor, which is good, but still an open-deck design so it probably won't hold up too well under supercharging. Since the seller states it has mechanical problems and an aftermarket supercharger, it's risky to believe that repairs will be limited to $1,000, or that the motor will hold up well after it's fixed. With the minor accident damage on top of all that, the prudent buyer wants to have this one thoroughly checked out by a top Subaru shop before laying out any cash.

Choosing Your Subaru

In the quest for the right ride, identifying the car in front of you is only part of the answer. A much more interesting question is: What kind of Subaru do you want?

Because of the great commonality in design between the Legacy and Impreza platforms, most performance parts can be installed on any chassis or grade of car. You can, for example, put an STI engine into a 1990 Legacy L, or install AWD components into a base-model FWD 1993 Impreza. It may take some compatibility research and a lot of fiddling, but it can be done. But as with any make of automobile, certain models are preferred by performance builders—and with good reason!

This is not to leave the impression that other cars can't be modified for performance. If you have a Forester, it's built on the Impreza platform and uses most of the same components. Outback and Baja models use different suspension components, but they are built on the Legacy platform and can be built up like any other Subaru. A unique ride is its own reward.

The following examples are those well-known and readily available Impreza and Legacy models that are frequently chosen for performance modification. Some comments about the strong and weak points of each model are included.

1993–2001 Impreza GC2/GC4/GF:
4-Door Sedan or Wagon with 1.8 or 2.2 liter engine.

This model is a low-cost starting point. These cars are all potential, which is to say there's little or nothing to start with. Many GC cars were delivered in FWD form, but all have the shape and the mounting points to convert to AWD. GC2 brakes are small (2-piston front calipers, rear drums), interiors are spartan, sway bars are usually nonexistent, and not all cars have mounting points for them! Trim levels include the rare base models, Brighton, and the most common L and LS versions. If you're considering any car in this range, plan to dismantle it completely and rebuild it with performance parts in every area. The GF variation is the hatchback wagon.

This car started life as a basic 2WD, 1.8-liter engine automatic transmission Impreza. At the moment it has a 3.0-liter H6 engine, 5-speed manual transmission, and coil-over suspension. Quite a difference from stock.

1998–2001 Impreza GM6/GC6:
2-Door Coupe or 4-Door Sedan with 2.5 liter engine

The GM6 is the early 2.5RS coupe. The GC6 is the 2.5RS sedan, offered in 2000 and 2001. These cars are very easy to find, not very expensive, and they already have much of the trim wanted in a performance car. The 2.5RS came with AWD, a basic 2.5-liter EFI engine, 5-speed manual or 4-speed automatic transmission, and limited slip rear differential. This car responds well to upgrades. Brakes are already better than the basic Impreza, with discs all around and 2-piston front and single piston rear calipers. Interior trim is upgraded as well, with white-face gauges and improved seats. These cars also came with the "basket handle" rear spoiler, fog lights, and usually a sunroof. For the tuner on a budget, this model is hard to pass up. If you are looking at a 1998 model year car, or even some 1999 models, check to see if the car has the early DOHC 2.5-liter engine. The DOHC units are prone to head gasket difficulties, and the later SOHC Phase 2 engine is a better choice.

This car is the four-door "GC" body style. This car might have started life as a GC2 with the 1.8-liter engine, a GC4 with a 2.2-liter engine, or a GC6 in 2.5RS trim.

This is the two-door "GM" body style. The two-door 2.5RS was the first real sports car in the Impreza line.

2002–2005 Impreza 2.5RS: *4-Door Sedan or Wagon with 2.5 liter engine*

This is the later-model 2.5RS with bodies identical to the WRX sedans and wagons of the same year. For a base model, it is well turned out with AWD, air conditioning, cruise control, CD player, 4-wheel disc brakes, and the same basic suspension (but not the rear sway bar) of the WRX. Since all of the relevant WRX (and usually STI) parts fit on these cars, they are a good lower-cost choice if you plan to build or buy a custom engine.

This is a 2004 model year 2.5RS in the "GD" body style, used in common with the WRX and the STI.

This is a 2002 or 2003 "Bugeye" 2.5RS wagon. This is the "GG" body style.

This is the 2006 2.5i wagon—it shares the 2006 and later grille work with the WRX and STI, but the engine and drivetrain are fundamentally the same as the 2.5RS that came before.

2006–2007 Impreza 2.5i: 4-Door Sedan or Wagon with 2.5 liter engine

This car's engine is basically unchanged from its 2.5RS predecessors. It shares the same front grillwork with the 2006 WRX. You still get AWD, air conditioning, cruise, CD, 4-wheel disc brakes, and generally a very nice car for under $20,000. As the years go by, this should be a very affordable and high-quality starting point. The front-end treatment did change to keep pace with the WRX in this year, and people either love or hate the new grillework. The 2006 2.5i has 2-piston front and single-piston rear disc brakes.

2002–2005 Impreza WRX: 4-Door Sedan or 5-Door Wagon with 2.0 liter turbocharged engine

This is the car that made Subaru a favorite among performance enthusiasts. The 2002–2003 model years are known as "bugeye" models because of

This is the car that really started the performance revolution for Subaru: the 2002–2003 WRX set a new performance standard. This is the "GD" body style

The WRX was also offered in a hatchback wagon version, hewing closer to Subaru's traditional Impreza lines, but under the surface it received the same engine and suspension and brakes as the WRX. This is the "GG" body style shown from the rear.

the oval headlights. People either love the bugeye lights, or they hate them.

2004–2005 models use different shaped headlights, but all WRX variants in the modern era have a rich aftermarket that is constantly introducing new products for every area of the car. In the wagon versions, you lose the "Boy Racer" fender styling and rear spoiler, making the 5-door an excellent choice for a sleeper hot rod. The 5-speed manual transmissions are a weak link in the WRX if subjected to greatly increased power over stock.

2006-2007 Impreza WRX: 4-Door Sedan or 5-Door Wagon with 2.5 liter turbo engine

This is the upgrade year for the WRX, moving to a DOHC 2.5-liter engine that shares the same semi-closed block with the STI, but uses different connecting rods and heads than its faster brother. The front-end treatment changed in this year, for better or worse depending on your taste. The 2006 model came from the factory with 230 hp and 235 ft-lbs of torque, mated to the same 5-speed (albeit with different gearing and final drive) as in prior years. Every 2006 WRX included a 6-disc in-dash CD changer, 17-inch wheels, some leather trim here and there, and some sportier suspension pieces than its predecessors, borrowed from the STI. Brakes are an inch larger in diameter than on the 2006 2.5i and feature 4 front and 2 rear pistons. The exhaust manifolds/headers have changed (along with the oil pan design) and are unique to the 2006 and later models.

The front view of the 2006 WRX wagon. Fender lines remain the same, but this car shares the grille treatment with all 2006 Imprezas.

2006–2007 WRX TR: *"Tuner Ready"* 4-Door Sedan with DOHC 2.5 liter turbo engine

The 2006 WRX TR is a stripped-down version of the sedan that costs about $1,000 less than a standard WRX. The TR designation indicates that the following features unwanted by tuners have been deleted:

- Automatic Climate Control (Replaced with standard air conditioning from the 2.5i)
- Fog lights (Replaced with STI covers)
- Body-colored outside mirrors (Replaced with black mirrors)
- Leather shift knob and e-brake handle (Replaced with plastic)
- Chromed inner door handles (Replace with black door handles)
- Performance Design front seats (Replaced with Sport Design front seats)
- 6-Disc CD changer with 6 speakers (Replaced by a single CD player with 4 speakers)
- Rear cup holders
- Passenger-side map pocket

This edition of the WRX follows a grand history in the automotive industry of recognizing and supporting sporting uses of popular cars. The legendary "delete radio" option on 1970s Pontiac Trans-Ams that caused a special engine and suspension to be installed is perhaps the best-known example of this phenomenon.

2004–2005 Impreza WRX STI: *4-Door Sedan with DOHC 2.5-liter turbo engine*

The STI (formerly STi) model has upgrades from the WRX in many areas, not the least of which is the semi-closed deck 2.5-liter DOHC EJ257 engine. With a 6-speed manual transmission that is substantially more durable than the WRX 5-speed, upgraded suspension, brakes, and Driver-Controlled Center Differential (DCCD), the STI starts at the highest level of performance. But don't be fooled—you can make plenty of modifications on an STI. Note that the hubs and wheels from a 2005 or later STI do not match the hubs and wheels used on other Subaru models because the bolt pattern is different beginning with that year.

The first generation of the STI (spelled STi at the time) included the powerful EJ257 engine, upgraded suspension and brakes, and the 6-speed manual transmission. This model was never offered in the wagon body style.

2006–2007 Impreza WRX STI: *4-Door Sedan with DOHC 2.5-liter turbo engine*

Apart from the front-end treatment, there were no major changes to the STI in these years, but plenty of minor upgrades. It remained Subaru's premium sports car offering, with improved suspension, transmission, brakes, center diff control, and other

The WRX was also offered in a stripped-down "Tuner Ready" version, on the notion that customers are happy to purchase a less expensive model that omitted trim and comfort items that are immediately discarded by the performance-minded.

Who or What is an STI or STi?

STI is a semi-independent business owned by Subaru that was formed in 1988. STI was created to improve Subaru's factory-backed motor sports operations and to produce high performance products for the enthusiast market. Eventually, this extended to special edition cars bearing the STI designation. The letters stand for Subaru Tecnica International. The acronym was officially spelled STi until 2006, when it was changed to STI. People who make a fuss over the difference in capitalization from year to year are just being pedantic.

Still the top of the line in Subaru's performance stable, the STI remains popular for both street and track purposes.

For 2007, Subaru issued a Limited Edition STI with a small lip spoiler in the rear, fog lights, special wheels, leather trimmed interior, heated front seats, and a glass sunroof.

other Imprezas. The exception to this is exhaust manifolds/headers, which have changed (along with the oil pan design) and are unique to the 2006 models. STI wheels and hubs are still unique to the STI.

2004–2007 Forester XT: 4-Door Wagon with DOHC 2.5-liter turbo engine

Because the Forester has always received a 2.5-liter engine, and the XT is a turbocharged model, Subaru gifted the 2004 and 2005 Forester XT with the same EJ257 semi-closed deck long-block found in the Impreza STI models of the same years. The Forester received a smaller turbo and intercooler than the STI, and less powerful ECU programming, but these are easily upgraded with the STI units or any aftermarket products you choose. Starting in 2006, the XT received the same EJ255 engine as the WRX. The Forester is built on the Impreza platform, and can be outfitted with virtually all performance parts that fit an Impreza of the same year. With its 5-speed manual transmission and advantageous 4.44:1 final drive gear ratios, the Forester XT can be a very fast car, and one that is unlikely to draw unwanted attention.

1991–1994 Legacy Turbo: 4-Door Sport Sedan or Sport Wagon with 2.2-liter turbo engine

Among older Legacies, this model is strongly preferred for performance

The Forester XT received a slightly detuned version of the 2.5-liter STI engine in 2004 and 2005, mated to the standard WRX 5-speed transmission, and a 4.44:1 final drive ratio. With a little work on the suspension and brakes, this soccer-mom car can take on the best of the boy racers.

use, and all others are much less popular, but also a lot cheaper. The desirable cars include the 1991–1992 Sport Sedan, 1993 Touring Sedan and Sport Wagon, and 1994 Turbo Touring Wagon and Sport Sedan. All of these cars offer AWD, upgraded brakes, wheels, suspension, bodywork, and trim. Manual transmission is available on the Sedans. This is all in addition to the desirable closed-deck 2.2-liter turbo engine. The tough part is that comparatively few of these cars were ever imported and sold in America. If you're shopping for a Legacy hot rod project, and you can find one, these are the early Legacies to buy.

2005–2007 Legacy 2.5 GT, 2.5 GT Limited, and Spec.B: 4-Door Sedan or 5-Door Sport Wagon with 2.5 liter turbo engine

This car has the same EJ255 2.5-liter DOHC engine found in the 2006

The Legacy Turbo is among the most affordable performance Subarus you can find. Parts are still readily available and upgrades are not generally difficult. These cars are pre-OBD II, so reflashing the ECU is not an option. This is the only early Legacy to carry a hood scoop.

The rear view of the Legacy Turbo shows its clean lines and attractive stance.

Impreza WRX, mated to a 5-speed manual or a 4 or 5-speed automatic transmission. Many ancillary engine components are different, however. Longer, sleeker, and generally more luxurious than the Impreza, most aftermarket performance parts can be installed on the Legacy GT platform. The Legacy wagon races in the Grand American Road Racing series, so its performance credentials are impeccable.

The Spec.B has been made in limited numbers in 2006 and 2007. It features the STI 6-speed manual transmission, a Torsen limited slip rear axle, upgraded 18-inch wheels, and Bilstein sport suspension.

The Legacy GT is designed to compete with the European sports sedans, and does so very effectively.

From the rear, you can see that this is a comfortable sedan to seat five adults.

Also offered in a wagon body, the Legacy GT is another example of Subaru making a classic "sleeper"— the car that no one expects to be fast.

THE SUBARU ENGINE

When building any car for performance, the engine takes center stage. This is where power is made, and where a great deal of money, time, and effort is spent. It's also among the most misunderstood parts of a car.

"There's no substitute for cubic inches," A.J. Foyt said famously—and he was right to a point. But you can make a little 2.5-liter Subaru engine into a powerhouse and still run it on pump gas. Modern technology such as Subaru's variable valve lift and timing, combined with real-time engine management based on data from multiple sensors gives the modern tuner a distinct advantage over the shade-tree hot rodder of days gone by—except that the shade-tree guy could sit and twiddle about three screws on a carburetor until the car ran right. Today, we don't have that option. It takes the right equipment, software, and knowledge to make power.

The EJ series engine has been delivered in a variety of sizes and formats. With 17 years of development since the first Legacy rolled off the line, this 2006 Outback has a great engine under the hood.

This is the first view most people get of a Subaru engine—in this case a 2002 WRX engine. Note the top-mounted intercooler and basic black plastic air ducts.

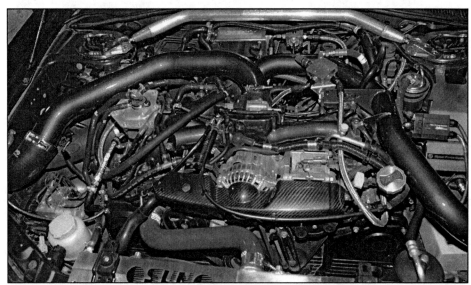

With a little work and a modest budget, you can dress up your engine bay and improve engine performance as well. Most performance enhancements are invisible, but everyone enjoys a nicely turned-out engine bay. Note that on this car, the intercooler has been moved to the front.

This chapter covers the basic engine variants available to you, what can be done with them, and some of the components that go into a Subaru engine. Detailed tables of the part numbers in recent WRX and STI models are provided in Appendix B to help you identify the parts that turn up in front of you.

The Subaru Boxer Engine

All Impreza and Legacy line Subarus use a horizontally opposed 4 or 6-cylinder "Boxer" engine design. This design is similar to the air-cooled engine used with great success for decades by Porsche, although Subaru's engines are water-cooled.

The design is simple enough: two aluminum crankcase halves come together around the crankshaft, and each side of the engine has a bank of pistons. The two banks of pistons are slightly offset from each other, accommodating the main and connecting rod bearing journals on the crank. A Subaru engine has five main bearings,

Here's a shot of a nicely done naturally aspirated 2.5RS engine. Note the lightened pulley visible on the power steering pump and the generally spotless condition of the engine bay. Small dress-up items such as the battery hold-down add to the appeal.

with thrust bearings in different locations depending on the model year of the engine. The engine case, crank, connecting rods, and pistons are collectively known as the "bottom end" of your engine.

Subaru uses a toothed belt (also known as a "Gilmer" belt) drive to turn single or double overhead camshafts in time with the crankshaft. Regardless of the number of cams, there are four valves per cylinder, either directly

actuated by the cam or using rocker arms. A separate sump pan is attached to the bottom of the crankcase to hold the oil reservoir.

Subaru's engineers offer several reasons for selecting this engine design, including:

• Light weight
• Good weight distribution
• Low center of gravity
• Low overall engine height

Additionally, horizontally opposed engines lend themselves to a very well balanced rotating mass, and can accommodate a larger bore (piston diameter) relative to the stroke (length of piston travel). The four-valve per cylinder layout also places the spark plug in the center of the combustion chamber, where it is most effective.

If you plan to exceed the stock performance on your engine, you're increasing the stress on all your engine components. With a 2.0-liter WRX, by the time you get to about 280 to 300 hp at the wheels, you're going to need a stronger bottom end. You'll need to consider lower horsepower limits with the 2.2-liter or 2.5RS naturally aspirated engine, and higher limits with the STI engine.

The following sections briefly discuss the components of your engine and their functions, and the considerations you should have in mind when thinking about upgrades.

This is the EJ255 as installed in the 2005–2007 Legacy GT. This one has an aftermarket front-mounted intercooler and short ram air intake, which reveals more of the engine. You can immediately identify the Legacy EJ255 by the plastic intake runners. Plain aluminum is used on most others, but the STI has a red crinkle finish.

Machine Shop Work

When you select an engine builder, find out which machine shop will be doing the measuring and fitment of your crank, rods, bearings, cams, and engine case. It may be that the engine builder has a machine shop in-house, but a general Subaru mechanic probably uses an outside machine shop to do the prep work, and then assembles your engine using parts prepared outside.

A good machine shop ensures that all the bearing journals in the engine case and crank line up and are the right size. They also balance and weigh the moving parts, including the flywheel and clutch plate. They install press-in bearings where needed, check all bearing clearances, and compare the combustion chamber volumes. Perhaps most importantly, a good machine shop "blueprints" your engine—that is, restores all clearances to their factory specifications.

Depending on the pieces you've purchased, the machine shop may also assemble your cylinder heads, install new valve guides, and cut the mating surfaces of the valves and valve seats in the heads.

When you go to have an engine built, remember the old racer's proverb: "If it hasn't been checked, it's wrong."

High-Performance Pistons

As your engine speed approaches the redline on your tachometer, the pistons in your engine are changing direction about 200 to 250 times per second. Combustion pushes your pistons with well over 5,000 times the force of gravity, and temperatures inside the combustion chamber are well over 1,500 degrees. So it follows that your pistons must be very well

Here's what happens when you run too much boost, too much spark advance, or your mixture is too lean. First the aluminum top of the piston starts to burn, and then detonation blows a hole right through the piston, sending tiny bits of aluminum, and then gasoline and compressed air into your oil.

made if they're going to last more than a few minutes under those conditions. Several considerations must be taken into account.

The most critical factor is the compression ratio. Simply put, this is the relative size of the combustion chamber at top dead center (TDC) compared to the size at bottom dead center (BDC). There's a complex formula to calculate the exact ratio, but generally if your chamber is 50cc at TDC and 500cc at BDC, your basic compression ratio is 10:1.

Anything you do to the chamber, such as machining the head, using a thicker or thinner head gasket, or changing the pistons, alters your compression ratio. If you've got a turbo, the amount of boost you're running changes your effective compression ratio as well. Turbocharged engines start out with a lower compression ratio because the cylinder pressure rises with your boost. So, the naturally aspirated EJ22 and EJ251 engines tend to have higher compression pistons than a turbocharged EJ205 or EJ257. For example, the native compression ratio on a 2007 2.5i is 10:1, while the 2007 WRX has a ratio of 8.4:1 and the 2007 STI has an 8.2:1 ratio.

If you put a turbocharger on a high-compression engine, you risk detonation and big holes in your pistons. The practical limit on turbocharging a high-compression Subaru engine is about 6 pounds of boost on pump gas. It is somewhat higher with racing gas, but you want to be careful.

So, selecting the right compression ratio for your pistons is critical. Your engine builder will be able to help you select the right ratio, taking into account your target boost and any other work. But there are other factors as well.

One of the factors to consider with your piston choice is the ring design. A piston has "ring lands" around its sides—these are the grooves where the rings fit and the walls between the grooves. Detonation can damage the rings and ring lands just as it can damage the piston's face.

Because the pistons are part of the rotating mass of the engine, you want a high-performance upgrade to be as light as possible, yet still strong enough to take the power you're going to make.

Some pistons are forged while others are cast. Both techniques have advantages, but as always, there are tradeoffs. Cast pistons are made by pouring (or sucking) molten alloys into a mold. The upside to cast pistons is that they do not expand much as they heat up. This allows an automaker to build a tight, quiet engine that will last a very long time. The down side is

This piston has had its ring lands broken out, probably by detonation. Compression goes to zero when this happens, and tiny pieces of metal are spread throughout your engine.

that cast pistons are not as strong, and don't hold up to the severe stresses of a high-performance engine.

Forged pistons, on the other hand, are made by taking a mostly molten lump of alloy and pounding it into a general shape, then machining the piston into its final shape. Forged pistons tend to be stronger than cast, but forged pistons also generally expand more than cast pistons under operational conditions. Because of this, they have a "loose" sound when they're cold, and so require more extensive engine warm-up before they seal completely. You can find forged pistons with the stock thermal expansion rate, however.

Because they cost less to produce, automakers tend to prefer cast pistons for mass-produced engines, and high-performance engine builders tend to choose forged pistons for their strength. However, some high-performance production motors use forged pistons. The recent JDM 2.0-liter STI motor uses forged pistons. The pistons in the USDM STI are made with a high-pressure casting technique called hypereutectic. This means that the pistons are made from an aluminum-silicon alloy and spun around until the alloy is completely homogeneous. Breaking down the silicon crystals helps eliminate tiny casting defects. The resulting piston is very hard, but also brittle.

Here are a couple examples of premium forged-pistons on the market today:

This is a well-made piston from Mahle Motorsport. Note how little material is used and how short the piston is overall. You can see the ring lands very clearly, and the hole where the wrist-pin fits in. (Photo courtesy of Mahle Motorsport)

Mahle Motorsport PowerPak Piston

Mahle Motorsport offers low expansion forged pistons made from 4032 aluminum alloy. The PowerPak pistons are designed for a hybrid WRX Stroker engine that uses the EJ257 crank in the EJ205 engine case to create a 2.2-liter high-performance engine. Mahle's pistons use two 1.2 mm compression rings and a 2.8 mm oil-control ring.

The top (or face) of a Wiseco piston. You can see the final machining that brings the piston up to the tight tolerances required inside a modern engine.

The ring lands and skirt area of a Wiseco piston. Every part of a piston has to be perfectly sized to fit and seal in the cylinder. Additionally, all pistons used in an engine should be precisely the same weight.

Wiseco Piston

Wiseco forges its pistons with a 2,000-ton press and then heat-treats them for maximum strength. It makes pistons for a variety of high-performance applications, and has a great reputation in the Subaru community.

It makes pistons for all Subaru EJ-series engines, including stroker pistons, and uses different alloys for naturally aspirated and turbocharged pistons.

Connecting Rods

Your pistons are connected to your crankshaft by the appropriately named connecting rods. These rods have three main parts. The "big end" is attached to the crankshaft and generally has a detachable section to facilitate the attachment. The opposite or "little end" typically has a simple hole through which the piston's "wrist pin" passes. The third part is the rod beam, which simply passes the piston's force from the little end to the big end and on down to the crankshaft.

Connecting rods have to be very strong. They take all the force placed on the piston and transmit it through a much smaller cross-section. When something bad happens and your engine "throws a rod," the results are spectacular and expensive. Usually the whole engine is a loss, as parts of your formerly hot-rod motor poke holes in the case on their way out into the air while other parts stay behind to ruin your crank and oil pump. Furthermore, when it is no longer limited in its range of motion by the connecting rod, at least one piston usually hits the top of its combustion chamber at ruinous speed, damaging the cylinder head and potentially the valvetrain, and even the cams.

So, given the absolutely critical function of the connecting rods, you don't want to skimp in this area any more than you would with your pistons or your cylinder heads. The ideal rods are light, strong, and identical down to a fraction of a gram. Automakers tend to opt for strong at the expense of light, because they want their engines to run reliably for a long time.

However, a great number of aftermarket rods are out there, and most of these represent an improvement in both power handling and weight over the stock units. You can use titanium or steel connecting rods, but whatever you choose, spend the money and get

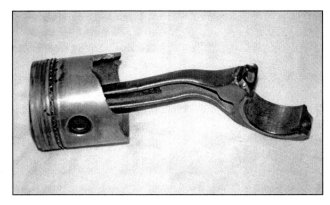

Another object lesson from the school of hard knocks: this rod used to be straight, until the big end gave way above 6,000 rpm. The piston hit the valves hard enough to break the rocker arms, and the loose part of the big end came through the side of the engine block.

been known to break, with predictably dire results. Subaru makes an excellent OEM crank—all Subaru cranks are forged and proven to hold over 600 wheel horsepower.

If that's not enough, you can get lightened cranks, cranks with enlarged oil passages, billet cranks, and other trick modifications as well. The rule to remember is that you should always get the best, most reliable crankshaft you can possibly afford, made by a reputable manufacturer, and checked for cracks by your engine builder.

Among the many great cranks out there, here's an example of one done right:

good ones with good fasteners. Here are a couple of good examples:

Carrillo Connecting Rods

Among the acknowledged leaders in high-performance connecting rods, Carrillo is almost always the first name mentioned. This company has been making rods for racing and high-performance applications since 1963, and it knows its business. One of the leading causes of engine failure is metal fatigue in the fasteners on the rods. Carrillo uses proprietary fasteners they have developed for strength.

This connecting rod is designed for extreme duty in turbocharged engines. It's a bit heavier, but it has to be. Note the large amount of material around the fasteners and up around the little end. (Photo courtesy of Manley Performance Products)

The H-Beam rod is lightened by removing material from the sides of the rod, while the Turbo Tuff product is a more traditional I-Beam cross section, with material removed from the front and back of the rod beam.

Cosworth Billet Crankshaft for the EJ25

No company has more experience building high-performance engines than Cosworth, and it makes a crank by machining a solid hunk of EN40B high-strength steel. The crank is counterweighted for smooth rotation and drilled for excellent oil distribution. Cosworth says that it has tested these cranks up to 1,000 hp.

Bearings

Bearings are an interesting part of your engine. Virtually all modern engines use "babbitt" bearings, which are plain bearings—meaning that they are a smooth metal surface, as opposed to ball bearings or needle bearings—made of an alloy of copper, tin, antimony, and lead.

Babbitt bearings rely on a thin film of oil to separate the steel of the crankshaft from the alloy surface of the main and the connecting rod bearings. This oil is delivered under pressure from your engine's oil pump and is distributed through passages drilled in the crank. If the oil stops flowing, it takes only seconds for the babbitt bearings to heat up, wear away, and potentially move (or "spin") in their bearing carriers. When this happens in a connecting rod journal, it's called "rod knock"—named for the distinctive sound your engine makes to tell you that your formerly expensive crankshaft is now a very shiny boat anchor.

This is a good example of an H-pattern performance connecting rod. Hollowing out the sides removes a lot of weight while maintaining the structural integrity when the piston pushes down with tremendous force. (Photo courtesy of Manley Performance Products)

Manley H-Beam and Turbo Tuff Connecting Rods

Manley Performance Products offers a variety of engine internal parts, including two rods designed for Subaru applications. These particular rods use two design alternatives that are representative of what is found on the market.

Crankshafts

The crankshaft is where up-and-down motion from the pistons is converted into rotational motion. The crankshaft is constantly being pushed on from opposite sides and spinning at thousands of RPM on a thin film of oil.

Like the other parts of your engine, the crank must be very well made to survive even for a short while in this environment. Crankshafts have

Most bearings on the market for your engine are good ones. Simply make sure that you get them in the right size and that they are measured for clearance and installed correctly. Above all, resist the temptation to look at a used bearing and decide that it's good enough to re-use. If it has a few thousand miles on it, it's better to replace that bearing than take a chance with engine failure.

Thrust bearings are a little different. These bearings carry the longitudinal loads that shove your spinning crankshaft against the sides of the bearing carriers. When you step on the clutch, you're using leverage to press a couple hundred pounds of force against the back of the crankshaft to push it forward . The thrust bearings (also known as thrust washers) take up this load. In the early (Phase 1) engines, the thrust bearings were positioned by the #3 (center) main bearing, but in Phase 2 motors, the thrust bearings were moved to the rear of the engine at the #5 main bearing to better isolate and manage the thrust loads.

Cylinder Heads and Valves

The bottom end of the engine does all the work, but it's the top ends—the cylinder heads—that make the power. A good cylinder head has well-formed and smoothed out intake and exhaust passages, and nice big valves. It's also important that the mating surfaces on those valves and their seats must be cut and ground together (also called "lapping") to seal well when closed and to flow well when open.

Engine builders use a device called a flow bench to measure how much air can flow through a head's ports and valves. A good builder makes sure all the ports on your heads flow at the same rate and with good gas velocity. Additionally, the engine builder should open up the area around the valve faces to reduce obstacles to flow. This is called "unshrouding" the valves.

Subaru heads are made of aluminum, and, depending on the

In this cutaway view of an EJ22 head, you can see how gases flow into the ports and into the combustion chamber. The smoother and larger this port is, the better your intake charge flows.

design, use bucket tappets or rocker arms to help the cam actuate the valves. Replaceable bronze valve guides are inserted into the valveways, and the valves themselves are made of steel. Some valves have hollow stems filled with sodium or other materials to aid in cooling and to reduce weight.

Cylinder heads mate to the bottom end of the engine with the aid of a head gasket. These are generally made of a "sandwich" of layers of metal and soft materials, with sealing surfaces added where needed on top. The head gasket must be able to hold the mixture in the cylinder during compression and combustion, so head gaskets tend to be expensive and precise. They are also made with the expectation that they will be "crushed" when you torque the heads onto the engine. A head gasket that has been crushed once generally does not seal well thereafter. So, as with bearings, resist the temptation to re-use a head gasket, no matter how good it looks.

The bottom line on heads is that unless you really know what you're doing, you're better off buying ones that have been prepared by expert shops, like COBB, Crawford, or Cosworth. Some example products are:

COBB Tuning CNC Ported Cylinder Heads

COBB offers a variety of cylinder heads in ascending stages of development. Stage 1 involves sending your heads to COBB for a hand-porting and

COBB Tuning has developed a line of CNC-machined cylinder heads designed for maximum flow. You can buy the heads fully assembled with valves and guides installed and ready to bolt onto your short block, or get a short block straight from COBB. (Photo courtesy of COBB)

multi-angle valve job. Using new seats, springs, and valves, COBB matches the volume in each combustion chamber and blueprints your heads before returning them to you. COBB Stage 2 cylinder heads use +1mm valves and are made from new Subaru castings. Porting is done on a computer-controlled CNC mill and improves intake flow by about 20% and exhaust flow by about 40%. Like the Stage 1 heads, everything is balanced, blueprinted, and assembled using top quality components.

Cosworth CNC Machined Big Valve Heads

Cosworth makes these heads by modifying new stock Subaru heads to use bigger valves. They also improve the flow characteristics and use their own upgraded valvetrain pieces. Additionally, they reshape and size-match the combustion chambers to unshroud the valves and improve the fuel burn characteristics.

Cams and Cam Timing

You can change your engine's performance characteristics substantially with a cam replacement, or just by changing the timing of the cams you've already got.

Your cams (two or four of them, depending on your engine) control the opening and closing of your intake and exhaust valves in time with the pistons and the crankshaft. You need your intake valves to open to let in fuel and air, and you need the valves to be closed in order for the engine to compress the mixture and harvest the energy released as the mixture burns. Then you need the exhaust valves to open to let the exhaust gases out. The cam controls the opening and closing of the valves by rotating a series of eccentric egg-shaped lobes against rockers or tappets (also called "cam followers" or "lifters" or "buckets"). The lobes are spaced around the cam to actuate the valves in precise order as the engine turns.

If you change the timing, duration, and height (known as "lift") of the cams, you change the way the engine operates. Most obviously, opening the valves farther allows an easier passageway into and out of the combustion chamber. Holding the valves open longer also allows the engine to breathe more efficiently. Stock 2-liter WRX cams use 208 degrees duration and 9.15mm of lift for the exhaust and 9.25mm for intake, and performance cams increase these numbers substantially.

You can also change the speed at which the valves open and close. This is accomplished with the cam *profile*, which is to say the shape of the cam

This piston has been striking something—either a valve or perhaps something dropped into the intake port. Either way, it's a complete engine teardown to get the piston out, and probably a ruined cylinder head as well.

This is what a piston should look like when it comes out of a well-used engine. There's a little scale and carbon build-up, but not a lot. The piston material is not burned, and there's no sign of detonation.

lobes. There is a danger associated with changing the cam profile on a modern engine. If you open the valves farther and hold them open longer, you run the risk of the piston striking the valves, especially at high RPM. This is because the time required for the valves to close may exceed the available time when the piston is coming towards the valves at several hundred miles per hour.

Also, when you change the way your cam works, you change the way your engine runs—a cam that makes great power at 6,000 rpm may not

allow your engine to idle at less than 1,500 rpm. Many high-performance cams actually make less power until the engine reaches a certain RPM. This phenomenon is known as "getting up on the cam" or "coming onto the cam."

In general, for street use, you want to limit your selection to those cams that allow a stock idle speed and have a good broad power curve.

More from the author's automotive hall of shame: this happened when the piston hit the valve repeatedly until the valve body broke off the stem, and lodged in the face of the piston. Shortly thereafter, the stem came down and poked its own hole in the piston. The cylinder head was just as ugly.

Another view of the results of incorrect valve/piston clearance. All the missing pieces of the piston face end up in your oil, oil pump, and every oil passage in your engine in a matter of seconds. Would you risk re-using a crankshaft that might have a piece of shrapnel in it, waiting to block oil flow to your new bearings?

Changing your cams can also affect your car's ability to pass emissions tests.

Cam timing is changed by altering the relationship between the rotation of the crankshaft and the rotation of the cams, advancing or retarding valve actuation relative to crank position. This is generally accomplished through the use of Subaru's Active Valve Control System (AVCS) in the EZ30, EJ255, and EJ257 engines.

Luckily, you can choose from many proven safe cam designs with a stock engine. If you have a custom engine, however, your engine builder will test your cams to make sure you don't have clearance problems. Some leading cam upgrades on the market are:

Crawford Performance Cams for WRX

Crawford Performance offers cams in Street, Rally, and Full-Race profiles for the WRX. Check with Crawford for implementation requirements.

COBB Tuning Billet Cams for STI

COBB offers a range of cams for the DOHC EJ257 engine. Its "Stage 1" cams work with stock heads and bottom ends and does not affect idle speed.

COBB Tuning 2.5RS/TS Street Performer Cams

These cams are designed to work with the naturally aspirated 2.5RS/TS engines and to improve top-end breathing without creating idle issues or requiring custom engine tuning.

Cosworth High-Performance Camshafts

Cosworth is one of the leading engine builders in the world. It offers a range of cams for the EJ205 and EJ257 engines with varying degrees of duration and lift heights. EJ257 cams feature a USDM profile with up to 278 degrees of intake and 274 degrees of exhaust duration and lift heights of 10.4mm on the intake and 10mm on the exhaust. EJ205 cams offer 272 degrees of duration and 10mm of lift on both intake and exhaust.

Lightened, Underdrive, and Overdrive Pulleys

Lightened and underdrive/overdrive pulleys are a common upgrade that can be made without disturbing the engine. A lighter pulley on the crankshaft, or anywhere on your belt system, allows your engine to spin up faster, and nicely dresses up your engine bay.

In addition to trading your stock steel crankshaft pulley for a nice light aluminum one, you can also choose an underdrive pulley kit. Lots of claims float around about underdrive pulleys making power, but the fact is that all they can do is reduce load—not actually make any new power. But reducing load is a great way to put more power to the ground!

An underdrive crank pulley reduces the amount of work your engine has to do in order to spin the power steering pump, water pump, and alternator. It does so by giving you a mechanical advantage—just like selecting a lower gear when your wheels are turning at a slower speed.

The tradeoff here is that your alternator generally needs to turn at a certain minimum speed to generate electricity, your power steering pump needs speed to work, and your water pump has a minimum speed to push coolant through your engine and radiator. Underdrive pulley setups are popular with racers—those cars rarely sit still and generally run at very high revs, so an underdrive pulley setup poses no problem. If you spend a lot of time in stop-and-go traffic, be mindful of your coolant temperature when adopting a pulley kit for "free power." Also, if you've got a bunch of electronics (like a huge stereo system) that place a big load on your alternator, you probably can't afford to underdrive it.

You can compensate for this effect somewhat with an overdrive pulley kit for your alternator and power steering pump. These kits restore RPM to your alternator and steering pumps, but your water pump will still turn at reduced speed. Keep an eye on your water temperature!

Your Subaru engine may use traditional V-belts or a serpentine belt system, depending on its age. If your car uses the serpentine belt system, make sure you understand the routing pattern before you attempt to replace any pulley. Regardless of your belt type, check to make sure that your belt length is correct for the pulley kit combination you're using. Finally, if you install a new crank pulley, be sure you know the correct torque for the bolt that holds the pulley on the crank.

This is the stock pulley on the Subaru water pump. It's a fairly heavy unit, made of stamped steel.

This is a good example of a lightened crank pulley. It's made of aluminum, and the anodized finish makes for a nice dress-up in the engine bay. Note how the machined holes reduce weight in the pulley, giving your engine that much less mass to turn. (Photo courtesy of Agency Power)

Choosing the Right Radiator and Oil Cooler

The stock Subaru cooling system should be sufficient to keep your engine running in the correct temperature range unless you are making well over stock horsepower. When you come to the point that you need to upgrade your cooling system, bear these considerations in mind:

1) Have you maximized airflow to your existing radiator and oil cooler?

2) Is your thermostat functioning as designed?

3) Are you underdriving your water pump?

4) Does your new radiator need to fit into the stock core support?

5) Can you use a thicker radiator of the same height and width?

6) Does your car have an automatic transmission, and if so, does the radiator you're considering include a compatible transmission cooler?

With the size of your radiator well understood, you can order a custom radiator or a direct-fit replacement. Some direct replacement kits already exist:

Fluidyne Direct-Fit Radiator for WRX and STI

Fluidyne makes direct replacement upgrade radiator for both the WRX and the STI. These radiators are all-aluminum, and use high-flow designs and improved heat transfer fins. Custom aftermarket radiators of this type have the same fittings as stock, allowing you to bolt the radiator straight into your car.

Radiator Cooling Plate

The market has several different kinds of radiator cooling plates available. In the stock configuration, some air is allowed to escape at the top of your radiator, limiting the amount of air flowing through the cooling fins. A cooling plate blocks this exit and forces all incoming air through the radiator to increase efficiency.

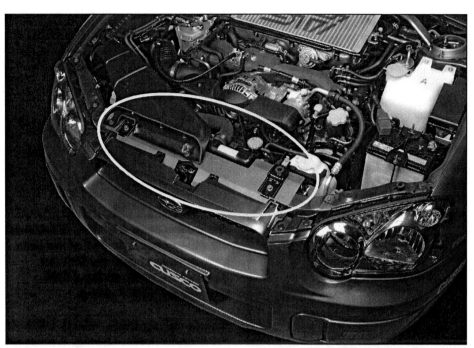

A cooling plate like this unit from Cusco is a low-cost addition that helps keep your engine cooler in summer. (Nukabe/Cusco)

Subaru Oil Cooler (all models)

Subaru makes a standard oil cooler that fits all Impreza and Legacy models, except the automatic transmission Forester. The kit comes with a water-transfer cooler that plumbs into your cooling system, and an extension that fits on your standard oil filter mount. As the oil passes through your filter, it is cooled to the same temperature as your coolant. This is a quick and easy installation that keeps your oil at optimum operating temperature.

Subaru Engine Types

This section lists the various engines that came with Imprezas and Legacies since the beginning of the product lines. More information about engine types and the years and models in which they were sold is found in the VIN code and engine plate tables in Chapter 1, and engine part number tables for 2.0 and 2.5 liter turbocharged models are presented in Appendix B. But in general, here's a short cheat sheet on the basic modern engine types found in common circulation and the models in which they were originally installed:

Subaru Engine Types
EJ18 – SOHC Impreza 1993–1997
EJ22 – SOHC Impreza 1995–1998 (Phase 1)
EJ22 – SOHC Impreza 1999–2001 (Phase 2)
EJ251 – DOHC Impreza 2.5RS 1998–1999 (Phase 1)
EJ251 – SOHC Impreza 2.5RS/2.5i 1999–2006 (Phase 2)
EJ205 – DOHC Impreza WRX 2002–2005
EJ207 – DOHC Impreza WRX STI JDM
EJ255 – DOHC Impreza WRX 2006–2007
EJ257 – DOHC Impreza WRX STI USDM (2004–2007)
EJ22 – SOHC Legacy 1990–1996
EJ22 – SOHC Legacy Turbo 1991–1994
EJ25 – SOHC Legacy 2.5 1996 (Phase 1)
EJ251 – DOHC Legacy 2.5 1997–1999 (Phase 1)
EJ251 – SOHC Legacy 2.5 1999–2004 (Phase 2)
EJ255 – DOHC Legacy 2.5GT 2003–2006
EZ30 – DOHC Legacy 6-Cylinder engine (2004–2006)

All EJ-series engines can be used in any Impreza or Legacy chassis. The rest of this chapter is a brief look at each engine you might choose.

EJ18

The EJ18 is the basic engine used in early Imprezas. The conventional wisdom is that the EJ18 is not a performance engine, but there is a small and dedicated group of EJ18 enthusiasts who are using these inexpensive and widely vailable engines to great effect.

Look at the engine plate, mounted on the left inner fender of most cars. If the engine hasn't been replaced, this tells you what you're looking at. In this case, look at the code stamped just to the right of "Engine Type," and you see that this is an EJ18.

EJ205

This is the WRX 2.0-liter DOHC engine. It uses an open-deck design, which means that it has only two supports (at 3 and 9 o'clock when viewed in the operating position) on the piston cylinders.

This design can allow for cylinder movement in high-boost, high-power implementations. This engine does not

The engine code stamping is towards the front of the right half of the case. Subaru stamps only the first two digits of the code, so the EJ205 receives an "EJ20" stamp.

include oil squirters, which lubricate the cylinder walls. Instead, it relies on oil splash, as do most engines. The heads of the EJ205 are known for their excellent flow characteristics and solid valve lifters. As a DOHC engine, cam profile and timing are easily tunable for good performance.

The EJ205 can be pushed to about 300 to 350 horsepower without modification. Beyond that, you'll want to upgrade your pistons, connecting rods, and crank. Most drivers who go past the stock limits upgrade to the EJ257 STI engine.

The EJ205 engine benefits most from increased flow in the exhaust and intake systems, followed by engine management tuning; this work is an absolute necessity before you replace the stock turbocharger or do more exotic work.

This is a view of the open-deck design used on the EJ205 WRX engine in the USDM. Note the supports for the pistons at 3 and 9 o'clock. But also note the thickness of the cylinder walls, which are made to handle turbo boost and increased horsepower.

EJ207

This is the JDM WRX and STI engine in the 1999–2000 model years. Previous to this, the JDM had seen examples such as the EJ20G and EJ20K, and these are frequently lumped together as JDM WRX engines. This line of engines has never been imported to North America by Subaru, but many examples have been imported by private parties. Due to Japan's strict emissions and inspection regimen, many JDM engines with substantial useful life remaining in them are removed and exported for the overseas tuner market.

The key features that make this engine desirable are the semi-closed deck, STI heads, special STI crankshaft with Tuftride impregnation to case-harden its bearing surfaces, and the STI pistons and connecting rods. The EJ207 includes "oil squirters" in the crankcase that squirt oil on the backs of the pistons to aid in cylinder wall lubrication and piston cooling.

The EJ207 can take more boost than the EJ205 without modification, but with the advent of the EJ257, the EJ207 has lost much of its desirability for extreme high-power applications.

Like all engines, the EJ207 benefits most from easily replaced intake and exhaust systems, and engine management tuning.

EJ22

The EJ22 engine comes in several versions. The Impreza EJ22 and the basic Legacy EJ22 are open-deck naturally aspirated engines making approximately 130 to 140 horsepower and generating about 140 ft-lbs of torque. Like the EJ18, these engines are best left in their stock configuration until they can be replaced with a 2.0 or 2.5-liter model.

But the EJ22 SOHC used in the 1991–1994 Legacy Turbo "Sport Sedan" and "Turbo Touring Wagon" is different. This block features a fully closed deck design, with excellent support for the cylinder walls. This design allows the block to support tremendous boost from an aftermarket

Looking very similar to other stampings, the EJ22 is marked in the same location on the right-hand case half. Note that there is no obvious way to tell from the stamping if you have an open deck EJ22, or the desirable closed-deck turbo EJ22.

Here's a look at what you'd see if you pulled a head off an ancient and dirty EJ22 turbo engine. Where the open and semi-closed decks have open coolant space, the closed deck turbo engine has smaller passages. This extra cylinder support material helps hold the engine components in place under high boost.

turbocharger, and that makes this engine an excellent candidate for performance modification. The EJ22 turbo engine also includes "oil squirters" to aid in cylinder wall lubrication and piston cooling.

Unfortunately, these engines were not widely sold in North America, and thus fall into the same category as the EJ207—highly desirable and somewhat difficult and expensive to obtain.

A common modification of the EJ22 turbo engine is to replace the original heads with heads from an EJ205 or EJ257 (WRX and USDM STI, respectively). The E205 heads flow much better than the EJ22 units and have solid lifters where the EJ22 has hydraulic lifters. With the EJ257 heads, you have to deal with the AVCS (Automatic Valve Control System) developed for the STI, so the EJ205 heads remain the most popular upgrade choice.

EJ251

The EJ25 is the most common Subaru engine found on the market. Like the EJ22, it's difficult to identify all EJ25 variations from the outside, especially when the engine is installed in a car.

The first Legacy/Impreza engine to carry the EJ25 designation came in the 1996 Legacy GT. It made 155 horsepower at 5,600 rpm and 140 ft-lbs of torque at 2,800 rpm. It was a sin-

Like the other engines, all 2.5-liter variants are stamped "EJ25," and you'll need to look further to identify an open-deck 2.5RS engine versus a semi-closed deck EJ255 WRX or EJ257 STI engine. One easy way is to check the cam covers—most EJ251 engines are SOHC, while the EJ255 and EJ257 are DOHC.

gle-cam, open deck, Phase 1 design, and provided the basis for the later SOHC EJ251 designs.

The most common EJ25 is the EJ251—an open-deck design, SOHC, 4 valve-per-cylinder design, although some early EJ251s were DOHC. In 1997, the Legacy GT went to the Phase 1 DOHC EJ251 design, and in 1998 the same engine was used at the introduction of the Impreza 2.5RS. This engine made 165 horsepower at 5,600 rpm, and 162 foot-pounds of torque at 4,000 rpm. These engines were sold from 1997 to early 1999, and they are known for having head gasket difficulties, ring land troubles, and thrust bearing weakness. Because the Phase 1 EJ251 engines used a DOHC design, they can be identified easily even when installed in a car.

If you have any choice in the matter, you want a Phase 2 engine. Phase 2 engines were introduced for the 1999 model year, and have several internal improvements over the earlier versions, such as moving the crankshaft thrust bearings from the middle #3 main bearing to the rearmost #5 main bearing for better load-bearing capacity, and a change to the piston skirts to improve piston ring longevity.

Phase 1 engines should be avoided if you are planning to increase the engine's output significantly. But there's no cause to panic if you have a Phase 1 engine, as long as you are not planning to add a turbo to it. It's not a desirable plant, but it's not necessarily a ticking time bomb, either.

It is important to note that model year 1999 is the transition point for Phase 1/Phase 2 engines. 1999 Imprezas and Foresters built in Japan (with JF1 as the first three letters of the VIN code) all have the Phase 2 engine, while 1999 Subarus manufactured in Indiana (with 4S3 or 4S4 as the first three letters of the VIN code) may have the Phase 1 engine. By the beginning of model year 2000 production in the spring of 1999, all Subarus received the Phase 2 engine.

The Phase 2 EJ251 is an open-deck SOHC design that has lasted

Look at the right side of this 1998 Legacy engine and you can see the cam timing belt cover on the front next to the battery and the oil cap. The shape of the cover tells you this is a DOHC engine. In 1998, that means a Phase 1 EJ251.

essentially unchanged to the present day in the Impreza 2.5RS and 2.5i models, and in the Legacy line through 2004. Through the years, the engine has made from about 165 to 175 horsepower, and 165 to 170 ft-lbs of torque. This engine has been made and imported in great numbers, and good examples are easy to find.

Because it was not designed for forced induction, the Phase 2 EJ251 can take only up to 6 pounds of boost on pump gas without modification. This is a crucial limit because the engine was made with high compression cast pistons that break under greater boost levels. Don't be tempted to exceed this boost level in an engine that was never designed or intended to be force-fed. If you want a turbo, get an

EJ205, EJ255, or EJ257.

But you don't have to give up on your naturally aspirated engine in search of performance. When people have a turbo, they look to boost in order to make power. Without a turbo, there's still a lot you can do. The EJ251 benefits greatly from exhaust and intake work, and a limited amount from engine management tuning. Because this engine is not designed for forced induction and has natively high compression, improving the flow produces dramatic results. Cams such as the COBB "Spicy" model also have great effects.

EJ255

Beginning in model year 2005, the Legacy 2.5GT was delivered with a

You can see the open deck-design in this EJ251 (no pistons in this one, though). Note the thinner piston walls that tell you this engine was never designed for turbocharging.

new EJ25 variation called the EJ255. This is a new DOHC engine with the Phase 2 improvements, a semi-closed deck, and it's built to be turbocharged. You can identify this engine (in its stock form) by its black plastic intake manifold. The WRX version retains an unpainted aluminum manifold.

There has been a great deal of conjecture about the similarities between this engine and the EJ257 STI unit. Subaru uses different part numbers for the engine case, heads, and pistons used in the EJ255 and those used in EJ257 engines. Different part numbers do not prove that components are not otherwise identical, but Subaru uses the same part numbers for the cams, valves, crankshaft, and connecting rods for both engines.

The 2005 Legacy EJ255 produces 243 horsepower at 6,000 rpm, and 250 ft-lbs of torque at 3,600 rpm. This engine uses Subaru's Active Valve Control System (AVCS).

For 2006 and later, the EJ255 was continued in the Legacy GT and it replaced the EJ205 in the Impreza WRX. In the WRX configuration, the engine is rated to produce 230 horsepower at 5,600 rpm, and 235 ft-lbs of torque at 3,600 rpm.

EJ257

The EJ257 is the hottest engine Subaru has ever sold in North America. Beginning in 2004, Subaru began importing a WRX STI Sedan functionally equal to the JDM STI Spec.C. The EJ257 is a larger-displacement version of the EJ207, but the EJ257 uses hypereutectic aluminum alloy pistons instead of the forged pistons provided with the EJ207. The EJ257's Active Valve Control System (AVCS) automatically adjusts the intake valve timing through a range of 35 crankshaft degrees. This keeps the timing of the intake optimized for power and torque at all times.

Statistics for this unit are impressive, with a semi-closed block, special connecting rods made from high-carbon steel, a high-boost turbo pushing maximum boost of 14.5 psi to a redline

Here you can see the additional cylinder supports at 12 and 6 o'clock that define a semi-closed deck engine, as used in the EJ255 and EJ257

You can easily identify the EZ30/H6 engine in any Subaru because it has six intake runners instead of the usual four. This installation was performed by Barrett Dash at All Wheels Driven in Bend, Oregon. It's a tight fit to put an EZ30 into a 1993 Impreza!

of 7,000 rpm. And that's all straight from the factory.

What that gets you is an engine with a factory warranty and peak power of 293 horsepower at 6,000 rpm and 300 ft-lbs of torque at 4,000 rpm.

EZ30/H6

The EZ30, commonly known as the H6, is a 6-cylinder horizontally opposed engine substantially similar to the EJ series in many ways. Beginning in 2003, Subaru introduced the H6 into certain Legacy Outback models, and it has also been used in the 2006 Tribeca SUV. Subaru has not yet sold a turbocharged version of this engine in North America.

The DOHC EZ30 is only 20mm (0.8 inches) longer than the EJ255. To achieve this short overall length, Subaru had to develop a new block and new heads, so the internals of this engine are all new. The EZ30 produces 220 horsepower at 6,000 rpm, along with 213 ft-lbs of torque at 4,400 rpm. Because of the engine's high compression ratio (10.7:1), you must replace the pistons with lower-compression models if you wish to add a turbo. On top of that, the EZ30's open-deck design makes turbocharging a generally risky proposition.

You can wedge an EZ30 into an Impreza with some work, and it fits well in the larger Legacy engine bay. It is becoming more popular as a tuner upgrade, although a great deal of expensive engine work has to be done to obtain better power than an EJ257. And that's on top of the great deal of

expensive work to fit the engine into an Impreza. Also, custom work is necessary to mate the EZ30 to any existing Subaru manual transmission. It is designed for use with the 4EAT transmission only.

Mixed-Source Engines

A mixed-source "hybrid" Subaru engine is one where the heads, engine case, and other components have been intentionally mismatched. This is typically done to obtain a larger displacement or other desired characteristics. An engine built with an EJ22 case mated with an EJ25 DOHC crank and rods and a pair of EJ205 heads is a perfect example—and such engines exist. Others have built engines using the EJ205 case and heads with an EJ257 crank and rods.

These unusual engines must be carefully designed and assembled by top professionals. If you are looking for an alternative engine design, COBB Tuning and Crawford Performance both offer a range of designs that they have researched for compatibility and increased performance.

COBB Tuning offers a 2.65-liter short block based on the EJ257. COBB uses a crankshaft with an 81mm stroke to achieve the displacement. COBB

offers an entire line of three stages of Tuner engines and two types of Pro series motors built to the highest standards in the industry.

Crawford Performance offers the R series—a set of racing short blocks set up for maximum power and speed. "Our R series blocks are made from the 2.2-liter turbo block which comes from the factory with a fully closed deck design and incorporates piston squirters to cool the pistons. This is the block of choice to make big power, but they are no longer available for purchase from Subaru," says engine builder Quirt Crawford.

The Crawford R series engines use replaceable wet sleeve cylinders, so that the sleeves may be replaced. The precious 2.2-liter block thereby becomes reusable. The Crawford R3 engine displaces 2.65 liters based on an increased bore size—another benefit of the wet sleeves. The 2.8-liter R4 engine uses a billet stroker crank and the larger bore size. If you don't need the full race kit, the Crawford S5 short block uses the stock bore of an EJ257 engine coupled with the Crawford 84mm stroke billet crank to achieve a 2.65-liter displacement. The stock EJ257 stroke is 79mm. Crawford also makes a destroked SR1 "Rally" short block with a 75mm stroke.

THE INDUCTION SYSTEM

Jeff Perrin's personal STI is a rolling R&D center for high-performance products. This car has it all, including a 6-cylinder engine borrowed from a Legacy and outfitted with a turbo. (Photo courtesy of Perrin Performance)

This and the next few chapters take a look at the engine components along the combustion path. At its most basic level, an internal combustion engine is an air pump. Air comes in the front, and goes out the back. We'll examine how air is sucked in through the intake filter and pulled onwards through the turbocharger, then pushed through the intercooler to the intake manifold and the combustion chambers. We'll look at the fuel system from the point where gas is pumped out of the tank towards the engine and is squirted in measured quantities into the airstream. Afterwards, we'll follow the exhaust as it makes its way through the manifold (or "header"), through the turbo again, through the catalytic converters and finally out the tailpipe.

Within reasonable limits, all products and upgrades discussed in this chapter are applicable to naturally aspirated engines.

How the Engine Does its Work

An internal combustion engine is a marvelous piece of technology. It runs, for years in most cases, under some of the most challenging conditions we could devise for it. Using pump gas that would have destroyed the engines our parents had in the 1950s and 1960s, our street cars make power that was until recently the sole province of expensive racing engines. For the most part, modern engines run longer, smoother, more reliably, and produce more power per cubic centimeter of displacement than any mass-produced engines ever sold to the public before.

A bewildering array of products out there claim better flow, more pounds per square inch (PSI) of boost, a cooler intake charge, and generally *more power*—which is what you're after. You can buy piggyback computers, reflashes, and replacement Engine Control Units (ECU), cold air and short ram intakes, upgraded turbochargers, and bigger, louder exhaust pipes. This book looks at the most popular and reliable upgrades being installed and tuned by some of the best shops in North America.

The main thing to remember is that all of these components function as a system. And because an engine is a system based on the flow of gases, the tightest point in the system generally governs the total output. The classic demonstration is to attempt to breathe through a drinking straw. What this means in real terms is that you may see an incremental improvement in power by relieving a restrictive component in your system, but real power gains require thoughtful modification to the entire system for the most efficient flow and greater energy output.

The Science of Combustion

A tablespoon of gasoline and a quart of air have a finite amount of energy potential held within them. We can change that potential into different forms of energy such as heat, motion, and light by putting the fuel and air into an internal combustion engine. We can theoretically create perfectly efficient engines and drivetrains, but we can never get more energy out of that spoonful of gas and bottle of air than the native elements hold. So to make more power in our cars, we have to put more of those elements through the system, and make the system as efficient as possible.

Inefficiency can include such flaws as not burning all of the fuel we put into the combustion chamber—these are the "unburned hydrocarbons" that are measured in many emissions tests. This happens when the air/fuel mixture is incorrect. The theoretically perfect mixture is called "Stoichiometric" (stow-ee-key-o-metric) and is about 14.7 parts air to 1 part gasoline. The reason you care is that if you have imperfect mixture, you're not getting all the energy you can out of your fuel and air.

Older cars relied on carburetors to feed fuel into the system. The carburetors were adjusted—generally by hand—until they achieved something close to the right mixture; nice enough to work on, but not tremendously accurate. The penalty for misadjusting the mixture on the rich side is fouled plugs, smelly exhaust, and low power. But the penalty for going too lean in the mixture is detonation—where the fuel/air mixture explodes in the combustion chamber. In any engine, this leads to piston failure, rod failure, burned valves, low power, and nothing at all that is good.

You can see that in a modern engine, the consequences of bad mixture are even worse. A modern high-compression engine coupled with pump gas requires that compression, spark, and mixture must be carefully controlled. We use computers and fuel injection to do this because the old tapered needles or sequential jets (little holes in brass tubes) simply aren't adaptable or accurate enough. If your engine is boosted with turbocharged air, you can blow it up before you even realize that there's a problem. Technology comes to the rescue with the modern car's array of sensors and probes that keep track of your engine's condition millisecond by millisecond. The information from those sensors allows your engine computer to make decisions about how much fuel to give, when to strike the spark, and in some cases such as the STI, when to open the valves and let gases flow.

A Word About Valves

The last part of your engine that the air and gasoline passes on the way into the combustion chamber is an intake valve. The first mechanical part of your engine that the exhaust gas passes on its way out of the car is an exhaust valve. These are important elements in the power equation because they are usually the tightest point in your flow.

All modern Subarus use a 4-valve per cylinder design. This means two intake valves and two exhaust valves to feed and exhaust each piston. Valves are moving parts, and they can wear out, break, bend, and burn. Most engines, even today, use two valves per cylinder because it's cheaper to make them that way. But there are good reasons to use four. The most important reason, highly simplified here, is that with everything else being equal, two smaller valves can flow more gas than one larger valve. This is because you can generally get more circumferential area out of two smaller valves—ergo, better flow.

But since you've already got four valves in your Subaru, what can you do to improve valve flow? You can get larger valves (within the limits of the head) and different valves are "cut" or "ground" in different ways. Some of those ways flow better than others. If you're having a custom engine built, talk to your engine builder. The correct grind for your application varies based on many other factors, but it's always good to ask the question.

Getting Air Into Your Engine

This section looks at some of the leading products for getting air into your engine.

Mass Airflow and Manifold Absolute Pressure

Naturally aspirated Subarus through 1999 and turbocharged Subarus through to the present day use MAF sensors in their intake flow. MAF stands for Mass Air Flow, and the MAF sensor is a delicate little device that tells the ECU how much air is coming in through the air filter. Positioning the MAF is crucial if you want to get an accurate reading—and you do want an accurate reading or your mixture will be wrong. Subaru MAF sensors use a "hot wire" design that measures the amount of air passing through by the "wind chill" on the filament. A secondary intake air temperature sensor corrects the MAF output for the temperature of the incoming air. Because the MAF output depends on accurate cooling of the hot wire, these devices are very susceptible to dirt and oil. It is vital that you use a high-quality air filter (and don't over-wet the oiled varieties!) to keep your MAF clean and functioning correctly.

MAP stands for Manifold Absolute Pressure. Naturally aspirated Subarus from 2000 to 2004 use a MAP device to measure airflow. In 2005, the naturally aspirated models went back to a MAF-based system. Turbocharged Subarus from 2002–onwards use a MAP device in addition to a MAF. This device works in concert with the intake air temperature sensor to perform essentially the same function as a MAF sensor. This redundant system helps to protect your car, and ensure accurate mixture control.

It's important to know what system your car uses because intakes are built to accommodate a MAF sensor or not. If your car uses a MAF, make sure your aftermarket inlet has a mounting point for one. Another factor to consider is the size and shape of the pipe where the MAF sensor lives. The MAF measures airflow by the cooling of the hot wire, and the ECU calculates how much air it has by assuming that you're using the stock intake. If you change to an intake that is even slightly smaller or larger, then the ECU will not make the correct calculation.

Finally this section talks about turbo inlet hoses. These are placed between the air filter/MAF assembly and the turbo. Turbo inlet hoses include several attachment points for vacuum lines that go to other places on the engine. These lines must be refitted correctly for the engine to run properly with an aftermarket inlet hose.

Air Filters, MAF and Inlet Hoses

Usually the first part of your car that the in-taken air encounters is the air filter. There may be a factory air intake that leads to the filter, or an aftermarket cold air pipe, and we'll consider these part of the filter assembly because they're generally upgraded as a unit.

What you want for an air filter is to have the least restrictive system you can possibly find that provides clean cold air to your engine. You really do need a filter, though, especially with a turbocharger, since all kinds of stuff can get sucked into your system otherwise. Nothing good has ever been reported about feeding a small rock to a turbocharger compressor wheel.

Another improvement you might consider is what racers call a cold air box. The stock system draws air from near the engine bay's right front corner—where a great deal of dust, water, and other yuck is flying around. Most aftermarket intakes pull in air that has passed through your car's radiator or intercooler (or both) and is hanging around your hot engine bay. To bring in truly fresh air requires a long intake to pull air from a protected pocket in the fender well or some ducting and separation of your intake point from the rest of your engine bay. This requires custom work, but if done right it sets you apart in both performance and engine bay dress-up.

Leading products for initial air induction include:

Perrin Performance Panel Air Filter

This is the most basic improvement you can make. Simply replace your stock paper or cloth filter with this drop-in upgrade for better flow through your stock system.

COBB Tuning SF Intake System

This intake system features an oiled-cloth filter element similar to a K&N filter. But the key feature of this system is a classically shaped velocity stack leading to an "airflow straightener." COBB says it designed the stack and the straightener grid to smooth out the incoming air as it passes the Mass Air Flow sensor for precise readings.

COBB makes some of best products on the market for Subarus of all kinds, and it has tested this product to make sure it won't throw off the MAF reading. (Photo courtesy of COBB Tuning)

This is what happens when you don't filter the air coming into your system. Some small rock or a loose washer turns your turbo into an impressive paperweight in a millisecond.

If you do nothing else, installing a filter like this one helps your engine breathe more easily. (Photo courtesy of Perrin Performance)

TurboXS Short Intake

The TurboXS intake system uses the K&N brand filter, with polished aluminum trim to dress up your engine bay. TurboXS says that its product is engineered to maintain the correct mass airflow sensor signal when the stock unit is plugged into the intake.

Perrin Performance Intakes

Perrin Performance offers a wide range of intakes for many Imprezas, Foresters, and Legacies. Perrin emphasizes correct placement of the MAF for correct readings. Perrin products are well known for quality, and use brightly colored silicone connector hoses for engine bay dress-up. The short intake is an easy install, while the long intake offers cooler air from a pocket in the fender well outside the engine bay.

Perrin Performance Inlet Hose

The Perrin Performance turbo inlet pipe is made of reinforced silicone. The stock inlet hose is made of plastic and has several design flaws, including a "bellows" section for flexibility that reduces airflow and tight places along the bend of the inlet. Perrin states that due to a smooth 3-inch profile maintained through all bends, its product increases intake airflow rate and air volume. A main feature of the Perrin product is that by shifting the auxiliary vacuum fittings forward, it has greatly simplified the installation process. The Perrin inlet pipe can be installed without removing the intake plenum, which reduces the installation time to less than one hour.

This photo shows the difference between the stock turbo inlet pipe and the Perrin aftermarket silicone pipe. The aftermarket unit offers smooth flow, without the bellows Subaru molded into its pipe for installation purposes. (Photo courtesy of Perrin Performance)

Throttle Bodies

When you "step on the gas," what you're really doing is opening up a throttle—rotating a plate in tube to allow more air to pass into your engine. The ECU then decides how much fuel to send along with this air. Every bit of air that makes power in your engine passes through the throttle body. By improving the airflow through the throttle, you help your engine make power smoothly. So, of course, it's an area where you can see some improvement.

This is the popular short intake that installs in minutes in any WRX, STI, or Forester XT. (Photo courtesy of Perrin Performance)

This intake pulls air from a pocket outside the engine bay for cooler intake temperatures. However, this kit does not fit if you're using a front mount intercooler. (Photo courtesy of Perrin Performance)

The stock throttle has a large shaft in the middle of the butterfly valve. That shaft is in the airflow at wide-open throttle, and the bore isn't smoothed out, either.

Proflow Design Throttle Body

Proflow Design modifies a stock throttle body, smoothing out the passage for increased airflow. These products use polished stainless steel throttle plates and low-profile fasteners to smooth the airflow.

Proflow machines the bore into a smooth-flowing horn, and eliminates the plate shaft for better flow.

Getting Fuel into Your Engine

The stock Subaru fueling system is based on the engine management map of the stock Subaru. The system has enough adjustability to let you improve your horsepower somewhat with intake and exhaust upgrades, but once you start changing to a larger turbo and really feeding more air to the engine, you also need to upgrade your ability to feed fuel. This means changing your injectors and fuel rails as well as your ECU. Your engine tuner should tell you when improving fuel flow is necessary, and many aftermarket products include information about necessary fuel flow requirements.

Fuel Pumps, Fuel Rails and Injectors

Among the upgrades to a Subaru fueling system, the first stage in getting gasoline from your tank to your engine is the fuel pump. In a performance engine, the stock pump may not flow enough fuel to keep pressure up. Aftermarket fuel pumps and pressure regulators are readily available to provide adequate fuel to the components down the line.

Once in the engine bay, the fuel

The stock air filter assembly takes up a lot of space; there's plenty of room to fit an aftermarket filter in the WRX.

travels to a distribution block—just an aluminum block drilled to divide the single pressurized fuel stream into four streams—one for each cylinder in the engine. These streams run through fuel rails that deliver the gasoline to each cylinder in your engine. Excess fuel is routed back to your fuel tank from the distribution block.

Finally, the fuel arrives at the injectors, which are valved jets that squirt a measured amount of fuel into each cylinder according to timing and volume instructions from the ECU. Injectors are generally measured by the amount of fuel they can inject into your

You're looking at the business end of an STI fuel injector. Fuel is sprayed out of those holes into the incoming airstream.

intake stream, and this measurement is expressed in cubic centimeters (cc). Factory injectors are rated to flow up to 420cc on the WRX 2.0-liter engine, and 550cc on the STI 2.5-liter engine.

Leading fuel delivery products on the market include:

Perrin Fuel Rail Kit for WRX and STI

Perrin's fuel rail kits are designed with an equal-pressure distribution

Fuel System Cautions

Whenever you work on your fuel injectors and the fuel injection system, you need to realize that this system depends on absolute cleanliness and perfect sealing. You should always work on this system in a clean environment and use new seals every time you remove the injectors from your car. A damaged seal, a poorly lubricated seal, or a small piece of foreign matter in the injector area can cause a high-pressure fuel or air leak into your engine, with disastrous consequences.

Perrin top or side feed fuel rails are designed to flow more fuel, and flow it evenly to meet the needs of high-flow injectors. (Photo courtesy of Perrin Performance)

block bolted onto the intake manifold. The factory fuel pressure regulator is retained, and the distribution block has a fitment for an aftermarket fuel pressure gauge sensor if you want one. The lines are all steel braided and coated with Teflon inside for better flow compared to rubber lines, and the system uses proven AN fittings for excellent sealing. The top-feed kits fit all years of WRX, 2007 and later STI, and 2006 and later Legacy GT, while the side-feed kits fit 2004–2006 Forester XT, 2004–2006 STI, and 2005 Legacy GT.

Perrin offers modified fuel injectors that increase flow to any Subaru application. Maximum flow rates are available according to your needs. (Photo courtesy of Perrin Performance)

740cc Perrin Fuel Injectors for WRX

Perrin provides a set of modified stock injectors that are tested to flow 740cc. Perrin recommends this upgrade for cars that are going beyond 300 wheel horsepower. Perrin modifies the injectors after first capping off the fuel inlet to prevent contamination. It

then removes the internal screen that limits flow, and finally it cleans up the injector tip to remove any machine filing, and to ensure a smooth surface that will not damage the seal.

816cc Perrin Fuel Injectors for STI

Perrin made this set of injectors to surpass the factory 550cc injector limitation of 350 crank horsepower on the STI. The Perrin STI Injectors flow 816cc. These injectors are designed for cars with large turbo kits making 400+ horsepower. If you use high-flow injectors, you should also perform a fuel pump upgrade at the same time you install this injector upgrade to compensate for the increased fuel-delivery requirements.

Controlling the Engine: ECU Upgrades

In an older car, fuel delivery and ignition tuning were controlled by the operation of mechanical parts. The car's gas pedal opened a butterfly valve in the carburetor, and manifold vacuum sucked some gasoline and air into the cylinders. Various pumps and reservoirs added a squirt of raw fuel to discourage balking as the system responded to increased throttle. Carburetor designs ranged from astonishingly simple to ingeniously simple. And you tuned them by changing the jets (little brass nozzles) or filing a tapered needle, or sometimes adjusting a tapered screw.

Similarly, the ignition system was a rotating distributor driven off of the camshaft, and an additional cam in the distributor actuated a set of electrical contact points that controlled how long the high-tension ignition coil was allowed to "fill" with electricity before it was discharged as a spark. You adjusted this system by twisting the distributor, setting the point gap with feeler gauges, and buying more or less powerful coils.

To find your car's ECU, you have to peel up the carpet in the passenger foot well and then unscrew a protective plate.

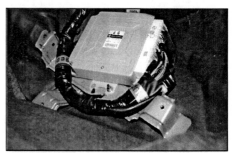

The stock ECU doesn't look like much, but it's the brains of the system, and this is where most of the tuning happens. Piggyback ECUs plug into this unit, and standalones replace it.

Today, all those functions are performed by the ECU—the Engine (or Electronic) Control Unit, also called the Engine Management System, the "chip," or the Computer. The ECU controls the timing and force of the spark, typically with individual coils for each spark plug. The ECU also controls the amount and timing of fuel delivery through the fuel injection system, and it controls the amount of boost pressure from the turbocharger.

The ECU almost always includes a top speed and maximum RPM governor. In some automatic transmission cars, such as the 2007 Legacies with SI-Drive, the ECU controls shift points as well.

The ECU is your car's brain, and it operates using input from various sensors throughout the intake, combustion, and exhaust systems. It adjusts mixture and timing-based indications of air density coming into the engine combustion performance, and exhaust gas composition and temperature. In cars with traction control and "fly-by-wire" throttle, the ECU may take input from the brakes or differentials to detect a loss of traction, and respond by making changes to reduce torque to get the car back under control.

Most 1996 and later OBD II-compliant ECU computers use "flash" memory—similar to the re-writable memory chip in a digital camera or thumb drive. Information is retained in the memory even if you completely disconnect its power source. There is a persistent myth that you are limited to 100 reflashes on your ECU, but this has been disproved in practice. If you are concerned about this potential problem, the COBB AccessPORT uses a reflash technique that does not increment your reflash count.

When an automaker builds a car, they play it safe with the ECU programming. They need to meet emissions standards, fuel economy standards, and perhaps most importantly, longevity standards for their products. So they program the ECU to accept whatever kind of fuel their cars may have to drink, a wide range of altitudes at which the cars may have to operate, and a big safety margin to keep the engines from blowing up.

Obviously then, the ECU is an excellent place to find some more performance. But it's also about the most difficult thing for the average car buyer to really understand. ECU programming is complex, and the vast majority of us are not qualified to tinker with it. But the market has many products with proven programs that optimize your car's performance with the specific hardware modifications you have made.

For the Subaru, you can choose from three levels of ECU upgrades. These are a packaged or custom reflash of the stock ECU, a "piggyback" unit that works in addition to your stock ECU, and a complete standalone replacement ECU computer. It is not fair to say that any of these options is natively better than the others—each

of these options has its place depending on your needs. Reflashing your stock ECU is cheaper than buying a piggyback unit, and a piggyback is generally cheaper than a full computer replacement, but you can get great performance improvements on the stock engine from a simple packaged reflash you can install yourself. A custom reflash such as the EcuTek or COBB's ProTuner generally requires an experienced tuner, but the result is customized to your car and your performance needs.

Legal Issues and Your ECU

There's one more thing you need to know about changing your ECU—it's an emissions-control device and covered under the same federal law that governs your catalytic converters—it's against federal law to tamper with an emissions-control device in any way on a car that is registered and driven on the public roads. These products should be considered for dedicated racecars only.

The ECU Lowdown with Sean Sexton of Rallitek/IPD

Sean Sexton is the man behind Rallitek Subaru Performance. His shop has built hundreds of high-performance Subarus of all kinds, and he knows his way around an ECU. I asked him to explain the pros and cons of the various ECU modifications available on the market today.

▶ *JZ: What's so great about a replacement standalone ECU?*
SS: Standalones allow real-time full programming of every aspect of your engine's performance. You've got complete control over anything and everything. They can also run peripheral devices like water sprays and shift lights for you.

The downside is that they're very difficult to program, because you've got to program everything. You really need to know what you're doing. You have to know your software very well, and you need to know what that motor's asking you for in terms of crank, cold

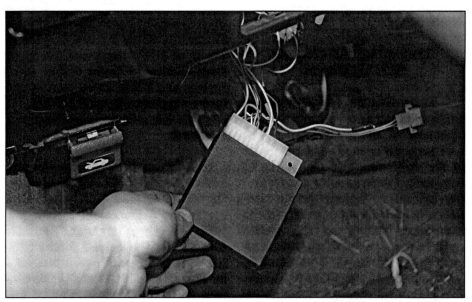

Even if you have a car without OBD II and a flashable ECU, you can still take advantage of tuning with a piggyback. This 1991 Legacy Turbo uses a Perfect-Power 6 from Rallitek/IPD.

THE INDUCTION SYSTEM

start, hot start, everything. They usually come with a base map that's got
some of that stuff figured out for you.
Usually with a standalone, you've got a
customer that comes in and you're
going to spend a day or a week with the
car getting that stuff down just right. If
you put standalone in your own car,
you're probably going to spend a year
getting it just right. The factory spent
millions of dollars get everything to
start and be smooth and be just perfect.
So a standalone has the most power,
and the ability to do multiple maps,
but it's also the most difficult.

Also, many standalones have no
OBD II or emissions information. If
you have to pass emissions tests by
reading the computer codes, they
might not be there. So the standalone
is definitely the best choice for a racecar that doesn't have to pass emissions tests.

JZ: What about the piggybacks?
SS: You're a little bit limited with a piggyback. They get difficult when you
change the fuel injectors. When you
put big injectors in, you now have to
go back and rescale everything that's
in the closed loop. You have to correct
the tuning for that. As the tune gets
complicated, you start running out of
tuning power from the little piggybacks. The advantage of piggybacks is
that for the first stage or two, they're
easy to program, you can program
them on the fly, and they can run your
peripheral toys.

The piggyback is the best choice
for the guy who's doing mild mods,
or who wants to get in and do his
own programming. They only come
into play under full load or high
RPM—all the light cruising stuff is
closed-loop, and you don't want to
get in and mess with that unless
you're doing corrective tuning, such
as if you put in big cams and now the
thing's running too lean and you
need to correct for that. But you
don't want to change the fuel target
from 14.7 to 16. The stock ECU
counter-corrects for that. The stock
computer is very sharp on that stuff.

JZ: And what about a reflash?
SS: The reflash has just as much
power as the standalones and they're
just as complicated as the standalones, but there's no external wiring
coming out of the ECU that you can
use to run any peripherals. Then also
with the EcuTek reflash, you can't do
anything on the fly. The car has to be
stopped, turned off, go under the
dash, plug some wires in—it's do a
flash, make a run, and log data, then
go back and do it again.

*JZ: Can you combine a reflash and a
piggyback?*
SS: Oh yes, a lot of times you'll use
both of them together. For example,
someone's got their piggyback, but
they want to go above stage 2 and now
they want injectors and the turbo and
all of that. Well, you can tune out all
the base parameters with your reflash,
like different injector sizes so you don't
have to rescale your injectors, and deal
with all of those basics. Then you can
stabilize your high-det and low-det
maps and make them all the same so
the ECU can't "walk around" on you.
Then you can let the customer do the
rest of his own programming on the
piggyback to run his water spray and
his shift light and even his open loop
programming at the high end.∎

Reflashes
The following popular reflash
products are widely available on the
market. Most reflash products consist
of an OBD II cable and a CD-ROM,
designed to work on a standard laptop
computer.

COBB AccessPORT 2.0
The AccessPORT 2.0 allows you
the ability to upload pre-programmed
maps to the Engine Control Unit
(ECU) via the OBD II diagnosis port
located below your steering wheel. The
system first makes a backup copy of
your stock ECU programming, so you
can come back to it at any time.
COBB's system uses a proprietary "lim-
itless" map changing system that does
not subtract from any reflash limit.

*The COBB AccessPORT is one of the
most popular reflash products on the
market because of its convenient
interface and great results. (Photo
courtesy of COBB Tuning)*

The AccessPORT is available for all turbocharged 2.0 and 2.5-liter Subarus.

The handheld AccessPORT can
hold up to 10 completely separate
maps at once, ready to be uploaded as
you drive. For example, you can drive
around with a high-performance map
in your hot rod, and switch it to a
"valet mode" to make sure others don't
over-work your car. Also, you can use
the AccessPORT for Digital Gauge Dis-
plays and Quarter-Mile Times, as well
as several other functions. You can
download new maps from COBB's
website and install them on your
AccessPORT as they become available.

The original AccessPORT 1.0 was
discontinued in October, 2006, with
the rollout of the 2.0 model.

EcuTek EasyECU
EcuTek's EasyECU product is limited to the "drive-by-wire" EJ255 and
EJ257 cars. This product also includes
EcuTek's Delta Dash product for diag-
nostic purposes. With the EasyECU,
EcuTek irrevocably links the software
to your car, so you can't use it to
reflash all your friends' cars, too. You
buy the EasyECU and a set of maps
from a tuner who deals in EcuTek
products, and then install it yourself.

Then you use the Delta Dash product to record your results, and send them back to the Tuner in an iterative process that does not require your presence at the Tuner's shop.

EcuTek ProECU

This is the original EcuTek reflash that thousands of people have used. EcuTek's ProECU is sold only to professional tuners, and you have to take your car to a tuner shop and have the tuner do the updates for you. The EcuTek reflash is limited to turbocharged cars.

EcuTek Delta Dash

Delta Dash allows you to display and log your engine's performance readout live on a laptop through your OBD II port and a special EcuTek cable. This allows you to send real-world information to your tuner to further optimize your car's performance.

Piggybacks

Piggyback ECUs were among the very first products available to alter your car's ECU programming in the days before the OBD II standard allowed reflashing. With the availability of reflash in the modern era, the popularity of piggybacks has fallen off. They are still a popular lower-cost choice for the pre-OBD II 1991–1994 Turbo Legacy. The following products are representative of what's available in piggyback ECU units today.

PerfectPower Smart Tuner 7

The PerfectPower line has been around a long time and is a popular product for both naturally aspirated and turbocharged cars, but one drawback is that it does require some wiring work. The PerfectPower is not a unit that an inexperienced user should try to install and tune. Consider this one if you have a good professional lined up for the installation.

TurboXS UTEC

The TurboXS UTEC piggyback also works for naturally aspirated as well as turbocharged cars. This unit requires no wire cutting or soldering—it simply plugs into your car's stock wiring harness. Like most piggyback units, the UTEC does not alter the factory ECU programming under normal driving conditions. The low-rev, low-power "closed loop" ECU control is maintained, and then the UTEC takes over when you go to "open loop" running above 4,500 rpm. TurboXS says that the UTEC is OBD II compliant and invisible to emissions-testing equipment that uses the OBD II port.

The UTEC comes with several pre-programmed maps, and you can program five different custom maps. The multi-map capability allows you to use the TurboXS remote map selector to switch between the five maps or stock mode on the fly. You can also run peripheral devices from the UTEC.

TurboXS DTEC

TurboXS also makes the DTEC Fuel Computer—known as the DTEC-FC. This unit is be used on cars with modified fuel systems (such as larger injectors) to restore the correct amount of fuel relative your MAF/MAP signals. The DTEC-FC intercepts and changes the main load signal to the factory ECU, correcting for your increased fuel delivery capacity. This product uses a Nintendo Game Boy as its user interface.

Unichip

The Unichip is a completely programmable piggyback ECU. This unit can channel over 53,000 fuel and ignition parameters through your stock ECU. Unichip says their products are compatible with OBD I and OBD II vehicles.

While Unichip has pre-programmed maps for many vehicles, it can and will put your car on the dyno and create a custom map and install it on its product in your car. The Unichip can be programmed to control virtually anything in your engine that the ECU controls and a few more things besides, such as nitrous-oxide delivery and launch control for drag racing.

Standalones

The following products illustrate the state of the art today in standalone ECUs. Dozens of base maps are available from the manufacturers and on the Internet to get you started with any of these standalones.

MoTeC M800

The MoTeC M800 and M880 are general purpose ECUs—they can be used with almost any EFI-equipped engine. The M800 can control up to eight high flow injectors. The M800 supports most of the existing sensors used in a Subaru, so you don't have to

The PerfectPower line is among the leading piggybacks for its ability to run peripheral products such as an intercooler sprayer or shift light.

buy a whole bank of replacements. The MoTeC M800 fully supports drive-by-wire as well.

MoTeC M4

The M4 is MoTeC's four cylinder sequential ECU. This unit is designed to provide you with the same programming capability as the M800 at a lower cost. The M800 is fully programmable to manage up to a 12-cylinder engine, while the M4 is scaled back for a 4-cylinder application (though it can support more cylinders if need be). The M4 uses a full real-time three-dimensional map of your engine speed, throttle position, and MAF/MAP inputs. The M4 supports sequential injector tuning for precise fuel delivery. This unit is also programmable to support launch and traction control. The M4 uses flash memory and can be reflashed at any time.

AEM

AEM offers a standalone ECU that plugs directly into your car's factory ECU harness. This "plug and play" unit requires no additional wiring or hardware. The ECU uses a Windows-based control program—it even has a "wizard" to help you create an initial base map customized to the modifications you've already made to your car. This system is fully programmable and includes support for factory sensors, traction control, boost control, rev limiters, two-step launch control, wet or dry nitrous control, and peripheral devices.

Link Engine Management WRXLinkG3

Link Engine Management in New Zealand has recently released the WRXLinkG3 direct replacement for 2002+ WRX and STI cars. Link's practical experience in rally and other motorsports brings its products a great deal of street credibility. Like the AEM unit, this product is a plug and play replacement for the stock ECU. The control software for this unit runs on Windows, and of course, it supports peripheral devices.

Hydra Nemesis

Element Tuning in Maryland is a distributor of the Hydra Nemesis ECU from Singapore. Additionally, its website contains several versions of tuning guide to help you use the Hydra to best effect. The plug-and-play Nemesis supports naturally aspirated cars since 1999 in addition to the turbocharged models. Advanced features in the Nemesis include a dedicated variable speed fuel pump signal for the WRX which not all standalone systems support. Like the others, this system uses Windows-based software for a programming interface, or you can download Element's proven "stage" maps and use those.

Finally, do hang on to your stock ECU if you ever plan to restore the stock setup.

About Dynamometers

One quick note about dynos—An experienced technician can assist you in fine-tuning your programming by using a dynamometer (also known as a dyno) to provide real-time power readings as the technician adjusts the programming.

There are bench dynos that measure the engine's power before it's installed in the car, there are chassis dynos where you park your car on a set of big rollers and drive with the tires on, and there are chassis dynos (as shown in the photo) that bolt to your wheel hubs. But all kinds of dynos operate by measuring your car's ability to overcome resistance and do work, and their readouts are adjustable. Given the same car and the same conditions, any dyno may read relatively higher or lower than another. This doesn't matter. What matters is the relative improvement you get on a given dyno when tuning your car. People love to brag on their dyno sheets, and tuning shops obviously want their customers to walk away happy and they want a reputation for getting more power out of the same car than their competitors. Choose your tuner carefully with good common sense.

An old-fashioned chassis dyno was a pair of rollers. You parked your car on it and drove the car to measure wheel horsepower. New dynos bolt right to your hubs to measure their turning power.

S-A DESIGN

TURBOCHARGERS AND RELATED COMPONENTS

This Legacy GT belongs to the folks at PDXTuning, which is home to some of the best Subaru tuners in the Pacific Northwest.

Forced Induction or Naturally Aspirated?

One of the decisions people make when selecting a car is whether to purchase a turbocharged or a "naturally aspirated" model. In a naturally aspirated model, air and fuel is sucked through the air filter and into the combustion chambers through the motion of the piston while the intake valve is open. No force other than the vacuum generated by moving pistons puts air into the combustion chamber. In a turbocharged engine, exhaust gases are used to turn a turbine wheel attached to a compressor wheel that pressurizes the air going into the combustion chambers. The effect of the turbocharger is to artificially increase the amount of air put through the engine. The stock WRX turbocharger, for example, boosts normal air pressure by about 11 to 13 psi. The engine computer can then add more fuel, which results in more power to turn the engine.

Of course, a turbocharged engine is also more complex than a naturally aspirated model, has more moving parts to break, and works under more extreme conditions.

About Turbochargers, with Robert Young of Forced Performance

Turbochargers are not generally well understood, so let's turn to the experts for a lesson. Robert Young is a scientist and engineer with Forced Performance, a well-known manufacturer of turbochargers. You can find out more by reading the FAQ at www.forcedperformance.com.

▶ *JZ: Tell us about Subaru turbochargers.*
RY: The factory turbocharger on the 2-liter engine is a Mitsubishi TD04 turbocharger. It's got a 14T compressor designation, and it flows approximately 350 to 370 cfm. The later 2.5-liter engines were equipped with a variety of IHI turbochargers such as the VF34 and VF39, which still keep you under the 450 CFM rating. Small turbos like that are very responsive on the big 2.5-liter engine.

Of course the factory likes it that way: it wants you to not notice turbo lag, it wants you to think you're driving a V-8 with no lag. That's why it

A cutaway view of a Turbonetics turbocharger: from left to right, you can see the turbine housing and exhaust turbine wheel, the bearings with threaded oil fittings, the compressor wheel and volute, and the intake.

configures the turbochargers with small nozzle areas in the turbine housing, small A/R ratios for the turbine housing, small turbine blades, and small compressor blades. The factory is running its turbos behind catalytic converters, factory air filters—things like that—which tend to be sort of restrictive. In order to get the turbocharger to spool up with those constraints, (factory manifolds, factory headers, factory catalytic converters, factory air filters) you need to size the turbo kind of small, so that it is responsive. And most customers are pretty satisfied with the response of their factory turbo on its factory engine with the factory exhaust system in place.

JZ: You've used several terms, like A/R, that I'm not familiar with. Can you explain?

RY: The A/R ratio of the housing is the ratio of the nozzle area of the housing to the radius outward of that area from the center of rotation of the shaft. It's the area that exists in the housing. Most IHI and Mitsubishi housings are not characterized in A/R ratio. They're just simply described as the A part of

This cutaway shot shows how the volute gets smaller as it circles the compressor wheel.

the A/R ratio. They're characterized by the square area of their nozzle. So when we say we have a 6, 7, or 8 centimeter housing, what we're actually meaning to say, for example, is that we have a 7 square centimeter nozzle in our housing. But due to the number of times we end up saying the name, we just call it a 6 or 7 or 8 centimeter housing.

But as far as A/R method of characterizing turbine housings, that's normally found only in Garrett turbochargers. Mitsubishi and IHI just use the square area of the nozzle.

Inside of a turbocharger exhaust housing, you have a very unique shape. It's very similar to a snail shell. And there's a very specific geometric pattern and formula that's used to determine what each cross-sectional area is at each changing angle as you rotate 360 degrees around the housing. Now, you characterize the size of the housing by the first cross sectional area of the volute. So a 7cm housing has a 7cm squared area to its first cross sectional volute in the housing. Each next cross-sectional area, each 5 degree or each infinitesimally small degree that the volute gets smaller as it turns around. It starts at 7 and then gets incrementally smaller all the way around. And it's the same with 8 or 9 centimeter housings—they start at 8 or 9 square centimeters and get incrementally smaller all the way around. They all end at the same cross sectional area at the end of the volute, which is zero. So the different size housings change the exhaust gas velocity according to the exhaust gas mass flow graph. If you graph exhaust gas velocity into the turbine wheel entry per mass flow, it would be very different for a 6-cm housing versus a 9-cm housing. It affects how fast your turbo spools up as well as when the flow "chokes" on the housing.

JZ: How should someone go about improving turbo performance?
RY: When you start changing parts, the first things you change are the exhaust system, the catalytic converter gets removed in a lot of cases, and aftermarket headers are put in place. Most people run a 2-3/4, 3 inch, maybe even 3-1/2 inch exhaust system on their cars, which really reduces the amount of pressure at the turbine outlet. Reducing the pressure at the turbine outlet makes it very easy to produce a

This is the turbine wheel. Note that the vanes are designed differently from the compressor wheel.

higher pressure ratio across the turbine. And when you do that, you accelerate turbine spool-up significantly. So what you can do is take out the small factory turbo and the restrictive factory exhaust system, and replace them with a larger turbocharger and a larger exhaust system, and you can get really similar spool up and torque characteristics to the stock

Compare this turbine wheel to the previous cutaway photo to see a difference in the design of the turbine blades and the overall size of the turbine.

turbo at the bottom end, but have tremendously improved power performance from the mid-range on out to redline. That's kind of the basic concept of going from the stock small turbo to the bigger aftermarket turbochargers such as the Forced Performance 20G or Forced Performance Green model or Red model for higher-horsepower applications.

And of course, the farther you take this, the more inclined you're going to be to modify things such, as maybe going to a front mount intercooler, replacing your factory 550cc injectors with larger 700 or 800cc injectors, depending on whatever your

ECU programmer recommends. Most people are going to install something like an ECU reflash or something like that. A variety of people are very proficient at reflashing these cars and have libraries of parts combinations. In a lot of cases, you can get a reflashed ECU through the mail that is a pretty good match for the combination of parts you have on your car.

JZ: So you're saying that in the quest for more power, it's not simply enough to change one characteristic, such as bolting on a bigger turbo. When you get a bigger turbo, you need to think about the fact that the engine produces power by burning air and fuel, and you can't just deliver more boost, you also need to deliver more fuel, hence the larger injectors. Generally, you need to de-restrict the flow of the air pump that is the engine.
RY: You can't lose sight of the fact that all the air that you're going to use to make your horsepower has to come in through the air filter, and go out through the tailpipe. The whole path has to be de-restricted. If you were watering your lawn, you wouldn't go right in the middle of your hose and splice in a soda pop straw. If you looked at your hose while you were watering your lawn and you realized not much water was coming out, and you looked at the length of hose and realized it was kinked in the middle, you'd unkink it and fix your problem. That's basically what you've got to do with turbocharged engines. You've got to figure out where the kink in the hose is, where's the restriction, and correct it.

JZ: You talked about selecting a turbo in consultation with engine tuner. Is that a requirement for any car as sophisticated as a Subaru?
RY: Correct. You're probably kidding yourself if you think you can do this all on your own. Most people are pretty capable of making a nice selection of hard parts. What most people are unable to do is achieve a software or programming solution to their prob-

lem, which is either going to come from a standalone computer or a reprogramming of the factory computer.

JZ: If a person shows up with a new Subaru and says they want to buy a Forced Performance turbo for it, what do you suggest as Stage 1 or Stage 2 products?

RY: I'll assume we're dealing with the STI and the 2.5-liter engine. It's the most popular avenue for hot rodders. The first thing you want to do is recognize that the factory turbo is already about 450 cfm, so it's already very close to what you would consider the first upgrade you'd do to the 2-liter. The small style, like 16G turbochargers, 500 cfm, 550 cfm, are not a real significant upgrade to the VF39 turbo that you'd find on the car from the factory. Your upgrade path for the 2.5-liter pretty much starts at the 600 cfm 18G, then the next turbocharger in line is the 650 cfm 20G, then the next turbocharger in line is the 730 cfm Forced Performance Green model, then after that you have the 850-cfm Forced Performance Red model. That takes you all the way from 350 to 400 wheel horsepower at the bottom end of the spectrum up to 520 or more wheel horsepower at the high end of the spectrum.

JZ: At those high horsepower levels, you need to think about bottom end improvements, right?

RY: Most people don't go beyond about 450 wheel horsepower with the factory engine in an unmodified format. As far as most consumers go, most bolt-on consumers aren't up for removing the engine and rebuilding and preparing it for high-boost pressure and leaded race gas. This is the bulk of the community. Most people have a car and they want to make some do-it-yourself tweaks to it, and maybe bring in a professional to help them with the ECU work. For the most part, most people are doing this because they get a kick out of it and they're really hands-on. Or at least they want to be the project manager. Maybe they don't want to turn wrenches, but they want to micromanage the whole project, and that is good.

In cases like that, most guys are going to leave the motor alone and stick with the bolt-ons. Assume that the end of the road for a factory engine is 400 to 450 wheel horsepower with a Green model on the car. Normally the parts that go on the car

in conjunction with that are the Green model turbocharger, 3-inch turbo-back exhaust system, an improved front-mount intercooler, some 800cc injectors, upgrade fuel pump, and modification to delete the Tumble Generator Valves. And probably an upgrade of the blow-off valve, an upgrade of the air intake pipe, and an ECU reflash by a company like PDXTuning, Perrin Performance, COBB and others.

JZ: That brings us to boost—you hear a lot of people talk about how much boost they run. We've talked about how the turbos make boost and the things you do to make your turbo flow, but what if I have a stock system and I put a manual boost controller on it and I pump up my boost—is that going to help me very much?

RY: You'll make another 10 to 20 horsepower doing that. If you do the exhaust system upgrades, put a manual boost controller on your car and turn the boost up, the factory ECU has enough width to its internal fuel trimming capacity to recognize that things are starting to run leaner than they used to and trim up the injector pulse width. There is a little bit of trim

This is the legendary Forced Performance Red model, which can help your engine make up to 520 wheel horsepower with the right combination of parts.

A blow-off valve releases the shock of a pressure wave bouncing through your intake system when you release the throttle.

adjustability inside the unmodified factory ECU to deal with 10 to 15 horsepower swings. Past that you've got to modify the ECU code. Once you get to the 350 wheel horsepower level, you'll find that the factory injectors are no longer adequate.

JZ: Where does the blow-off valve come into the picture?

RY: You've got a column of air, and if you've got a front-mount intercooler, this column of air is about 6 or 10 feet long. And this column of air is moving very fast. It takes a fraction of a second for that air to make it from one end of that tube to the other. So you have a lot of inertia in the air, and when you get to 7,500 rpm and you lift your foot off the throttle and the throttle plate closes, where's that air going? It's got to come to a complete stop, and it doesn't take long for that pressure wave to bounce all the way back through the intake system and back to the turbo, and try to bend the shaft and the blades on the turbocharger, and cause other havoc there. The turbo goes from 110,000 to 120,000 rpm down to 10,000 rpm at that same instant in time. When you shift into the next gear and apply wide open throttle, suddenly your turbo has to accelerate from 10,000 rpm all the way back up to 110,000 rpm again. That's lag. With a very high capacity blow off valve in the system, that air doesn't just stop, and it doesn't cause the turbocharger to lose 100,000 rpm of shaft speed instantaneously. That blow off valve can open, the air can exit the blow off valve, and the turbocharger loses much less shaft speed in the process. Recovering boost pressure after a shift can be much more rapid if you use a large blow-off valve.

JZ: What about a waste gate? We don't often hear people talking about improving their waste gates.

RY: A lot of people get turned around on waste gate function. Here's why—a lot of people think, "Oh, I run really high boost, I need a really big waste gate." That's not true at all. If you run

really high boost, you probably want to reroute very little of your exhaust gas around your turbine. You need to run most of your exhaust gas through your turbine to maintain 100,000+ rpm on your turbo shaft to get the highest performance out of that compressor that's attached to the other side of your turbine.

So, in race applications where you're trying to maintain 25 or 30 psi, you actually need a waste gate that does not have a high flow rate, but has a lot of tension in it to keep the valve shut. And when you get to the 20G and FP Green and Red model turbochargers, we actually stopped using a stock 6 or 7 psi actuator, and replaced it with a 15 psi actuator. There's more

The turbine wheel and wastegate are clearly shown here, looking at the turbo through the downpipe flange.

spring tension maintaining the valve-closed position when your boost controller is calling for the valve to be closed, like during spool up and high boost near redline.

Once you get to the last 1,000 rpm of your engine operating range, you're reaching the maximum capacity of your compressor. That's when you need more turbine flow to maintain that very high shaft speed in the turbocharger. So the waste gate flapper

valve is going to need to begin to close back up at that point. You need extra spring tension to close that valve in the face of the high amount of flow coming through the waste gate passage. With a weak spring and a factory-weight actuator, it is very difficult to get that flapper valve to creep more towards a closed position in the upper RPM range, especially if you're using a factory boost control solenoid in a bleed configuration, because a bleed configuration never removes all the pressure from the actuator. All the bleed is doing is leaking off a percentage of the signal going to the waste gate actuator.

Manual boost controllers operate the opposite way. Manual boost controllers let no signal go to the actuator until a particular boost pressure is reached. You get a little bit better spool up performance and a little reduction of your boost drop-off on the upper end using a manual boost controller in most cases.

JZ: One of the problems a lot of early turbos had was the need to sit and let it idle for 30 seconds before you turned it off to allow oil to flow in and cool everything down. I had a 1982 car with a turbo, and I had to do that.

RY: That was a very good recommendation because in 1982, you didn't have oil that cost $7 or $10 a quart. Today, most people are using a very high-quality synthetic motor oil, and it's virtually impossible to get it to burn. The reason they told you to let the car run for half a minute before you turned it off was the fact that if you turned the car off when the turbocharger was glowing red, the oil stopped flowing. Suddenly the oil is just sitting inside of something that's glowing red. It's just going to burn in place and turn into a carbon deposit right where it's sitting. So your oil feed line, for example, starts to develop arteriosclerosis—carbon deposits building up in your oil line and in the internal passages inside the turbocharger. If you do that for a year, the next thing you know is that there's no more oil flowing through the turbo. So instead of having a heart attack, you have a turbo attack where the turbo just gives up the will to live.

JZ: So should I replace and upgrade the oil lines when I upgrade my turbo?
RY: Generally speaking, any time you're going to remove the factory turbocharger from the car and replace it with an aftermarket upgrade turbocharger, you're going to need a different oil line anyway just for thread compatibility. Most of the time when you run into anyone selling an upgrade turbocharger, you'll notice that they also offer some gaskets, some nuts and bolts, and an oil line at the same time.

Our Forced Performance turbochargers come with new water lines already attached to the turbocharger because the factory water lines are not going to be compatible. Things that bolt onto a Ford won't necessarily bolt onto a Chevy, and things that bolt onto an IHI turbocharger won't necessarily bolt onto a Mitsubishi turbocharger. All of our turbochargers are Mitsubishi-based, and they replace the factory IHI turbos that come on the STI. They're flange-compatible turbochargers, really similar in appearance and footprint, that require very little fitment to get them to install.

One of the things you do want to change, though, is the oil feed line because the factory hard-steel line, in addition to having a small orifice drilled into it, is also very difficult to re-bend and refit to the new turbocharger. You don't want to run the risk of trying to bend your steel line, because you might kink it and reduce its performance.

JZ: I've heard about different vane designs. What do you do to design the vanes on the turbine and compressor wheels?
RY: Generally speaking— and this is universally true with the Subaru turbochargers that we offer— we use high performance blades that already exist

from other applications. We borrow certain blades from other motorsports programs from Garrett and Mitsubishi, and use those blades rather than using the factory blades. For example, if you look at the little turbo that comes on the Subaru Legacy, it is even smaller than the VF39 turbocharger. The entry width on the turbine blade is very narrow, but it serves a purpose. The Legacy is more of a luxury sedan than a performance vehicle, and they need to shift the torque curve even lower in the RPM band than they do in the STI. How do you do this? You get the turbocharger to spool up faster. How do you do that? You increase the exhaust gas velocity as it enters the turbine wheels. You put a small A/R turbine housing on it, and you put a very narrow entry width turbine wheel in it, and that's exactly what you see in the Legacy. In addition to running select Garrett and Mitsubishi blades, we have also begun designing and manufacturing our own unique blades from billet bar stock using a CNC machining process that gives us very accurate control over the exact shape of the blade.

JZ: It seems like a lot of brand names float around, but few actual turbo manufacturers.
RY: The actual manufacturers of turbo housings are IHI, Mitsubishi, and Garrett. You're not going to find anything that's not based on those three brands of turbochargers. What you see is a lot of little micro shops all over the place who decide to rename a product. It may be the same as another product, but they just decide to call it by their own name.

At Forced Performance, we use a mixture of Mitsubishi castings and Garrett castings. In addition, we manufacture some of our own castings and compressor wheels. But we make everything to be basically Mitsubishi compatible. One of the primary design constraints on any turbocharger project that we work on for mass production is that we want it to be able to fit the vehicle with the least amount of modification possible.

So for example on the STI, the car's equipped with IHI and Mitsubishi turbochargers. You don't usually find Mitsubishi here in the USA, but in Europe and Asia, you do find TD05-based Mitsubishi castings. So as a result of that, the castings that are available are either the IHI castings or the Mitsubishi castings. That's what fits the up pipe, that's what fits the down pipe. You use these castings because the customer has already spent $1,500 on an exhaust header and downpipe that fits their factory turbo. If you want to have a product that's useful and performs well, you need to find a way to make these factory-compatible castings perform well and fit the car. This is what we specialize in doing. ∎

Some Example Turbochargers

As mentioned, there are just three major manufacturers of turbo bodies, but many companies put together kits that include components such as intakes, inlets, up and down pipes, and so on. This section looks at a few of the most popular turbos and kits on the market.

Forced Performance 16G Turbocharger for WRX
This water-cooled TD05H-16G-7cm2 turbocharger is a direct fit for the WRX. It has a compressor flow rating of 510 cfm and compressor efficiency

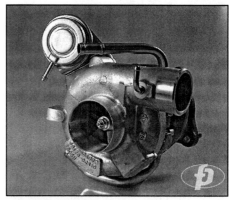

The Forced Performance 16G is a Mitsubishi TD05 body, modified by FP for increased flow. It bolts right on to your 2002–2005 WRX. (Photo courtesy of Forced Performance)

of 77%. This unit is designed as a low-cost easy-install option for your 2.0-liter Subaru up to about 330 wheel horsepower. The FP16G comes fitted with brand new coolant lines and an 8 psi wastegate actuator.

Forced Performance 18T Turbocharger for WRX

The 18T WRX upgrade turbocharger from Forced Performance gets its power from a larger compressor wheel and clipping the stock turbine wheel. Forced Performance says its WRX testers have reported that the turbo provides a substantial increase in mid-range and top-end power, while sacrificing very little boost response. FP says their dyno tests yielded 247 horsepower to the wheels at 15.5 psi. At that level, the power output is approaching the limits of the stock fuel system, so this is about as much turbo as you can use without changing injectors, fuel pump, and ECU mapping. Larger power gains are possible with an upgraded fuel system and higher boost levels.

The FP 18T is about as big a turbo as you can use on a WRX without substantial upgrades elsewhere in the system. (Photo courtesy of Forced Performance)

Forced Performance Green Turbocharger

The Forced Performance Green model is a very large and powerful racing turbocharger that features a 49lb/minute compressor and a huge TDO6 turbine wheel. The FP Green retains the stock Subaru flange pat-

When you get into serious racing power, the FP Green model is a good choice. This turbo can give you over 30 pounds of boost! (Photo courtesy of Forced Performance)

terns. An internal wastegate is standard with an adjustable 15psi high-pressure actuator. This unit is capable of over 30 psi of boost. This turbo features a 2.4-inch compressor-housing inlet as standard. An optional 3-inch cover can be selected for those intending to run 3-inch air inlet tubes such as the Perrin product.

Forced Performance says that the Green model typically produces 400 to 450 wheel horsepower with "astounding spool up response and efficiency." Internal modifications to your engine are required to use this product.

Forced Performance Red Turbocharger

The Forced Performance Red model is an extreme high-power turbocharger. You don't get into one of these unless you've substantially modified your entire engine, including very low compression pistons to handle the boost, and expensive bottom-end improvements to handle the power without snapping your crankshaft like a pretzel stick.

The experts at PDXTuning have taken the FP Red model about as high as it can go. Here's what they had to say about one instance: "We took the car over to the local Dynapak dyno for some more tuning. Our goal was to push the midrange boost a bit more, and refine some of the fueling. We targeted getting a bit over 30 psi in the midrange, as well as having it hold to 30 psi at redline. We set the boost con-

troller (AVCR) to 90% duty cycle the entire run (learn and feedback off), so this is about the max of what the internal wastegate combo will run. The results: 510 ft-lbs of torque at 4900 rpm, and 521 horsepower at 6,700 rpm. This is with C-16 fuel, AFRs in the 12.0 to 12.5 range."

When too much is just barely enough, the FP Red model is the turbo for you. This turbo is capable of over 520 horsepower and 500 ft-lbs of torque. (Photo courtesy of Forced Performance)

Perrin GT35R Complete Turbo Kit for WRX/STI

Many turbo kits for your Subaru WRX or STI use a Garret GT35R turbocharger. Most kits also include an up pipe and a 3-inch down pipe, wastegate dump pipe, and an intake pipe with a MAF sensor mount. Most kits

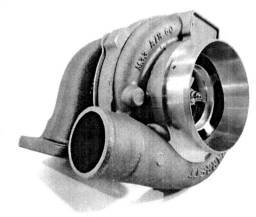

This is the Garrett GT35R from the Perrin kit. This is a major upgrade unit from the stock turbo that came with your car. (Photo courtesy of Perrin Performance)

also come with a K&N air filter, hoses for coolant and lubricant, intercooler adapter pipe, a Tial wastegate, silicone couplers, and stainless steel bracketry and fasteners. A GT35R turbo kit is usually designed to maximize performance for street, drag, or the ultimate road racing needs. The GT35R is a complete ball bearing turbine that has a 0.63 A/R ratio for fast spool up.

AVO 2.5 Turbo Kit for 2.5RS and 2.5i

Turbocharging a 2.5RS/2.5i engine is a delicate operation. Because the engine was not designed for turbocharging, the amount of boost you can run safely is extremely limited—to about 6 psi on pump gas. However, you can get a good performance enhancement with this limited amount of boost. This AVO kit is designed to use an aftermarket Perfect Power piggyback ECU. The kit includes a Garrett water cooled ball bearing turbo, top mount intercooler, blow off valve, up pipe, down pipe with catalytic converter, pre-programmed engine management electronics, braided stainless steel oil lines, air filter and intake pipe, hood scoop ducting, high-quality hoses, and a set of installation instructions. This kit is designed to work with aftermarket headers and cat-back exhaust or with the stock exhaust.

Intercoolers and Other Turbo-Related Parts

Turbochargers require some additional parts to perform their functions correctly, or to increase performance. Among these parts are intercoolers, blow-off valves, and boost controllers.

When you compress air, it gets hot. Hot air is not as good for combustion as cold air, so it helps performance to cool the air after it has been compressed by the turbocharger and before it enters your engine. Cooling the compressed air is the function of the intercooler—it's just a radiator for air. Subaru mounts its stock intercoolers on top of the engine and provides a hood scoop to collect cool outside air and direct it through the intercooler. This is a pretty good setup, but mounting the intercooler at the front of the car is very popular with tuners, because the increased air collection area and better rearward venting improve cooling efficiency.

Here are just a few of the leading turbo-related products on the market today:

Perrin Performance Top Mount Intercooler

Perrin Performance makes a top-mount intercooler that is a direct replacement for the stock unit. The larger core offers more surface area for a higher cooling capacity for your air

Buying a Front-Mounted Intercooler

Before you invest in a front-mounted intercooler kit, be sure to ask these questions:

1. Can I use this kit with my front bumper and bodywork? (If you have a body kit, this is a crucial question.)
2. What sort of blow-off valve can I use with this product?
3. Does this intercooler work with my intake and air filter system?
4. Do I have to change anything else to fit this on my car?
5. Does this require any special mounting work?

If you have answers to these questions, you'll have no problems getting your intercooler installed.

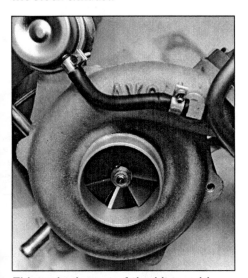

This turbo is part of the kit to add forced induction to your EJ251 engine. Rallitek has done a number of these upgrades with great success.

A front-mount intercooler looks racy, it can be larger than a top-mount, and it certainly gets airflow, but it's also in a prime position to take a hit from road debris unless you protect it.

The Perrin top-mount intercooler is available for Impreza, Forester, and Legacy. These intercoolers offer more surface area per square inch—more than 200% of the OEM unit. (Photo courtesy of Perrin Performance)

charge. This intercooler retains the stock bypass valve mounting-flange, which allows you to use the stock blow-off valve or any direct replacement product. This intercooler works with almost all aftermarket turbos on the market today.

Perrin Performance Front Mount Intercooler

A front mounted intercooler offers better airflow and cooling performance, and this unit is designed to resist damage from road debris. This intercooler stretches across the entire width of the bumper skin opening to maximize surface area. The tubes that connect this intercooler to the engine are mandrel bent. Silicone couplers with special hose clamps secure all piping. This intercooler kit also includes a brand new silicone coolant reservoir. Perrin recommends that this product should not be used on vehicles driven on public streets and highways.

Blow-Off Valves (BOV)

As Robert Young pointed out, blow-off valves (BOV) are necessary to relieve pressure when you lift off the gas, to avoid a reverse shock wave hitting your turbo and reducing turbine speed. As you increase boost, and especially if you use a higher-rated turbocharger, you'll want to invest in a more capable BOV to protect your system from boost spikes. A related device that performs the same function as a BOV is called a bypass valve. The difference between the two is that most blow-off valves vent pressure to the outside world, while a bypass valve routes the released air back into the intake stream after the MAF/MAS, but before the turbo. For our purposes, the differences are really recirculating valves versus vent-to-atmosphere valves.

On a street car, it is preferable to maintain strict air/fuel ratios and a smooth idle. For that application, you want to use a fully recirculated valve. An aftermarket recirculating valve allows you to change the volume of recirculated air and the spring tension that controls when the valve activates. For racing, or if you just like a nice racing sound, a vent to the atmosphere valve gives you the "Whoosht" sound, but in the process it's taking air that your MAF has already metered into the engine and releasing it—altering your air/fuel ratio.

Top-mount intercoolers are subject to heat buildup from the rising engine heat, reducing their effectiveness. A front-mount intercooler puts the radiator right out in the cool air stream, and it looks great, too. (Photo courtesy of Perrin Performance)

Perrin Performance offers both fully recirculated and vent-to-atmosphere (VTA) blow-off valves to let you choose the best solution for your application. (Photo courtesy of Perrin Performance)

Perrin Performance Blow-Off Valve

Perrin Performance offers both fully recirculated and vent to atmosphere (VTA) blow-off valves that work with every aftermarket intercooler available today. Its valves are capable of managing any boost you can possibly throw at them. The Perrin adjustable spring tension helps reduce rough idle, and stalling sometimes found in other products.

Unlike other blow-off valves, the piston in the Perrin unit is actuated by vacuum in the intake manifold, not by increasing boost pressure. The reasoning behind this design is that vacuum in the manifold happens before the boost shock wave hits the valve, so opening the valve sooner helps avoid boost spikes.

TurboXS Blow-Off Valves

TurboXS makes a line of blow-off valves in a variety of sizes and applications. Its Type-S is designed for small to medium sized turbochargers running 12-psi boost or less—for example, on a turbocharged 2.5RS engine. The TurboXS Type-H provides greater venting flow than the Type-S and is designed for turbocharged engines running 10 to 25 psi boost. The TurboXS Type-H34 is recommended for racing, and designed to be plumbed to recirculate air back into the intake stream.

TiAL Sport Blow-Off Valve

The TiAL blow-off valve body and all internal components are machined from 6061 aluminum alloy. It features an extra large 1.98-inch (50.5mm) valve, and flows as much or more than any valve on the market. This product is also available made of stainless steel, at extra cost. TiAL is also well known for its high-quality waste gates.

Manual Boost Controllers

Finally, manual boost controllers are used to coax a little more boost out of a turbocharger. But be aware that in

The Hallman manual boost controller has an easy interface, but you can't adjust it while you're driving. (Photo courtesy of fastwrx.com

a Subaru, boost is controlled through the ECU, and a reflash or ECU upgrade should really be your first choice for modest increases in boost pressure because that also remaps your fuel program and ignition at the same time, maintaining balance.

Hallman Pro Manual Boost Controller

Fastwrx sells a standardized Hallman manual boost controller, usable with most turbocharged vehicles, including Subarus. Just twist the adjustment knob to raise your boost several PSI. This controller is a bleed-valve design, which means the device bleeds pressure off from the waste gate to generate higher boost pressure. Tighten the knob down and restrict the bleed flow to restore pressure to the waste gate and reduce your boost.

The Perrin manual boost controller is easy to install and adjust. It uses a progressive spring and a ceramic ball to control the pressure signal to the waste gate. (Photo courtesy of Perrin Performance)

Perrin Performance Manual Boost Controller

The Subaru factory boost management system adjusts boost levels based on gear, RPM, and throttle position. This controller allows you to

increase low-end boost response in all gears, and it enables upper end increases in boost level without sacrifices to drivability. This controller adjusts with a twist of the main body, and uses an internal progressive rate spring and ceramic metering ball to manage pressure release. This controller can be used in any turbocharged Subaru.

Turbo Timers

A Turbo Timer is a device that idles the engine for a set amount of time after you turn the key off and leave. The thought behind this comes from older turbocharged cars that required a cool-down period to bring the turbo's RPM down and allow fresh, cooler oil to lubricate the bearings.

Subaru issued a technical bulletin in 2001 that says, "FHI's position is that it is not necessary to perform a cool down/idling procedure, as was recommended with past turbo models. Our current 2.0L turbo engine has a far greater cooling capacity and, coupled with technology advances, makes this practice no longer necessary."

The WRX and other turbocharged Subarus are designed to use an evaporative cooling system. By placing the coolant reservoir above the turbo and providing a tube down to the turbo, gravity feeds fresh coolant to the turbo even when the engine is off. If the turbo is hot, the coolant boils and the steam rises, only to be replaced by fresh coolant!

You can buy a turbo timer if you want some extra security for your turbo. Many have done so, and it certainly won't hurt anything, but the consensus of the experts at Subaru is that you don't need one.

Intake Manifolds

Finally, we come to the intake manifold. You can sometimes tell what engine you're looking at from

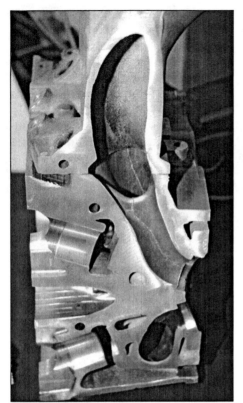

This cutaway shows the intake path on an older EJ22 manifold and head.

This is a Subaru JDM injector housing for the EJ20 engine. In Japan, they don't use the Tumble Generator Valve on the 2-liter engine.

its intake manifold—for example, the EJ255 on the Legacy GT has a plastic intake manifold, while the EJ257 STI engine uses an intake with a red crinkle paint finish. The EJ251 and EJ205 use a plain cast aluminum manifold.

The Subaru WRX intake manifold has one area for substantial improvement. The stock WRX intake manifold assembly incorporates Tumble Generator Valves (TGV) to "stir up" the air on its way to the cylinders. The TGV is simply an additional butterfly near the fuel injectors that partially blocks the intake manifold path as air moves towards the combustion chamber. As you might expect, this reduces flow, and so the TGV is frequently removed and smoothed over in high-performance applications. For street operation, this is not generally required, as the valve operates mainly at idle and opens as the engine revs up.

The TGV is an emissions-control device, so be aware that tampering with it is against the law. Also, be aware that the engine includes a TGV position sensor, and if you simply remove the TGVs and disconnect the sensor, your ECU will throw a Check Engine light, and there is no way to turn it off. The APS kit listed below has a bracket to mount the TGV sensor and its servo motor to work around this problem.

Here are a few example products that delete the TGV:

TGV Deletes for the WRX and STI from Crawford Performance

Crawford's Tumbler Generator Valve Delete intake is a modified stock intake housing that replaces the stock injector housing assembly.

APS Tumbler Delete Injector Manifold Assembly from Dyno-Comp

The bolt-on APS Tumbler Valve Delete Housing is a precision-machined aluminum part that replaces the stock injector housing. This kit also includes two precision manufactured Throttle Position/Servo couplings to offer the correct reading back to your ECU.

JDM TGV Deletes from Rallitek

Rallitek imports the Subaru factory JDM intake housing, which has no TGV, replacing the stock USDM injector housing assembly.

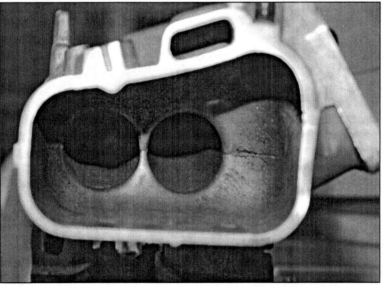

Here's a look inside an EJ22 intake manifold. You're looking in the main plenum, towards the individual runners.

EXHAUST COMPONENTS

A complete Kakumei exhaust system set up next to the Revolution Motorsports car. It's really just a simple pipe, as straight as possible to the back of the car. (Photo courtesy of Revolution Motorsports)

The fuel charge in an engine does its work by pushing a piston down in the cylinder as it burns. Once it has accomplished this task, the main thing you want to do with the products of combustion is get them out of your car as efficiently as possible—although turbocharged cars scavenge a bit more energy out of the gas on the way out. This very simple function is accomplished by your exhaust system. We already talked a bit about the exhaust valve and the ports on the cylinder head, so we pick this story up where you can easily bolt on some improvement—at the header.

You can see the Kakumei unequal length headers that give the Subaru its distinctive sound, the flexible up pipe, the turbo and down pipe with catalyst, and the cat-back exhaust system— all the components you need. (Photo courtesy of Revolution Motorsports)

About Exhaust Gaskets

A note of common sense—always replace all gaskets and worn fasteners when replacing exhaust components. Exhaust leaks are easy to avoid and a pain to fix.

Catalytic Converters

The catalytic converter has been the cornerstone of automotive emission controls for the past 30 years or so. Controlling emissions from street cars is an important environmental concern. Cars today are cleaner than ever before, thanks in large part to improvements in catalyst technology. While extreme high-performance applications generally include removing one or more catalysts from the exhaust system, it is a violation of U.S. federal law to do so on a car registered for use on public roads. Moreover, removing the catalysts makes it harder, if not impossible, for your car to pass emissions testing. Keeping your catalyst is no bar to high performance. Your entire engine management system is designed to work with the catalyst and provide good performance.

The catalytic converter is a muffler-type device that uses a ceramic or stainless steel alloy web that holds reactive catalyzing material (usually palladium or rhodium). When the exhaust gases pass through the catalytic converter and heats up the catalyst, a chemical reaction occurs that helps change carbon monoxide to carbon dioxide, and helps to burn off any unburned hydrocarbons that remain in the exhaust stream before it exits your car.

Q&A On Catalytic Converters

Perrin Performance has developed an excellent Q&A on the subject of catalytic converters and the legal issues with upgrading your exhaust. Perrin has graciously offered permission to reprint some of it here.

When can I install an aftermarket converter?

Generally, an aftermarket converter can only be installed in three situations. They are:

1. If the converter is missing from the vehicle when brought in for exhaust system repair.

2. If a state or local inspection program has determined the existing converter has been lead poisoned, damaged, or otherwise needs replacement.

3. If the vehicle is more than five years old or has more than 50,000

miles (eight years/80,000 miles for 1995 and newer vehicles) and a legitimate need for replacement has been established and appropriately documented (such as a plugged converter or unrepairable exhaust leaks).

What should customers know about buying converters for their cars?

First and most importantly, the original converter on a car or truck was designed to last the life of the vehicle if it is properly used and maintained, and is fully warranted by the vehicle manufacturer to last for at least five years or 50,000 miles (eight years or 80,000 miles on 1995 and newer cars and trucks), whichever comes first. See the vehicle warranty booklet for more information.

It is illegal to remove a functional catalytic converter even to replace it with a new one.

It is illegal to tamper with emission-control devices. The Anti-tampering Law applies to individuals as well as to businesses. Individuals may be fined as much as $2,500 for each vehicle tampered with, and businesses are subject to fines of up to $25,000.

How can I tell if an aftermarket converter meets EPA requirements?

Any converter that meets EPA requirements and is an acceptable, legal substitute must be properly labeled and warranted to meet federal durability and performance standards.

Manufacturers of new aftermarket converters are required to have a five-year/50,000 mile warranty on the converter shell and end pipes. They are also required to be warranted to meet EPA's emission performance standards for 25,000 miles when the vehicle is properly used and maintained. All manufacturers who meet the requirements also must state that fact in writing and obtain an individual manufacturers EPA code. Usually this is stated in the warranty information or application catalog.

EPA requires that a new, legal replacement catalytic converter must be properly labeled. Required labels on the converters have a series of letters and numbers in the following format:

N/XX/YYYY/ZZZZ

Here's what that label means:

- N: indicates a new converter
- XX: is the manufacturer's code issued by EPA
- YYYY: is usually a numerical designation of the vehicle application or part number
- ZZZZ: is the month and year of manufacture (i.e., "0187" for January 1987)

Note that converters manufactured for sale in California may have the letters "CA" in place of the "N" or "U." Since California standards are more stringent than EPA's, these converters also meet EPA requirements. If your new catalytic converter does not have this label it may not be a legal replacement part for your application, placing you in violation of federal law.

What are the requirements for businesses installing an aftermarket converter?

Besides installing aftermarket converters only in the three situations outlined above, other requirements and restrictions also apply. These include completely documenting the need for converter replacement, properly installing the correct one on the vehicle, and informing the customer of his rights and certain restrictions.

What may happen if I don't use the correct converter?

Vehicle performance can also be affected by the use of the wrong converter and, in some severe cases, converter or engine overheating can occur, resulting in unsafe operation and possibly engine damage. The conditions or even simply the use of the wrong part on a vehicle may allow the converter manufacturer to not honor the 25,000 mile or the 5 year/50,000 mile warranty.

Exhaust Headers

The headers (also known as the exhaust manifolds) attach directly to the body of the engine at the exhaust ports on the cylinder heads. In a naturally aspirated car, these lead directly to the catalytic converter, and then through the exhaust pipe to the mufflers and out the back of your car. On a turbocharged car, the headers lead to the turbocharger components before finding their way out of the car.

The main thing you want in a header (and throughout your exhaust system) is efficient flow of gases on their way out of your car. This means a pipe with a few smooth bends and no restrictions. It's good for this pipe to be wrapped or coated on the outside to keep heat in the exhaust gas until it exits your car. It's good for this pipe to be made of stainless steel, or coated on the inside, to reduce friction and more efficiently move the gas through the system to the exit.

You can buy unequal-length headers or equal length. With unequal-length headers, the driver's side pipes are longer than the passenger side. Equal-length headers, as the name implies, are the same length on both sides. The benefit with equal length is increased power across the RPM band and 300 to 500 rpm faster spool-up on the turbo. Many tests show huge gains in power and torque with equal-length headers. The other difference is in the sound produced. Subaru EJ-series engines have a distinctive "burble" sound that is largely a result of the odd timing of exhaust pulses coming through the stock unequal-length manifolds. Equal-length headers give the engine a more conventional exhaust note.

Here are some of the leading headers on the market today.

Kakumei Unequal Length Headers for WRX/STI

These headers fit the 2002–2005 turbocharged Imprezas. They're made of stainless steel and the kit includes all gaskets necessary to complete the swap.

Perrin Performance STI Equal Length Headers

These headers are specific to the EJ257 and Legacy EJ255 engines. Instead of being a 4-into-1 design (which are not equal length) they use the large cutout in the STI oil pan and route the primaries in such a way that they are truly equal length.

COBB Tuning Equal Length Headers for Impreza 2.5RS/2.5i

COBB Tuning manufactures a set of equal length headers that are a racing pipe designed for use with a high-flow catalytic converter, and their stainless steel performance cat-back exhaust system. Optimizing exhaust flow in a non-turbocharged application is one of the best performance improvements you can make.

Borla 2.2 and 2.5 Liter Stainless Steel Headers from SPO Motorsports

It's rare to find performance parts for the earlier EJ22 engine, but SPO motorsports stocks exhausts for both the 2.2 and the later 2.5RS engines. This newly revised header is rerouted, and has fewer bends for improved performance and increased strength. These headers are made from aircraft-quality T-304 stainless steel and Borla offers a very confident warranty.

Up and Down Pipes

In a turbocharged Subaru, the turbo generally sits high up relative to the engine, although the aftermarket has exceptions to this design. But regardless of the location of the turbo, the up pipe comes from the header to the turbo, and the down pipe returns to the exhaust system from the turbo. Like the header, the goal for these pipes is to efficiently flow gases to the turbo, without losing velocity.

The stock factory up pipe on any Subaru restricts gas flow, and thus engine performance, because it houses the first of two restrictive catalytic converters in the exhaust system, and also uses a corrugated bend to clear the engine. Look for smooth bends or a flexible section. Some up pipes eliminate the car's initial catalytic converter to increase gas flow in any aftermarket up pipe. As noted previously, it's against federal law to

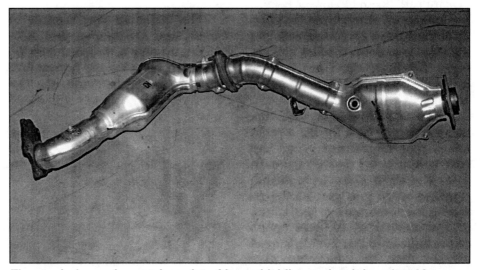

The stock down pipe carries a lot of heat shielding and weighs a lot. Aftermarket pipes are more efficient, but many eliminate the catalyst, which is illegal on a street car and doesn't help performance very much.

The stock down pipe has a flat face, and gases that come through the turbo's wastegate have to bounce off that face and then rejoin the main flow. This is not good for your exhaust flow.

This is COBB's catless up pipe for racing applications. It's made of a special "super alloy" to resist heat and corrosion. (Photo courtesy of COBB Tuning)

tory ECU uses the EGT sensor reading to kill the motor if exhaust temperatures exceed 1,800 degrees F. Once temperatures exceed 1,800 degrees, internal engine damage has already occurred, so Perrin recommends that you mount an EGT sensor within the header system, closer to the engine, and monitor the temperature yourself.

remove a working catalyst from a car, and beyond that, using such an up-pipe on a street car may affect your car's ability to pass emissions testing—check your local laws to be sure. The Impreza STI does not use a catalyst in this location, so this is not an issue for those models.

Also, somewhat counter-intuitively, the up pipe is one location where increasing the diameter of the exhaust path doesn't help you. Because the turbo relies primarily on the velocity of the exhaust gas stream, enlarging the pipe slows down the flow and prevents fast spool-up. The designed inside diameter of a Subaru up pipe is 1.62 inches.

On the down-pipe side, one major feature to look for is a separate return pipe for exhaust gasses that have been diverted through the waste gate. The stock down pipe directly combines waste gate gas with the gas exiting the turbocharger. This mixing of gas moving at different speeds causes turbulence that inhibits smooth exhaust flow. By combining these streams later in the exhaust system the turbocharger works against less output pressure, which helps it spool up faster.

Most up and down pipes fit all models, but some are optimized for a specific model. The 2006 model year WRX has a longer down pipe that also includes the catalyst. In prior years, these were two separate parts. Check with the manufacturer before you purchase. Leading products for up and down pipes are:

Perrin Performance Legacy GT Up Pipe

The Perrin up pipe is made of mandrel bent 321 stainless steel. Note that this up pipe is designed with no installation bung for the factory EGT sensor. According to Perrin, the fac-

COBB Up Pipe

COBB Tuning offers two different up pipes to suit different needs and budgets. COBB states that its standard series up pipe is constructed of investment cast T304 stainless steel. This alloy handles heat cycling very well, has excellent corrosion resistance, and does not expand or contract to the same extent as other alloys more commonly used. COBB describes its Pro series up pipe as being constructed from investment cast Inconel 625. Inconel is considered

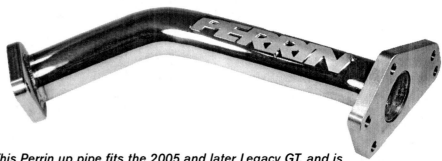

This Perrin up pipe fits the 2005 and later Legacy GT, and is made of mandrel-bent 321 stainless steel for a long and useful life. (Photo courtesy of Perrin Performance)

to be a "superalloy" due to its superior strength, corrosion resistance, and stability under extreme heat.

Kakumei Up Pipe

This up pipe features a double-layer flexible section to isolate torsion and vibration in the system. It's made of T304 stainless steel and includes a machined EGT bung. Its 2.25-inch internal diameter means that you should consider this product when using upgraded turbos that do not rely on the stock up—pipe diameter. The kit includes all necessary gaskets.

The COBB Tuning down pipe works much better than the stock unit for mixing waste gate gases with the main flow from the turbine. You can see the oxygen sensor bung and the catalyst towards the end. (Photo courtesy of COBB Tuning)

The mating face of the COBB down pipe includes an EGT bung and a wide mouth to collect and flow exhaust gases. (Photo courtesy of COBB Tuning)

COBB Down Pipe

The COBB down pipe features full T304 Stainless Steel construction. Starting from the turbo, exhaust

Paul Eklund's 2004 Forester XT

Paul Eklund is a past SCCA National Champion autocrosser and accomplished Open Class performance rally driver in his Impreza STI. He's also the owner of Primitive Enterprises, a leading supplier of Subaru performance and rally parts. After taking one of Subaru's factory-prepped Turbo-Foresters above the Arctic Circle on the 2004 Alcan 5000 winter rally, the man who knows performance and knows Subaru chose a 2004 Forester XT as his daily driver. Here's what Paul keeps in his garage:

- Factory "Mica Red" paint
- 2.5-liter EJ257 engine
- VF-39 Turbocharger (as used in the Impreza STI)
- Perrin Performance Silicone Y-Pipe
- STI Intercooler
- Perrin Performance up pipe
- TurboXS downpipe
- 3-inch cat-back exhaust

- STI muffler
- COBB AccessPORT
- STI "Pink" springs all around
- Syms rear strut bar
- Primitive Racing front strut bar
- Forester 5-speed transmission
- Group N transmission mount
- 4.44:1 final drive gears

Subaru racer Paul Eklund has modified this Forester with a larger turbo, exhaust system, larger intercooler, ECU reflash, springs, and suspension bars, and can hold his own with any hot rods out there.

Under the hood is where Paul put the few parts that brought his Forester XT up to STI performance.

gasses enter a cast stainless steel bell-mouth housing followed by 3-inch mandrel bent stainless steel piping. The pipe features a metallic substrate catalytic converter. COBB says, "These metal substrate cats are designed for optimal durability and flow so well, they pose virtually no horsepower reduction on most street cars."

Perrin Performance Legacy GT Down Pipe

Perrin has developed one of the highest flowing 49-state legal down pipes on the market, including a down pipe designed specifically for the 2005 and later Legacy GT, which has fewer options for performance products than the Impreza line. This mandrel bent, 3-inch diameter, two-piece down pipe is constructed of mirror polished, T304 stainless steel. Bends are minimized throughout the entire length of the down pipe smoothing exhaust flow.

This Perrin down pipe is designed specifically for the 2005 and later Legacy GT, but of course Perrin has pipes to fit any Subaru application. (Photo courtesy of Perrin Performance)

Kakumei WRX/STI Metal-Catted Down Pipe

This 3-inch T-304 stainless steel down pipe features an American-made metallic catalyst for legal installation on street cars. It's designed to work with the Kakumei cat-back exhaust

Perrin offers a full line of single and dual-tip cat-back exhausts, and single and dual-tube exhausts based on your model and application needs. (Photo courtesy of Perrin Performance)

and be a direct bolt-on replacement for your stock down pipe.

Cat-Back Exhaust Systems

As the name implies, a cat-back system replaces your factory exhaust from the last catalytic converter (generally in the down pipe, or just past it) to the exhaust tip at the rear of the car. This is where the muffler(s) are found. Because the exhaust has done all its work at this point, the desirable features in this part of the system are velocity and free flow with as few bends as possible.

Because of differing vehicle wheelbases and underbody configurations, exhaust systems are generally not shared among different platforms. Make sure the system you buy fits your car, especially if you buy an increased-diameter system.

Perrin Single or Dual-Tip Cat-Back Exhaust System

Perrin's WRX cat-back exhaust is constructed of full 3-inch diameter, CNC mandrel bent, and 304 stainless

steel. This exhaust bolts directly to stock and after-market down pipes using all existing mounting-hangers. The product comes with a straight-though, 3.5-inch inside diameter Perrin muffler and features single or dual 2.5-inch slash cut stainless steel tips.

Borla Cat-Back Exhaust

SPO Motorsports sells this Borla stainless steel cat-back exhaust. Borla is one of the leading exhaust manufacturers in the world, and SPO stocks cat-backs to fit 2.2-liter Imprezas, as well as the 2.5RS/2.5i, WRX, and STI, Legacy GT and Outback, and Forester. Made of T304 mandrel-bent stainless steel, this system comes with Borla's million-mile warranty.

Kakumei Cat-Back Exhaust

This kit uses 3-inch (76mm) internal diameter T304 stainless steel pipe, matching resonator and muffler, and STI-style exhaust tips. The system is entirely TIG welded and fitted to Kakumei's project WRX.

AVO Cat-Back Exhaust

This high-quality AVO Stainless steel cat-back is designed for the 2005-6 Legacy GT. This mandrel-bent polished stainless steel system was designed for North American cars and made by AVO in Japan. This kit comes with a straight-through resonator and two straight-through mufflers.

CLUTCH, TRANSMISSION AND DRIVETRAIN

"I just don't get it," says the disappointed autocrosser. "I have all the good go-fast parts—I've got the big turbo and tuned ECU, the fancy exhaust, and the great intake. That other guy has less horsepower than my car and he's not a better driver, so how did he beat me?"

In the automotive performance world, the best speed secret is one of the easiest to improve: gearing. Just like riding your bike up a hill when you were a kid, choosing the right

gears makes the difference between power pedaling and bogging down.

As with every performance decision, choosing gears involves trade-offs. Lower-ratio "tall" gears give you faster speed at a given RPM, while "short" gears sacrifice top speed to improve acceleration off the line. The correct gearing answer for best performance depends on your engine's torque and horsepower. Torque helps your engine pull the car "out of the hole" at low speeds, while horsepower

helps your car maintain top speed at high engine revs.

The right answer for your gears depends on where and how you drive, and what you want to achieve. Autocrossers typically want the shortest gears they can find to maximize acceleration between corners. Land speed record seekers go to the opposite extreme—they want the tallest gears they can find to maximize top speed. Most of the rest of us like something in the middle.

The main place to set up gearing in any car is in the final drive. In a Subaru, you have two sets of final drive gears—one for the front wheels and one for the rear. Each set of final drive gears has its own differential. Differentials are the devices that allow your wheels to turn at slightly different speeds during cornering. You've got three diffs in a Subaru: one for the front axles, one for the rear axles, and one in the center to split power between the front and rear wheels.

Another variable in the drivetrain is the total number of gears in a transmission. In the past, three-speed transmissions were the norm. Then four speeds came along, followed by five and now six speeds. Some very high-end automakers are now offering 7-speed automatic transmissions. All modern transmissions include at least one overdrive gear—where the ratio is

A great deal of your car's performance potential resides under this stick. Gearing can help you make the most of the power your engine is giving you.

taller than 1:1 (expressed as 1.000). Generally these overdrive gears are about the same ratio—somewhere about 0.7:1 or 0.8:1. At the other end, most first gears are about 3.5:1. Automatics can have taller first gears because their torque converters allow more slip than a clutch. But the important thing is that the more gears you have between first gear and top gear, the closer together the gear ratios are. This allows you to keep your engine in its power band by shifting gears, so you won't bog down on an upshift.

In a Subaru, you've got very few choices to make among stock transmissions. The 5-speed manual transmission has several minor variations—each with its own set of gear ratios. Ratio changes over the years are tiny, and inconsequential for most purposes. Also, note that changes were not always made precisely on model year cut-overs, so dates are approximate. If five gears just aren't enough for you, there is also the six-speed manual transmission from the WRX STI, and a 4-speed automatic transmission that is common to both the Legacy and Impreza lines. Late model Legacies can also be obtained with a new 5-speed automatic.

Table 6-1 lists the some of the transmissions that have appeared in the Subaru Impreza and Legacy lines.

The Easiest Way to Improve Your Gearing

The gears you choose—transmission and final drive—control the speed at which your wheels turn at a given RPM. They are both difficult and expensive to replace. But there's one other gearing factor that affects your car's speed and acceleration that is easy to change: your wheel/tire combination. By far, your car's shoes are the easiest place to make changes to the overall drive ratio.

By changing to a larger-diameter wheel/tire combo, the increased circumference effectively makes your final drive ratio taller—which is to say, every time that wheel turns around, you're bound to cover just a little more ground. Conversely, choosing a smaller diameter combination shortens your gearing. Racing teams that cannot change transmission or final drive gears frequently carry several different diameters of tires to fine-tune their gearing for track conditions.

We'll talk more about the issues surrounding wheel and tire choice in another chapter. For now, just keep in mind that while bigger rims may look cool, they can make your final drive ratio taller than you want it to be.

Manual Transmissions

Most, but not all, of the cars used for performance driving are equipped with manual transmissions. Manual transmissions allow you to use the clutch and select your own shift points based on everything that is happening, or is about to happen, to you and your car. But manual transmissions aren't for everyone—those who have to commute through long stretches of stop-and-go traffic quickly grow tired of three-pedal driving. Still, almost anyone can learn to manage a clutch, and most people with an interest in performance driving do so.

Anyone can learn to drive a manual transmission, and for performance, it's night and day compared to any automatic.

Subaru has offered several internal variations on its 5-speed manual transmission through the Impreza and Legacy years. The gear ratios don't change significantly, but each generation has generally been an improvement over the previous. So the later the transmission, the better it is, generally speaking. For example, the gears and synchronizers on the 1997 and later models are tougher than those that came before. Similarly, the WRX from 2004 onwards received a tougher gearset. So, all the transmissions may fit in all the cars, but in general you want your transmission to be as new as possible.

For the builder who wants to be different, it's worth noting that some early JDM Imprezas were offered with a dual-range manual similar to earlier Subaru 4WD systems, where pulling a lever engaged reduction gears and

Table 6-1: 1990-2007 Transmission Gear Ratios

Approximate Model Year	First	Second	Third	Fourth	Fifth	Sixth
1993 - 1997 5MT 1.8L	3.636	2.105	1.428	1.093	0.825	
1995 - 2001 5MT 2.2L	3.545	1.947	1.366	0.972	0.780	
1990 - 2001 5MT Legacy	3.545	2.111	1.448	1.088	0.825	
1998 - 2001 5MT 2.5RS	3.545	2.111	1.448	1.088	0.780	
2002 - 2006 5MT WRX	3.454	1.947	1.366	0.972	0.738	
2007+ 5MT WRX	3.454	2.062	1.448	0.880	0.780	
1990 - 2007 4EAT	2.785	1.545	1.000	0.694		
2005+ 5EAT	3.545	2.264	1.471	1.000	0.834	
2004 - 2006 STI 6MT	3.636	2.375	1.761	1.346	0.971	0.756
2007+ STI 6MT	3.636	2.375	1.521	1.137	0.971	0.756
2007+ Spec.B 6MT	3.636	2.235	1.521	1.137	0.891	0.707

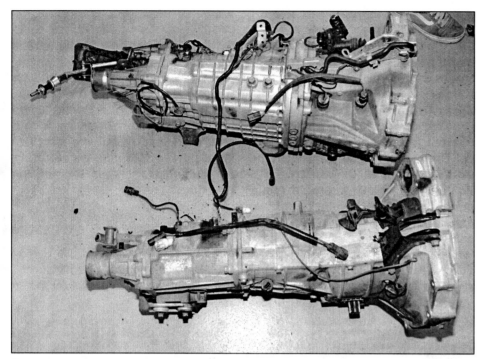

This photo shows the STI 6MT (top) and the 2.5RS 5MT transmissions. The 6-speed is bigger, and includes an extra layer between the bellhousing and the gearbox to house its internal oil pump.

simultaneously raised the suspension. However, as with most JDM options, these cars are rare and not generally used for performance applications in North America. The 1991–1994 Legacy Turbos also have transmissions reputed to be tougher than their naturally aspirated counterparts.

How Not to Drive Your Transmission to Death

The Subaru 5MT in the Impreza has generally gotten a bad rap as being weak and unreliable. This is only a little bit true. Like everything else in the car, the transmission was designed to handle the power output of the stock engine. When you introduce an engine that has been modified to put out a great deal more power, the stock transmission is just the part that breaks first.

Many transmissions break for another far more common reason: bad driving. Your transmission is made of steel and aluminum, and it's not indestructible. Your smooth shifts rely on a set of synchronizers that gently press against each other to encourage the motion shafts to spin together as you

select your gears. As the gears come together and you release the clutch, torsional and shear forces are applied to the various bearings, gear teeth, and axle joints throughout the drivetrain.

If you stop and think about it, being rough with your gears makes no sense at all. Abusing your gearbox does not help you go faster. Slamming a car into gear at full throttle at the moment the clutch is engaging makes the car jump, upsetting traction as well as applying a hammer blow throughout your engine, drivetrain, and suspension. I have watched in horror as a guy destroyed the transmission on his brand new Audi during the course of a single 30-minute open track practice session. He did it by hammering each shift until the third and fourth gear synchros just gave up and died.

Conversely, the best racing drivers in the world are silky smooth with their shifts. They hold the shift lever lightly in their hands, and they touch it only when selecting a gear. Their shifts are not slow, but not faster than the machinery can handle, either. You can hear race drivers making lightning

shifts when you watch a race, but remember that those are exotic dog ring gearboxes, which are built for that kind of treatment—and they get rebuilt after every race.

When you drive, treat your clutch and your shift lever like they're made of thin glass. You can learn to shift your car both quickly and smoothly. If the car jerks or the gears don't want to engage smoothly, back off, slow down, and make sure you're doing it right. You will be rewarded with years of reliable service from your clutch and gearbox.

Manual Transmission Upgrades

There aren't a whole lot of options for upgrading manual transmissions. You can get an exotic dog box transmission or a set of aftermarket straight-cut gears for racing, but these options are very expensive and make normal street-driving somewhat tricky. These units are properly considered Exotics, and some sources for them are mentioned in Chapter 11.

A far better and less expensive option is to obtain a set of RA (Race Altered) gears and fit them to the 5-speed case. Many racers who are rule-limited to five forward gears have done this to help them handle increased engine power, and enhance transmission reliability. RA gears are a closer ratio than stock and have a lower tooth count, and both of these features add to their reliability.

Aftermarket replacement gears tend to be stronger than stock or RA gears. Among the most popular products are the Pfitzner Performance Gearbox (PPG) gearsets available through www.gearboxtech.com.

But if you're headed north of 280 wheel horsepower and you don't mind quite a bit of work, you can get an STI 6-speed transmission. The STI 6-speed comes with several key benefits. Among these are a tougher gearset, an internal oil pump that keeps the gears positively lubricated, an improved and cockpit-controllable active center differential, plus an extra gear that your basic Impreza never had before.

This shot shows the extra segment between the bellhousing and gearbox on the 6MT. This extra "slice" in the transmission houses the oil pump, and is where you can connect an external oil cooler through those plugged holes in the side.

Downsides are that the 6MT has a different final drive ratio, so you need a matching rear end. You can achieve this by installing the correct rear ratio, or you can get an STI rear end. But the STI rear end also requires STI rear axles and STI hubs. The STI hubs have a different bolt pattern than other Imprezas and Legacies, so your brakes and wheels are up for replacement at that point as well. You also need to install a means to operate the Driver Controlled Center Differential (DCCD). The DCCD has a special computer control unit and its own set of sensors, which are expensive and must be correctly wired.

Aftermarket Manual Transmission Upgrades

For the 5 and 6-speed manual transmissions, a few products are available to improve performance:

Transmission Hard Mounts

You can buy the STI "Group N" transmission mount from many dealers. This mount is less flexible than the stock unit, and holds your transmission firmly in place where drivetrain torque can twist the stock unit. The firmer mount gives you better power transfer, and a more solid feel to the powertrain. The downside of this modification is that more vibration is transferred from the drivetrain to the chassis and its occupants.

The 6MT stock shift linkage uses rubber bushings—a set of poly bushings is a definite upgrade. (Photo courtesy of Perrin Performance)

Shift Bushings

The stock shift linkage bushings on the 6MT used in the STI and Legacy Spec.B cars are made of soft rubber that gives a squishy imprecise feeling when shifting. You can upgrade to a set of poly bushings and get a crisp shifter feel.

This is one of the most popular short shifters on the market. The kartboy shifter is well made and designed for strength. (Photo courtesy of www.fastwrx.com)

Kartboy Short Shifter

The Kartboy short shifter kit is the most popular kit with tuners and performance enthusiasts. By changing the relative lengths of the ends of your shift lever on either side of a fulcrum, you can reduce the throw length between gears. This allows you to shift gears more quickly, but you must first know how to shift your car smoothly, or you'll damage your transmission over time.

Rallitek recommends this AVO short shifter with the polymer ball for the shift socket.

AVO Short Shifter

Rallitek sells this AVO short shifter, which improves shift feel and shortens your shifter throw by 30% compared to the stock unit. Unlike the Kartboy unit, the AVO uses a polymer ball for the shift socket and a slightly different shape to the lever.

This is the adjustable Perrin short shifter for all Imprezas since 2002 and the 2005 and later Legacy GT. (Photo courtesy of Perrin Performance)

Perrin Short Shifter

Perrin makes an adjustable short shifter, so you can adjust the lever to your shifting preference. This unit is made from steel and billet aluminum, and includes all necessary mounting hardware and instructions. Variations are available for all Imprezas since 2002 and Legacy GT since 2005. The STI version includes the reverse lock-out détente.

RA Gear Sets

You can buy RA gearsets from many STI dealers. These are wider, stronger gears that retain the original 5-speed transmission case. For racing applications where you are rule-limited to five forward gears, these gears are an excellent choice.

Kaaz Performance Gear Sets

Kaaz makes an aftermarket performance gear set for the Subaru 5MT. In this setup, first and second gears are both straight-cut while three, four, and five are the quieter helical cut. All five gears use synchromesh engagement. Kaaz recommends these gears for applications up to about 400 wheel horsepower.

Transmission Coolers

On the STI cars with the 6MT, Subaru installed the automatic transmission radiator in order to use a pump in the transmission to circulate oil to the transmission cooler integrated with the radiator. With an aftermarket cooler, you can potentially keep your transmission oil too cool to do its job effectively. The in-radiator cooler keeps your oil warm enough to flow well, but not so hot that it loses its effectiveness. The 5MT relies on splash to lubricate its gears, and it has no oil pump or fittings for an external cooler, but if your oil is getting hot in your 6MT, 4EAT, or 5EAT, external transmission oil coolers are easy to find and generally easy to install.

Clutch & Flywheel Upgrades

Subaru's manual transmission cars all use the industry-standard clutch design. The clutch disc is usually a round plate faced with an organic asbestos-like surface material. The disc has a splined hole in its center, and it slides onto the splined transmission input shaft. The pressure plate

and flywheel are connected to the engine's crankshaft. The clutch disc is like the meat in a sandwich made by the pressure plate and flywheel. The pressure plate is spring-loaded and squeezes the clutch disc when the

sure plate and clutch actuation system in your car.

Your clutch disc (also known as a driven disc), pressure plate, and throw-out bearing are a team, and they should always be replaced together.

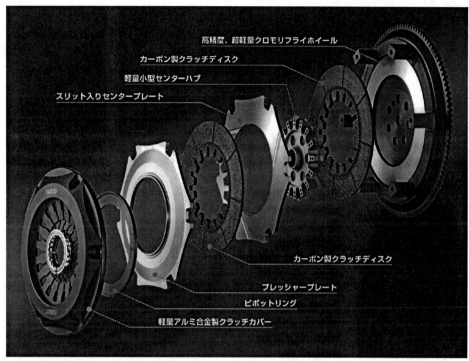

This diagram shows the components of a Cusco twin-plate carbon racing clutch. This upgrade uses two friction plates and multiple mating surfaces for maximum torque-carrying capacity. Note that this clutch requires the use of a special lightened flywheel as well. (Photo Courtesy of Nukabe USA).

clutch is not engaged. As you step on the clutch, the pressure plate face is pulled away from the clutch disc, thereby disconnecting the transmission input shaft from the engine's crankshaft.

Subaru has used two types of clutch actuation—cable and hydraulic. The cable-actuated style pulls on a lever to release the clutch, while the hydraulic style pushes on a lever. The only time this matters is if you are changing from one style of transmission case to the other, in which case you need to obtain all the parts right back to the clutch pedal, and you might have to do some fitment work to get it in and adjusted properly. As always, make sure you buy the correct kind of throw-out bearing (also known as a clutch release bearing) for the pres-

You should also resurface your flywheel when you replace your clutch components. Since you have to separate the engine and transmission to replace any of these components, it just makes sense to do them all at the same time.

The most common upgrades available to improve your clutch and flywheel system are lighter flywheels and stronger clutches with improved clutch discs. An engine with a lighter flywheel spins up faster because it has less mass to accelerate. The tradeoff here is that the mass of the flywheel helps you get the car moving smoothly. Lighter flywheels can tend to judder on takeoff and make the engine easier to stall, but the advantage in throttle response is dramatic. The STI flywheel is an easy "mostly

This kind of clutch uses a hydraulic system to push the release lever. This transmission is a 6MT from an STI.

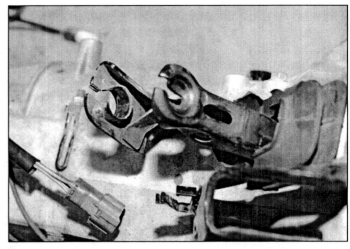

This type of clutch actuation uses a cable to pull the release lever. This transmission is from a 2.5RS.

This is a Cusco aftermarket flywheel. It's lighter than stock, but still a solid chunk of steel. The lightest fly-wheels use a steel ring gear (where the starter motor engages), an aluminum body, and a steel friction surface for the clutch disc. (Photo Courtesy of Nukabe USA)

This photo shows a greatly lightened Cusco flywheel. The large holes spaced around the outside reduce weight and keep the weight close to the center, reducing the moment of inertia. This flywheel and a grabby clutch make it very easy to stall the engine! (Photo Courtesy of Nukabe USA)

This is very much like a stock Subaru pressure plate. Used properly, this unit is perfectly adequate for the stock output of the engine, but can be overwhelmed quickly as you increase torque values.

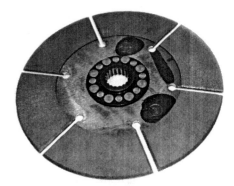

Here is a good example of a metal-faced racing clutch. This is a full-face springless design with a rough metal friction surface. Slots are cut into the disc to dissipate heat and dust.

stock" replacement for the WRX and other heavier flywheels.

As you increase the torque output of your engine, you can overwhelm the ability of the clutch sandwich to hold together. When this happens, your clutch begins to slip and very rapidly wears out altogether. As the Beach Boys told us: "To get the traction I'm riding the clutch. My pressure plate's burning, this machine's too much!" Your stock 5MT clutch should be able to handle up to about 300 ft-lbs of torque, while the stock clutch in the STI 6MT should be good up to about 400 foot-pounds when new—but you can kill any clutch quickly with abuse.

If you're in danger of overpowering your clutch, the solution is to get a stronger pressure plate and a better clutch disc. An improved pressure plate is designed to squeeze the clutch disc with greater force, and the clutch plate is made of tougher stuff to better grip the pressure plate and stand up to the torsional forces that are exerted when you release the clutch under power. Most clutch upgrade kits don't look (or behave) much different from your stock unit, but you may notice that your clutch pedal takes more effort to engage, and your new system

Cusco makes a strong line of after-market performance clutches. This is the single-plate high-performance model. These clutch kits install right onto your car with no modifications necessary. (Photo Courtesy of Nukabe USA).

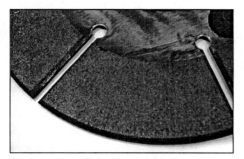

A close-up of the metal friction material on this unsprung clutch disc. Engaging one of these discs is extremely jumpy.

This four-puck clutch uses springs—a compromise for a dual-purpose car, perhaps?

This four-puck design is unsprung—a good strong light racing clutch disc.

This is very much like a stock Subaru clutch disc. It's a full-face design, with grooves for heat and dust dissipation. The material is organic, shaped and held in place with resin. The center is sprung for smooth engagement. This type of clutch disc is the most gentle to your transmission.

This clutch disc shows a partial or segmented design. Larger spaces between the ceramic friction surfaces allow for more heat dissipation, and the ceramic friction surfaces can also handle high heat. Bear in mind that these discs will wear out your fly-wheel!

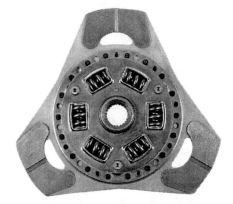

This Cusco clutch disc is a 3-puck design with metal friction surfaces and springs to smooth the engagement. (Photo Courtesy of Nukabe USA).

may feel more "grabby" than your stock clutch.

Several kinds of clutch discs are available. There are clutches where all the organic material has been replaced with kevlar, iron, bronze, ceramic, or carbon fiber composite materials. Each of these materials has different friction characteristics. Ceramic clutches, for example, are designed to handle high heat, while metal clutches offer the most friction.

There are clutches with and without springs between the splined mounting hole and the friction material. The stock clutch has small coil springs sur-rounding the mounting boss that help smooth out some of the rotational force when you let out the clutch. They damp the shock as the clutch disc starts moving. A racing clutch disc is made without those springs, and thus can be noisy and "grabby."

The friction surfaces of clutches are different. "Full face" clutches have a full surface of material with grooves.

These are commonly used in OEM designs because they engage smoothly. "Segmented" or "partial" clutches have several pads of material with gaps in between. "Puck" or "button" clutches use ceramic or bronze buttons as the mating surface. The thing to remember is the smaller the surface area on a clutch, the more pounds of pressure will be applied by the pressure plate to the surface area that is there. This is why button clutches are sometimes "grabby" where OEM clutches are smooth.

You can also get racing clutch sys-tems that are smaller in diameter than

This is an extremely strong racing clutch, made to handle maximum torque and horsepower without slipping. This clutch is also available with carbon discs. (Photo Courtesy of Nukabe USA)

the stock unit. These clutches are designed to work with lightweight flywheels to further reduce mass and moment of inertia to allow your engine to rev up faster. These units are much more jumpy than stock and you really don't want one for street driving.

Some good options for upgraded clutch kits are:

Cusco Twin Plate Clutch

A twin-plate clutch kit is an excellent choice for high-torque applications. The Cusco product has a self-leveling system that balances equal wear on both the flywheel and transmission side of the two discs to promote longer clutch life. The pull-type kit for the WRX does not require you to install adjuster kits and fits easily in the car. It is available in carbon-disc and metal-disc options.

Carbonetic Single Clutch

Carbonetic offers a single-disc clutch with a three-puck design. The friction surfaces of the clutch disc are made from Carbonetics' proprietary

C/CMC—Carbon/Carbon Metal Composite compound. Carbonetics says that its clutch offers nearly double the clamping force of the stock unit and reduces weight—easing the burden on your synchros. Carbonetic also offers twin and triple-plate clutches.

Automatic Transmissions

The Subaru 4EAT (Electronic Automatic Transmission) is the automatic transmission common to most Legacies and Imprezas. Late-model Legacies also offer an optional 5EAT 5-speed automatic. The Subaru 4/5EAT is a technologically advanced unit compared to most automatic transmissions from other manufacturers. The 4/5EAT

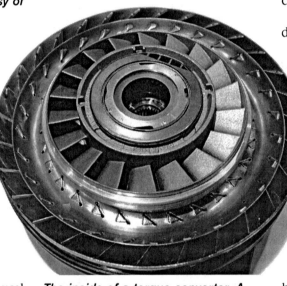

The inside of a torque converter. A whole working torque converter looks like a doughnut, but inside is where the action happens. The "fan" spins in a bath of automatic transmission fluid, which forces another fan to spin through hydraulic action.

uses a TCU (Transmission Control Unit) computer that works in concert with the ECU to control shift points, and increase fuel economy and transmission lifespan. The TCU is aware of your throttle position and the current load on the system, and makes shifting decisions based on those inputs.

Regardless of the manufacturer,

most automatic transmissions use a device called a torque converter to perform the same function that a clutch performs for a manual transmission. The torque converter is attached on one side to the engine, and on the other side to the transmission. A torque converter has two internal turbine fans, like propellers facing each other, and the unit is filled with transmission fluid. There is an input turbine connected to the engine, and an output turbine connected to the transmission. When the engine side of the converter begins to spin, the turbine moves the fluid around in the converter. Hydraulic motion forces the transmission turbine to spin as well, passing power to the gearbox. There's more that happens inside a torque converter than this describes, but suffice it to say that they get the job done, and you can't work on them.

A key thing about torque converters is that at low speeds, the fluid allows the system to slip somewhat, which is why you can hold an automatic transmission car at a stop by keeping your foot on the brake. As you offer more engine revs, the engine propeller begins to move the fluid faster, which forces the transmission propeller to move as well, transferring motion to the transmission. The Subaru torque converter is a "lock-up" type that eliminates all slip at sustained high RPM.

In the racing world, automatic transmissions are most popular with drag racers. Drag racers use custom torque converters that allow their drivers to rev the engine into the power band without moving the car, then lock up quickly to deliver maximum power to the wheels. These are called "stall" converters, and unless you're building a dedicated drag racing car, you won't need one of these.

All Subaru automatics use a system called Active All Wheel Drive to deliver limited slip power to the front and rear wheels. A multiplate wet clutch in the transmission is electronically controlled to maximize traction at all four wheels. Under standard operation, power is biased towards the front wheels, but all four wheels receive some power at all times. Under acceleration, power is biased back to the rear wheels, and under braking, more power is transferred to the front wheels. Wheel speed is measured by sensors on the four axles. In the event the front wheels begin to slip, the system directs more power to the rear wheels until traction is regained.

Automatic 6-cylinder Legacy Outbacks since 2001 and the automatic Impreza WRX since 2002 use the Variable Torque Distribution system. Under this system, about 55% of your engine's power is directed to the rear wheels, and about 45% to the front under normal driving conditions. If any wheels begin to slip, the system directs more power (up to a 50/50 split) to the front wheels.

Several products on the market improve the performance of the 4/5EAT:

This exploded diagram shows the stacks of friction discs inside a rear axle Cusco type RS Limited Slip Differential. You can also see the bevel gears at the center. The friction discs are squeezed together, and resist when your wheels try to spin at different speeds. (Photo Courtesy of Nukabe USA)

Level Ten Transmission or Upgrade Kit

The leading automatic transmission upgrade products come from a company called Level Ten in New Jersey. It makes a kit with all-new internal components and an optimized valve body. It also sells upgrade torque converters and full transmissions built for performance.

Transmission Cooler

Any automatic transmission benefits from a cooler. In the stock configuration, the transmission fluid is routed through a special part of the car's radiator for cooling. If you have a high-power engine, you may want to consider plumbing in an aftermarket transmission cooler. You can generally use the stock plumbing, or run braided steel lines. Many outlets sell quality transmission cooler kits.

ProTorque Custom Torque Converter

There's a company called Pro-Torque in New York. ProTorque's specialty is custom-built high-performance torque converters. It says that its products are designed for performance street and occasional track use, with stall speed increases of 300 to 1,000 rpm. ProTorque also offers racing converters that increase your stall speed from 1,000 to 4,000 rpm. It makes a street converter optimized for the WRX.

Differentials

As stated at the beginning of the chapter, differentials ("diffs") are the devices that allow your wheels to turn at slightly different speeds during cornering. This is achieved by a set of four bevel (also called "spider") gears that come together in the axle housing. As the axles rotate, the bevel gears can counter-rotate relative to each other to allow for different axle speeds.

With an open diff, a slipping wheel always spins freely, while the other wheel just sits there. Inside the axle housing, the little bevel gears are spinning madly to allow power to go down the path of least resistance. This is great for smooth cornering on dry pavement, and very frustrating when you're stuck in snow or mud.

When you have a limited slip differential (LSD), the differential is designed to bind up when a certain amount of slip is reached. Generally

These bevel gears can freely rotate around each other to take up the motion when your tires rotate at different speeds. Gears like these are the heart of a differential. (Photo Courtesy of Nukabe USA)

Table 6-2: Differential Options

Model Year	Model	Front	Rear	Center
1998–1999	2.5RS	open	open	viscous
2000–2001	2.5RS	open	limited	viscous locking
2002–2007	2.5RS/2.5i	open	open	viscous locking
2002–2007	WRX	open	limited	viscous locking
2004	STI	limited	limited	6-level DCCD
2005–2006	STI	helical limited	limited	6-level DCCD
2007	STI	helical limited	Torsen limited	6-level DCCD
2000–2007	Legacy GT Manual	open	limited	viscous locking
2006–2007	Legacy GT Spec.B	open	Torsen limited	viscous locking

The center differential lives in the transmission case and splits torque between the front and rear axles. Normally this differential is limited by viscosity of oil in manual transmission cars, but the Cusco unit uses the same friction surfaces as the RS front and rear diffs. (Photo Courtesy of Nukabe USA)

this is accomplished through some kind of friction device—either conical or flat plates rubbing together. There are many other designs as well—each with their own strengths and weaknesses. A fully locking differential that forces all drive wheels to turn at the same speed at all times is not a differential at all, but instead is called a "live axle."

When you're on gravel, mud, snow, or other limited-traction surfaces, control is enhanced by forcing all four wheels to turn at the same speed, distributing power equally. Each wheel can then slip or grip as moment-to-moment conditions allow,

and you are unlikely to get bogged down. Conversely, on dry pavement, all wheels are likely to have grip and you want to direct more power to the rear wheels for better handling. Additionally, it's a bad idea to run a locked torque split on dry pavement because your wheels need to turn at slightly different speeds during cornering. A live axle creates resistance and torsional stress in your drivetrain, and loses speed as well as tires are forced to scrub on the pavement.

You've got three differentials in a Subaru: one for the front axles, one for the rear axles, and one in the center to split power between the front

and rear of the car. The 2006–2007 Legacy Spec.B and the 2007 STI both come with a special Torsen limited slip rear axle. The center differential on the Legacy Spec.B is preset to a 45/55% front/rear power split.

Table 6-2 shows the differentials on the most popular Subaru models.

The Subaru 5-speed manual transmission uses a bevel gear center

This RS limited slip differential is designed for use with the older GC-bodied Imprezas. (Photo Courtesy of Nukabe USA)

Ring and pinion gears are used to set the final drive ratio, and to help rotation force "turn the corner" from your driveshaft to your rear axles. (Photo Courtesy of Nukabe USA)

Procedure for Checking a Car's Final Drive Ratio

You can check the ratio of a final drive like this:

1. Get a friend to help you.

2. Jack up one rear tire of the car and place a jackstand under the car. Place the transmission in neutral and the parking brake down.

3. Make a chalk mark on the 6 o'clock position of the tire and then slide under the car and make a similar mark on the bottom of the drive-shaft input yoke.

4. Now turn the driveshaft by hand and count the number of rotations until the mark on the tire returns to six o'clock. About three and a half rotations is a 3.54:1, just less than four rotations is a 3.9:1, a little more than four is a 4.11:1, and about four and a half rotations means a 4.44:1. Easy!

Table 6-3: Subaru Final Drive Ratios

Model Years	Model	Transmission	Final Drive Ratio
1991–1994	Legacy Turbo 2.2L	All	3.90:1
1995–2001	Impreza 2.2L	Manual	3.90:1
1995–2001	Impreza 2.2L	Automatic	4.11:1
1998–2005	2.5RS	Manual	4.11:1
1998–2005	2.5RS	Automatic	4.44:1
2006–2007	2.5i	Manual	3.90:1
2006–2007	2.5i	Automatic	4.11:1
2002–2005	WRX 2.0L	Manual	3.90:1
2002–2005	WRX 2.0L	Automatic	4.11:1
2006	WRX 2.5L	Manual	3.70:1
2006	WRX 2.5L	Automatic	3.90:1
2007	WRX 2.5L	Manual	3.90:1
2007	WRX 2.5L	Automatic	4.11:1
2004–2007	STI	Manual	3.90:1
2004–2005	Forester XT	All	4.44:1
2000–2007	Forester	Manual	4.11:1
2000–2007	Forester	Automatic	4.44:1
2001–2007	Legacy 2.5i	Manual	3.90:1
2004–2007	Legacy 2.5i	Automatic	4.11:1
2001–2007	Legacy GT	Manual	3.90:1
2001–2007	Legacy GT	4 Speed Automatic	4.11:1
2005–2007	Legacy GT	5 Speed Automatic	3.27:1
2006–2007	Legacy GT Spec.B	6 Speed Manual	3.45:1

differential with a locking viscous coupling that splits torque 50/50 between the front and rear wheels at all times. Because the center differential works with thick oil, if it begins to spin as either pair of wheels loses traction, the system binds up and power is automatically directed to all wheels equally.

The STI 6-speed manual transmission has an active Driver Controlled Center Differential (DCCD). The system allows you to set the torque split manually between the front and rear wheels or let the transmission decide. Set in automatic mode, the system directs power to the front or rear wheels to maximize traction as it perceives conditions moment-to-moment. If you choose to manually adjust the torque split, you have a range of adjustment. At one extreme, about 60% of the power

is delivered to the rear wheels and 40% to the front. Adjusted to the other extreme, torque split is 50/50, and the center differential locks, preventing any slip at all. The DCCD also opens the diff entirely when the ABS is engaged.

As mentioned previously, Subaru 4 and 5-speed automatic transmissions use a system Subaru calls Variable Torque Distribution. According to Subaru, VTD uses a planetary gear center differential that splits the power 45% to the front and 55% to the rear wheels. The variable part is that an electronic clutch controls power distribution between the front and rear wheels, and is activated when any of the wheels start to spin.

Some aftermarket products include:

Cusco Type RS LSD

The Cusco Type RS LSD utilizes coil springs located between the pressure rings to develop initial torque,

and features full engagement during acceleration and deceleration. The type RS is available for both front and rear differentials. Cusco says the use of coil springs rather than cone plates helps to promote engagement and durability.

Quaife Front and Rear LSD

Quaife offers a high quality limited slip differential for both the front and rear of the WRX, though it should also fit the Legacy or other Impreza with the correct rear axle housing.

Cusco Limited Slip Center Differential

Cusco also offers their own RS-type limited slip center differentials. They have an MZ model that works when the car is under acceleration (which is when you need a limited slip the most) and a "tarmac" center diff that guarantees a 35/65 front/rear torque split.

This is the Nissan R160 rear end used in the Impreza, 2.5RS, WRX, and Legacy cars.

This is the Nissan R180 rear end used in the STI sedans.

Vermont Sports Car DCCD Controller

If you have an STI, you have the factory DCCD control, which is a scrolling wheel. But if you're retrofitting an STI transmission to a different car, you need an aftermarket control. A few of these are on the market, but no one has more experience than Vermont Sports Car. It has a custom computer-controller for the center diff that allows you to enter six programmable maps, or switch the control to manual. The controller also opens the center differential when the driver pulls the handbrake, facilitating handbrake turns.

Final Drive Gears

Every AWD Subaru has a pair of final drive gearsets. One set lives in the transmission case to drive the front wheels, and one lives in the rear differential to drive the rear wheels. You have a few options for final drive ratios, and this is the main place where you can match your gear ratio to your engine's power characteristics for your best benefit.

Most final drives come in 3.70:1, 3.90:1, 4.11:1, and 4.44:1 ratios. The 4.44:1 gears are the shortest, but most manual transmission USDM cars came fitted with the 3.9:1 gears because of our generally higher highway speeds, and to improve fuel economy. USDM automatic cars usually received the 4.11:1 or 4.44:1 final drive gears because of their higher transmission gear ratios. 2.5RS manual transmission cars received 4.11:1 final drive gears. The 2004–2005 turbocharged Forester XT uses 4.44:1 gears, as does the naturally aspirated automatic transmission Forester. The manual transmission naturally aspirated Forester uses 4.11:1 gears. Foresters since 2006 use either 4.44:1 or 4.11:1 gears depending on their trim level.

The WRX has a unique gear set. The final drive ratio for the front wheels is 3.90:1, while the final drive ratio for the rear differential is 3.54:1. The discrepancy is resolved in the center differential, which has a 1.1:1 ratio. The STI uses 3.90:1 gears with no center differential reduction.

Changing the final drive gears is a job for a professional shop. The gears have to be installed properly, including setting the correct free-play and bearing tolerances. These gears have to take a tremendous amount of force during both acceleration and deceleration, and failures are catastrophic—imagine all four wheels locking up at high speed. If you decide to change your final drives, your most affordable path is to look for a matched set transmission and rear axle from a single low-mileage parts car, or ordering a new set from a reputable source. One of the most popular replacements for final drive ratios is the 4.44:1 gear set used in the JDM STI vehicles.

The Impreza, 2.5RS, WRX, and Legacy all use a Nissan R160 rear final drive and differential housing, while the STI uses a larger and tougher Nissan R180 unit. For extreme high-horsepower applications, you're going to want the R180 or the even tougher R200, and this makes a compelling

These cast aluminum diff covers fit all R160 and R180 cars and look great while helping to keep your gears cool. (Photo courtesy of Perrin Performance)

argument to just adopt the whole STI drivetrain.

The main consideration if you decide to change any drivetrain component is to make absolutely sure that the final drive ratio for your front axle is the same as your rear axle—WRX peculiarities must be taken into account here. Otherwise your wheels will always try to move at substantially different speeds and your center differential spins until it fails. For the same reason, your Subaru must always have the same size wheels and tires on all four corners of the vehicle, or you will wear out some or all of your final drives and differentials.

Table 6-3 shows common final drive ratios for many USDM Subarus.

Final Drive Dress-Up

You can dress up your rear differential case with a finned aluminum cover from Perrin Performance. The fins help shed heat from your rear diff and final drive gears and they add 30% more oil capacity, but the best benefit from this item is that it looks great. One model of this cover fits all R160 cars, and another covers the R180 on the STI.

Front and Rear Axle Upgrades

The last pieces of the drivetrain to talk about are the axles. Subaru axles are simple pieces of hardware, and they don't do anything except turn as driven by the final drives and differentials, transferring power to the wheels. Each axle has two Constant Velocity (CV) joints and a solid shaft joining them. Depending on the year, model, and position of the axle, one or both ends may terminate in a splined and threaded shaft, a receptacle, or a mating surface with bolt holes.

Because you divide your drive torque four ways in a Subaru, rather than two ways as with most cars, axle failures happen less often than in other brands—but you can still break an axle, especially if you have a high-torque drivetrain, and a harshly locking differential.

Axle failures frequently happen at a worn CV joint. Stock axles are relatively inexpensive and easy to replace, so make sure yours are always in good condition. If you have an extreme drivetrain, you can have upgraded axles made at a custom axle shop. Stronger axles weigh a bit more, but if you have reason to suspect you might break them, it's well worth the weight and expense to perform the upgrade.

The Driveshaft Shop in North Carolina (www.driveshaftshop.com) offers a range of upgraded axles for both the R160 and R180 housings. They say their top of the line axles can handle up to 1,000 wheel horsepower, which should be sufficient for most cars.

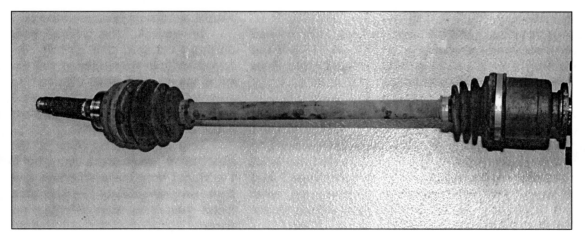

The axles used in the R160 and R180 axles are different from each other, which makes a rear axle upgrade somewhat challenging. You can get adaptive axles, or transfer the hubs from an STI to your car.

SUSPENSION & STEERING

Note: *If the subject of general suspension development interests you, there are several good books on the market that go into far greater detail about the science that governs suspension than this one. Carroll Smith's* Tune to Win *and Fred Puhn's classic* How to Make Your Car Handle *are good places to start.*

One look tells you this car has definitely got a suspension package—in this case from Progress Technology. This car belongs to Kris Hanson. (Photo courtesy of the Progress Group)

WARNING: Automotive suspensions use tremendously powerful springs that are held under compression when normally installed. Do not attempt to release any automotive spring without the proper tools and instructions, or you could seriously injure yourself or even be killed. It costs just a few dollars to have a professional shop install front springs, and it's money well spent.

Chances are good that one major reason you bought a Subaru is that it has all wheel drive. The Subaru symmetrical AWD system has been the brand's primary selling feature for over a decade, and even if you bought a FWD model, you can convert it to AWD.

But AWD doesn't mean anything if you can't put that drive to the ground. We've talked about the engine and the drivetrain, and the next system in your car on the way to the ground is your suspension. High-performance drivers from all disciplines

agree that a good suspension is crucial to top performance. Even in straight-line drag racing, suspensions are carefully set up to maximize traction factors such as weight transfer and high-speed stability. In disciplines such as rally racing, road racing, and autocross, suspension development is just as important as engine development in the quest for speed.

Hint: A weak car can build up and maintain speed if it handles well, but a poor-handling car has to slow down for every corner.

This chapter looks at the major factors involved in Subaru suspension development and tuning. Like the engine, a car's suspension is an amalgamation of interrelated and interdependent systems, and what you do to one feature affects all the others as well.

Sprung and Unsprung Weight

When talking about suspensions, you'll hear the term "unsprung weight" from time to time. What this means is simply that portion of a car's total weight that is not supported by a spring. Usually, this means the wheel/tire combination, the hub, brake, a portion of the lower suspension arms and bottom of the strut/shock assembly on each wheel.

In general, the higher your unsprung weight, the greater the impact on your suspension as you traverse bumps and other "upsets" to your vehicle. The reason is simple—your suspension has to control more bouncing mass as you drive.

Your tires take up some of the shock when you go over a bump, but if you've got very low-profile tires and high unsprung-weight, be prepared when your tires start skipping on bumps.

So for better handling and steering, you want to keep your unsprung weight as low as possible through the use of lighter wheels and other suspension components. But as always, there are tradeoffs to think about. For example, you might decide that larger brakes are a good investment despite the increase in unsprung weight that they carry.

Camber, Caster & Toe

Three terms you hear frequently in any discussion of suspension are camber, caster, and toe. There are other, more advanced concepts, but along with ride height, these three measurements are the basic building blocks of suspension alignment. The terms are broadly defined as follows:

Camber: Camber is the angle made by the plane of the wheel and a truly vertical line drawn next to the wheel when viewed from the front or rear. Simply put, if the wheel angles in at

the top, this is called "negative" camber. If the wheel angles out at the top, it's "positive" camber.

Generally you want "zero" camber *while you're cornering.* That's key, because you have to account for suspension compression and tire deflection while the car is sitting still. Most suspensions move towards positive camber as the suspension compresses

This diagram shows a front wheel and strut viewed from the side. The caster angle follows the turning axis of the wheel through its centerline, and is shown with the dashed line.

and the front wheels turn, so you start with a bit of negative. Also, your tires deflect a bit under cornering (taller 60 and 70 series tires much more so than low-profile tires) and you have to take that into account, too. With aftermarket parts, all four wheels on a Subaru can be adjusted for camber.

Caster: Caster is the angle between the actual steering axis (a line from the upper ball joint to the lower ball joint and through to the floor), and a true vertical line drawn up the diameter of the wheel. Generally the top ball joint is set slightly farther back than the lower ball joint. A rolling wheel naturally tries to follow its steering axis, which is why if you release the steering wheel in a turn, the car begins to straighten itself out. For ordinary driving purposes, caster has a wonderful effect—enhancing stability and helping your car go in a straight line. Caster is a function limited to wheels used for steering. For Subarus, that means front wheels only.

Too much caster can make a car harder to steer and sluggish to turn down into corners, but on a Subaru, you've got only about six degrees of caster available so you can't really go overboard. Caster also affects camber as your wheels turn.

Toe: Toe is the angle between two lines drawn parallel to the planes of a pair of tires. This is the easiest of the three to explain—if the fronts of a pair of tires are closer together than the backs, that's toe-in. If the backs are closer together, that's toe-out. Look at your feet if you're not sure. Put your heels apart and toes in; that's toe-in. Heels together and toes apart; that's toe-out.

Your toe settings have a few different effects on your car. For straight-line speed, you ideally want zero toe—all wheels exactly parallel. Front wheel toe-in adds to straight-line steering stability because it takes a bit more steering input (whether from your steering wheel or bouncing over a bump) to get both the wheels pointed

This diagram shows positive, zero, and negative camber, with a dashed line showing negative camber.

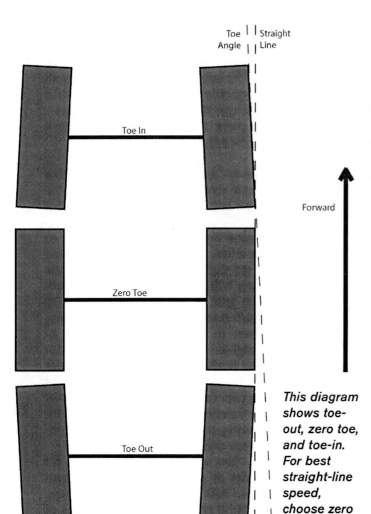

Toe Angle | | Straight Line

Toe In

Zero Toe

Toe Out

Forward

This diagram shows toe-out, zero toe, and toe-in. For best straight-line speed, choose zero toe, or a very slight toe-in.

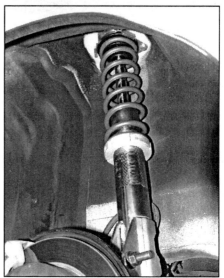

Above: This underbody picture shows the lower A-arms, sway bar, steering rods, and axles. There's a front subframe brace as well. (Photo courtesy of Nukabe USA)

Progress makes each strut by hand in their own shop, using a twin-tube shock design for compliance and great handling. (Photo courtesy of the Progress Group)

in the direction of a turn. Similarly, rear wheel toe-in helps keep the rear end planted and tracking behind the front, since both rear wheels are trying to drive to the centerline of the car. Conversely, toe-out makes your car want to turn, because the slightest movement of the steering wheel gets both front wheels describing an arc in one direction or the other. Rear-wheel toe-out means your rear tires are constantly trying to drive away from the centerline of your car, which can make the rear end wander, especially on a rough surface.

Note that your steering arm angle changes your toe setting when you change the ride height of your car because you are changing the relation-ship of your wheels to the fixed point of steering attachment on the chassis. Ideally you want the steering rods level—parallel with the ground—to minimize bump steer problems.

The next two subsections describe the design of the front and rear suspensions, and the rest of this chapter takes a look at the improve-ments that you can make and some of the more popular suspension products on the market.

Front Suspension Design

A Subaru front suspension is rela-tively simple, as suspensions go. Each side of the car has an L-shaped lower A-arm attached to the chassis in two places. The part is called an A-arm (or wishbone) for historical reasons—on most cars they are actually shaped like a capital A. The A-arm is made from thick stamped and welded sheet steel, or cast aluminum, and it supports a hub and bearing carrier assembly on a ball joint.

The bearing carrier includes a flange to attach the steering arm and a flange on which to attach the brake caliper. The brake disc slides loosely over the wheel studs on the hub and is held captive by the caliper and the wheel. The front axle comes through the bear-ing carrier assembly to spin the hub, and it is held into the hub by a large nut. At its top, the bearing carrier attaches by two bolts to a MacPherson Strut assem-bly, which includes a support structure, a spring, a shock absorber, and a top mount that bolts into the chassis of the car. A sway bar runs between the outer parts of each A-arm and is attached to the chassis in two places. The bar runs above the transmission support beam and below the bell housing of the transmission.

With the stock front suspension, camber and caster are mostly set for you. There's some camber adjustment at the strut/hub bolts, but the suspension is built with squishy rubber bushings that allow a lot of motion that you don't necessarily want. That's why there's an aftermarket for performance products.

Rear Suspension Design

Each side of the rear of the car has a hub and bearing carrier assembly. Each side also has two lateral control arms that attach to the chassis inboard of each hub assembly, and these attach to the hub assembly at its bottom, fore, and aft of its centerline. These arms limit the lateral movement of the rear wheels, and provide a small amount of toe-in adjustment by means of an eccentric bolt on the forward lateral link.

Additionally, a trailing arm is attached to the chassis in front of the hub. The trailing arm supports the hub/bearing assembly, and limits its fore and aft motion. These control arms have been manufactured in different ways for different years and models, but are generally made of tubular steel, stamped steel, or cast aluminum.

The rear bearing carrier includes a flange on which to attach the brake caliper. Some early models are designed to receive a drum brake assembly. The brake disc slides loosely over the wheel studs on the hub and is held captive by the caliper and the wheel. On AWD models, the rear axle

This is the stock rear strut. It is very easy to replace with a coil-over, and not as expensive to do so as you might think.

This is a stock rubber suspension bushing after a few years. You want to replace this with a nice polyurethane bushing or a Heim joint.

This is the stock trailing arm after a few thousand miles. Not a pretty sight, but help is available in the aftermarket.

This is the eccentric bolt that you can use to slightly adjust the rear toe-in. Note the index marks stamped into the bracket.

This picture illustrates the control arms of the rear suspension in convenient Cusco blue. The trailing arm, lateral control arms, and rear sway bar are all visible. (Photo courtesy of Nukabe USA)

This is a rear coil-over strut installed. Note that the strut is mounted off-center to the front of the hub.

This rear sway-bar link is designed to work around the stock rear lateral control arm. Note the pillow-ball design on this one. (Photo courtesy of Primitive Racing)

The stock rear sway bar is held in place with a rubber bushing and this stamped clamp. Aftermarket solutions vary, but are more substantial than this.

comes through the bearing carrier assembly to spin the hub, and it is affixed to the hub by a large nut. On the forward side of the hub, the bearing carrier attaches by two bolts to a MacPherson Strut assembly, which includes a support structure, a spring, a shock absorber, and a top mount that bolts into the chassis of the car. The rear sway bar is attached to the chassis in two places towards the center of the car, and uses C-shaped drop links to attach to the rear lateral control arms at either side of the car.

With the stock rear suspension, camber is set for you, and toe is slightly adjustable with the eccentric bolt. But again, remember that it's all put together with those soft rubber bushings. You can tighten up your suspension quite a lot with just a little effort and expense.

Sway Bars

Perhaps the biggest bang for your buck in suspension development comes with a set of replacement sway bars. You'll notice a difference right away with a new set of sways, and they're relatively easy to install yourself. The front bar can be tricky because it runs up above the transmission cross member, but the rear bar is easy. You can set a preload on your sway bars if you get adjustable drop links, sold by many aftermarket shops.

Sway bars are designed to reduce "body roll" during hard cornering, but that's not all they do. Depending on the particular size and position of the sway bar, you can set your car up with a tendency to oversteer or understeer. Simply put, to increase understeer, get a bigger or stiffer front bar. To increase oversteer, get a bigger or stiffer rear bar. As always, oversteer and understeer tendencies are affected by many factors in addition to your sway bar choice, but if you get a big stiff rear bar then get ready to have your rear tires get loose.

Lots of companies make sway bar kits for all years and models of Subaru. Here are just a couple of manufacturers:

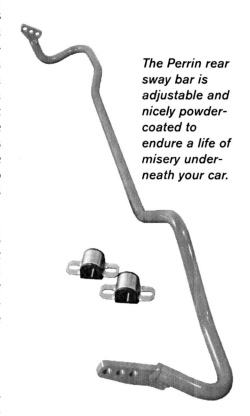

The Perrin rear sway bar is adjustable and nicely powder-coated to endure a life of misery underneath your car.

Perrin makes two sizes of front sway bars in 7/8 and 1-inch varieties for street and track use. Poly bushings are included, and upgraded drop links will complete the package.

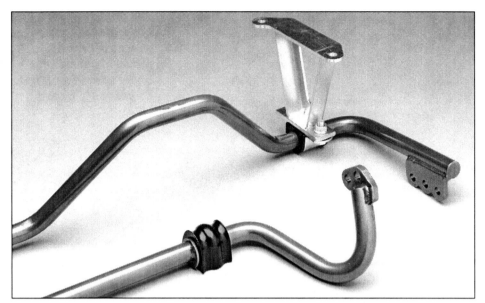

These sway bars from Progress Technology are adjustable, and offer nice polyurethane bushings for a nice tight steering feel. (Photo courtesy of the Progress Group)

Strut Bars and Suspension Braces

In hard cornering, your chassis is subjected to a great deal of pressure, and it flexes. Ideally, you want your chassis to be as stiff as possible. The main points of flex are at the strut towers and subframes, where the force from the suspension is concentrated. Strut tower bars bridge your strut towers across the top of your engine bay, making an arch that helps stiffen your chassis.

Bars are also available to bridge the rear strut towers, the lower A-arms, and other points on the underside of your chassis. These bars help stiffen the chassis, and improve steering and suspension response. All of them can be installed at home in minutes using ordinary hand tools. For ultimate chassis stiffening, however, you can't beat a good roll cage.

Here are some representative products for strut and chassis stiffening:

Perrin Sway Bars

Perrin makes two sizes of front sway bars and one adjustable rear bar for your Subaru. Perrin also sells upgraded drop links with pillow ball bushings for the tightest control. The 22mm (7/8-inch) front bar is an ideal choice for street performance. Those with racing applications usually prefer the 25mm (1-inch) front bar.

Progress Auto Sway Bars for Impreza

Progress Auto makes these sway bars for the 2002 and later Impreza. They have several holes on which you can mount the drop links. This allows you to adjust the stiffness of the bar by selecting different holes. The hole at the very end of the bar is the softest setting, and each hole farther in is a little stiffer. The rear bar includes a triangulated mounting brace for extra firm hold.

COBB Tubular Sway Bars

What makes the COBB tubular bars unique is their hollow construction. Tubular sway bars have long been popular with racecars because a hollow bar is much lighter than a solid bar of the same diameter. These bars are 50% stiffer than stock and fit into the stock mounting points. The kit includes new poly bushings, and fits your stock or most aftermarket endlinks. COBB makes these bars to fit Legacy GT since 2005 and all years of Forester, WRX, and STI.

Perrin Stout Mounts

The stock rear sway bar mount is simply a bracket of stamped metal. Perrin has developed a set of billet aluminum mounts for the Impreza, and a tougher bracket of cold rolled steel for Legacies. These braces hold the rear sway bar firmly in place during cornering.

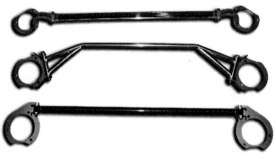

These billet aluminum braces put an end to the sheet metal flex you get on the rear sway-bar mounts. This is the Impreza design, but there is a comparable product for the Legacy. (Photo courtesy of Perrin Performance)

These attractive bars are made by Primitive Racing and are available in traditional cherry blossom red or a gold-tone end finish.

Primitive Racing Strut Bars

Primitive Racing makes this line of high-quality strut bars. You can order a bar with an aluminum brace or carbon fiber. The aluminum set offers both front and rear tower braces with ends in STI cherry blossom red. The carbon fiber bar is lighter, and features gold-toned ends for a nice dress-up to your engine bay.

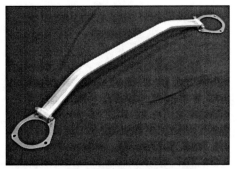

This bar from Tein is well made with a flat cross-section. (Photo courtesy of Tein)

The front strut bar connects the tops of your strut towers, reducing chassis flex under cornering. (Photo courtesy of Nukabe USA)

Tein Performance Strut Bars

Tein offers a line of performance top strut bars for all Imprezas back to 1993. These are available in an oval or round cross section. The bars are made of aluminum, with Tein green mounting plates. These bars do not interfere with the Tein Electronic Damping Force Control system.

The bright red crinkle coating on this Perrin strut bar matches the STI intake manifold. The cast aluminum feet are also a nice dress-up for the engine bay. (Photo courtesy of Perrin Performance)

Perrin Strut Bars

This product utilizes cast aluminum feet and mandrel bent aluminum tubing. The Perrin strut bar is lightweight, strong, and especially attractive in the STI engine bay with its bright red crinkle coating and aluminum plates. This product fits Impreza, WRX, and STI since 2002.

Cusco Titanium, Type 40 and AC 40, and Type OS Strut Bars

Cusco's product line includes the titanium bar, designed for high strength and low weight, starting at 1.3 pounds. The Type 40 is a 40mm bar, made of aluminum, and featuring gray end plates. The Type AC 40 is the same aluminum bar as the Type 40 but is wrapped in carbon fiber. The most popular Cusco bar is the Type OS. This product features an oval aluminum shaft with a high polish finish. The end plates are painted the traditional Cusco blue. All Cusco bars come with all required hardware for installation.

These bars connect your lower suspension mounting points, further reducing chassis flex by tying these points together. Made for both Legacy and Impreza (Photo courtesy of Nukabe USA)

Cusco Type I and II Lower Arm Bar

Cusco's lower arm bars are made of aluminum to help keep weight down without compromising strength. The bar is painted Cusco blue for a nice dress-up to your undercarriage. The Type I bar is a simple 2-point setup, and includes all the required hardware for installation. It bolts on easily using normal hand tools. The Type II is a multi-point setup and includes all the required hardware for installation. Both bars install easily using normal hand tools.

Carbing Chassis Stiffener

This underbody lower arm bar chassis stiffener fits Imprezas back to 2002 and Legacies back to 2000. This kind of product helps reduce chassis flex, and thereby improves suspension and steering feel.

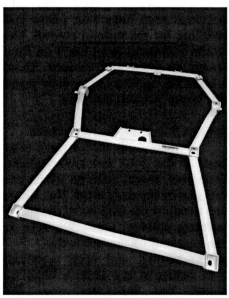

The Carbing chassis stiffener is a longer, more comprehensive piece from Tein. It ties together lower suspension mount points and other fixed points on the chassis. (Photo courtesy of Tein)

Perrin Cross-Lock Subframe Brace

This cross-lock subframe brace system allows you to remove up to 36 pounds from the front end of your

You can remove the stock heavy front subframe brace and replace it with this lightened and strengthened cross-locking brace; it saves up to 32 pounds. (Photo courtesy of Perrin Performance)

Regardless of the name, what you're dealing with is a spherical steel bearing in an enclosing bearing race. There is a hole through the sphere to allow you to fasten it at one end, and usually a male or female threaded end for the second attachment point. Pillow ball strut tops usually come assembled with the entire top structure. You generally buy these bushings premade, keep them lubricated, and throw them away when they're worn.

The reason these bushings are so highly prized is that the rotation of the ball in the socket allows a good range of motion for a control arm, while allowing virtually no unwanted "slack" in that motion. Where a rubber bushing compresses and deforms, a Heim Joint holds firm. The effect of Heim Joints on steering and suspension response is nothing short of amazing.

Impreza by replacing stock subframe parts. Cross-lock means that each mounting point of the engine cradle is tied to the subframe system, adding strength and preventing chassis flex under hard cornering. This kit fits Imprezas since 2002.

Suspension Bushings and Control Arms

All of the control arms and sway bars on a Subaru use rubber bushings to attach themselves to the chassis and hub assemblies. Among the first things any performance enthusiast does to improve handling is replace these rubber bushings with a firmer material such as polyurethane. Similarly, the top mounts of the struts use rubber bushings that may be replaced with firmer materials (hardened rubber, polyurethane, or even metal) to tighten up steering response.

A metal bushing may go by several different names—pillow ball is popular among tuners, while racers call the same item a Heim Joint, or spherical bearing. Some mil-spec or aviation applications call the same item a Mono-ball bearing.

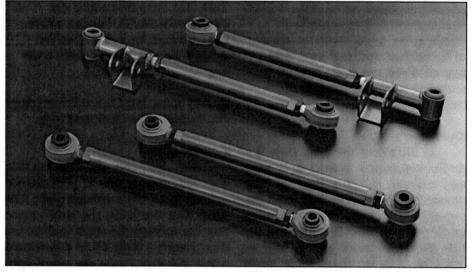

A Heim joint and poly bushing control arm allows your suspension to move only within the range designed by the engineers—it's like night and day for your feeling of car control. (Photo courtesy of Nukabe USA)

Heim joints, or pillow-ball joints, are used on performance applications for their strength and rigidity, while providing easy motion within their range of travel. (Photo courtesy of the Progress Group)

Replacement Bushings

Upgraded replacement bushings are available from a wide variety of performance Subaru parts suppliers. Getting these bushings installed in your stock suspension components is challenging even if you own a hydraulic press, and impossible if you don't. You'll save blood, sweat, toil, and tears if you take these out and have them pressed into your control arms. Sway bar bushings are easy, and any sway bar kit you buy should come with nice poly bushings.

Replacement bushings made of Delrin, nylon, or polyurethane are one of the easiest and least expensive upgrades you can make to your suspension. (Photo courtesy of Nukabe USA)

Strut Tops

At the top of the strut, there is a device commonly known as a strut top, but also called a "hat" or "top mount." This is the cap that holds the top of the shock and holds the spring under compression. The strut top fits into the strut tower and is held in place by two or three fairly small studs—just enough force to keep it located.

Because rally racing rules prevent the use of metal bushings in strut tops, Subaru manufactures "Group N" strut tops with hardened rubber bushings to keep struts in place. The stock units allow a comparatively great deal of play in order to make the stock ride comfortable, and the Group N tops eliminate most of that play. Cusco, Tein, and several other manufacturers make true metal-bushing "pillow ball" tops for tuners and those not limited

This Cusco top mount uses a rubber bushing, and is not adjustable for camber. (Photo courtesy of Nukabe USA)

These top mounts are also not camber-adjustable, but use pillow-ball bushings for a more positive suspension mounting. (Photo courtesy of Nukabe USA)

by rally rules. Most full coilover setups also feature pillow ball strut tops.

Camber Plates

The other part of a strut top that you can change for a performance upgrade is to add a camber plate. The stock strut top holds the strut in one position to keep the stock camber setting. There's a little bit of adjustment where the strut meets the wheel hub, but just a little. Camber plates are slotted, so you can move the top of the strut in or out, and tighten it in place to set your camber. Most full coilover setups also include camber adjustment in their custom strut tops. There's a small tradeoff here—you'll notice increased noise, vibration, and harshness (commonly called NVH) in the car with a fixed top like this.

Anti-Lift Kits

Anti-lift kits help soften the resistance of your suspension to lifting

This picture shows an installed camber plate top with pillow-ball bushings. To adjust camber, this racer simply loosens the four Allen-head bolts and moves the strut in or out. The pillow-ball bushing and metal strut top make this a very firm suspension mounting.

under acceleration. Newtonian physics tells us that the reaction to acceleration and deceleration has to go somewhere, and if it doesn't go to the suspension, it goes to the chassis. The suspension is made to absorb bumps, and the chassis is supposed to be rigid. So the main advantage is that your springs get to absorb the lift rather than your chassis, and this helps keep your tires in good contact with the ground. With your tires in better contact with the ground, you've got more cornering capability, and fewer tendencies for the front wheels to lose traction under acceleration because of weight transfer through the chassis.

Finally, virtually all anti-lift kits come with upgraded bushings for your A-arms, so you score a point there as well. The A-arm bushings are large, and made of soft rubber. The bushings deflect quite a bit under braking and accelerating and this deflection is expressed as a surprisingly large toe-in/toe-out change. You can feel this through the steering wheel as a "wandering" feeling.

The two most popular steering response/anti-lift kits are:

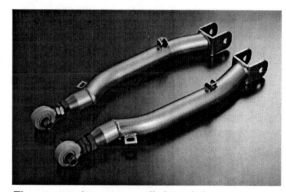

Perrin Positive Steering Response System

Perrin's kit includes anodized aluminum blocks with upgraded bushings to relocate your A-arms about an inch, increasing caster by 1 degree and preventing lift. This kit comes with everything you need to install it yourself. The Legacy kit is slightly different and fits into the lower A-arm of all Legacy models since 2005.

The Perrin Positive Steering Response System adds about 1 degree of caster by changing the location of your lower A-arm. The effect is dramatic, and you'll wonder why Subaru didn't design their cars this way in the first place.

The kit for the Legacy is slightly different—this kit fits all Legacies since 2005. (Photo courtesy of Perrin Performance)

This is the Whiteline Anti-Lift Kit. This kit is made in Australia and marketed through several vendors in North America.

Whiteline Anti-Lift Kit

The Whiteline kit drops the back of the A-arm by approximately 20mm for a gain of about 1 degree of caster. It uses large polyurethane bushings, and is very well regarded as an easy suspension upgrade.

Adjustable Control Arms

A friend of mine who raced a Formula Ford once observed that the car had so many adjustable suspension components, he tended to adjust himself into complete oblivion. Subaru gives you lateral links and trailing arms of a fixed length, but with rubber bushings. For the performance-minded tuner, many lightened, strengthened, and well-bushed control arms are available on the market. You can easily upgrade your suspension one piece at a

These are ultra-strong, lightweight, fully adjustable rear trailing arms from Cusco. Together with a set of adjustable lateral links and a good set of coil-overs, they give you a fully adjustable rear suspension. (Photo courtesy of Nukabe USA)

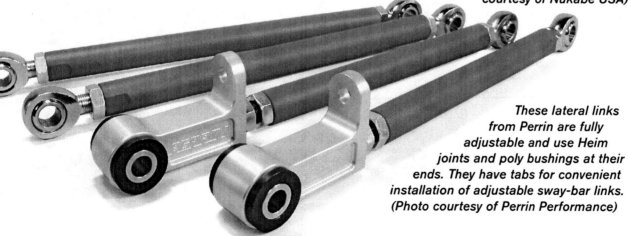

These lateral links from Perrin are fully adjustable and use Heim joints and poly bushings at their ends. They have tabs for convenient installation of adjustable sway-bar links. (Photo courtesy of Perrin Performance)

time, but bear in mind that you need to get the right adjustment into these parts once you get them on the car. Start with the stock measurements, or find someone with experience with your particular model and ask them about their preferred settings. You may end up with one set of figures you use for autocross or track day events, and a more conservative setup for day-to-day driving.

Steering Rack Upgrades

All Subarus in the modern era use rack and pinion steering. Various years and models have differing steering ratios—meaning more or fewer turns lock to lock. Generally, performance enthusiasts prefer "quicker" racks with fewer turns lock to lock. The desirable rack for this purpose is the STI model—with 15:1 ratio as opposed to the standard WRX rack at 16.5:1, and a ratio as high as 19:1 on some Legacies. If you're swapping racks in an older car, be sure to pick up a set of poly steering rack bushings—it's one more place you can eliminate a little bit of play in the system.

Shock Absorbers and Struts

In any modern car, you'll hear the word "strut" used synonymously with the work "shock." In many cases this is accurate enough—if they need new shocks, most folks go buy a new strut assembly. But the strut is properly the assembly that functions as the upper control arm of your front suspension, and the shock absorber simply the insert that damps suspension motion.

Shock absorbers (also called dampers) are a critical part of your suspension. More than anything else, they keep your wheels in contact with the ground by absorbing the spring recoil when you drive over a bump. Without shocks, your springs can literally launch your car into the air when they are suddenly compressed by a bump and then release their energy. The shock absorbers "catch" your car and make the springs release their energy

over time. Moreover, your shocks make your car's ride more comfortable and confident. You should always keep your shocks in good condition.

When people talk about shock absorbers, they sometimes use the terms "jounce" or "bump" and "rebound" to describe compression and extension resistance, respectively. Your shock absorber resists both jounce and rebound, but it may not resist both motions equally. If you have adjustable shocks, you can set the resistance level to harder or softer settings, but sometimes only in the rebound direction. If you have purchased double-adjustable shocks, you can set jounce and rebound resistance separately.

A common mistake people make with adjustable shocks is to set them up as stiff as possible. Stiff shocks "feel like" high performance because you can feel every bump—you may feel like you can tell the difference between driving over a dime and a nickel, but that's not necessarily helping keep your tires on the ground. Most adjustable shocks are quite stiff to begin with, so start with them on their softest setting and work your way up through the range. Chances are you'll find that a medium-soft setting gives you the best all-around results, especially if you've gone to stiffer and lower springs.

Checking for Worn Out Shocks

You can take your shock absorbers to a racing shop and have them tested on a shock dynamometer. You get a readout of performance across a range of jounce and rebound characteristics, and throughout the motion range of the shock, but this is not strictly necessary to find a worn-out or broken shock. For every time your shock is completely compressed or extended, it moves across the first inch of its travel literally thousands of times. It is in the first inch of travel that most shocks wear out. If you can move the shock easily by hand back and forth through that first inch, it's worn out no matter how stiff it is at its limits.

Shock Absorber Upgrades

In the case of the Subaru, the shock and strut body are usually sold together, unless the unit is a coil-over design, so we call them struts for the purposes of this chapter. A wide variety of struts are made to fit your Subaru. As mentioned before, your best bet is to have your new struts installed by a professional. In order to install new struts, the old strut must be removed from the

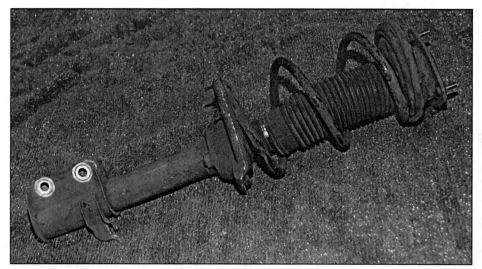

This is a basic strut. Depending on the brand of shock you buy, you might have to cut your stock strut body to use an insert, or just buy the strut with a new spring perch and mounting bracket already attached.

car, losing the alignment settings. You can carefully mark the strut positions before removal and attempt to match them when you reinstall, but a good suspension shop realigns your car for you when they install your new struts.

Some of the leading strut assemblies on the market include Bilstein, Tokico, Koni, and KYB. Different people prefer different brands, and some people have really strong preferences, but each of these brands has a dedicated following. Some of these require you to cut your stock struts and insert a new cartridge—others just sell you the whole strut.

Suspension Upgrades

You can make a number of suspension upgrades—here are some of the available options, in order from the least expensive to the most:

Spring Upgrades

At the easy and low-cost end of the suspension upgrade spectrum, you can buy spring kits that install into the stock strut body and are known to have pretty good spring

These are the classic spring upgrade for most Subarus—a set of STI springs in "Cherry Blossom Red"—a color most people simply call "STI Pink"

rates for most Subaru applications. The STI "pink" springs and numerous other manufacturers' kits fall into this category. It's a good idea to replace your shock/strut assemblies at the same time as your springs.

These Cusco coil-over adapters require you to cut your stock strut body and install these with set screws. They have a spring perch that allows you to use stock-size coil springs. (Photo courtesy of Nukabe USA)

These Cusco coil-over adapters are sized for aftermarket springs used with most coil-over kits. They still require you to cut your stock struts and install these adapters with their set screws. (Photo courtesy of Nukabe USA)

Threaded Sleeve Kits

If you want to go with an aftermarket adjustable spring setup, but you don't have the money for the full coil-over setup, you can buy a set of sleeves. These products require you to cut up your stock struts—usually removing the spring perch, and then you slide the threaded sleeve over the outside and weld, or screw, it to the strut body. Sleeves have the advantage

of accepting stock-compatible shock bodies and allowing you to use the same kind of springs used with coil-over setups. Sleeves also allow you to safely release spring tension, but they are not as strong as purpose-built coil-over units. Consider buying your coil-overs in stages (front first, then back) or just saving up your money. Entry-level coil-over kits are not that expensive, considering the labor involved in a sleeve kit.

Coil-Over Suspension

At the top of the suspension hierarchy, you can buy coil-over suspension kits. These kits replace the stock strut body with a threaded-body unit that accepts springs of a specific coil diameter and shock bodies of a specific diameter and/or design. Large adjustment nuts move up and down the outside of the threaded bodies to allow you to assemble and disassemble the unit and set ride height, corner weight, and spring preload. With a coil-over system, you can generally remove and install springs on your own, and this opens up the possibility of multiple sets of springs of varying rates for your different driving events.

Virtually every suspension manufacturer offers a kit designed for your car, including a set of springs chosen for your car's weight and the kind of driving you do. Larger manufacturers have product lines ranging from non-adjustable entry-level kits to full-race kits with multiple adjustments. The best coil-over kits include adjustment

This photo shows the bottom of a coil-over strut that has an independent ride height adjustment. By turning this nut, you can extend or contract the total length of your strut between the top and the bottom mounts. (Photo courtesy of Nukabe USA)

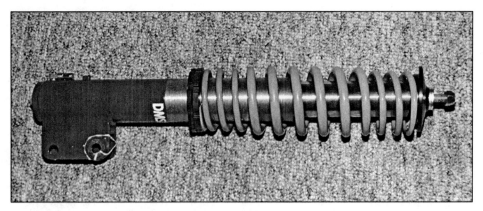

Primitive Racing sells these DMS shocks for rally and tarmac use. When the going gets really tough, you just can't beat DMS. The rebound damping is adjustable on these shocks, and the inverted design is very popular with rally racers. (Photo courtesy of Primitive Racing)

The Cusco Z2R is a popular inverted design shock, and it has total ride height adjustment as well as adjustable rebound. (Photo courtesy of Nukabe USA)

This shot shows the pillow-ball top, camber adjustment, and rebound adjustment on the top of a Cusco Zero-2 coil-over strut. This strut is also total ride height adjustable. (Photo courtesy of Nukabe USA)

This strut is special because it allows a remote unit in the driver's compartment to adjust the shock damping electronically. You can go from smooth road driving to stiff competition valving at the push of a button. (Photo courtesy of Nukabe USA)

nuts that let you set the total height of the assembly as well as the compression on the spring. This allows you to set ride height and retain the full travel of the suspension while separately adjusting your effective spring rate.

Coil-over kits are frequently designed for specialized purposes. For example, the 50mm Drummond Motor Sport (DMS) coil-over kit is designed to handle the extreme rigors of rally racing, where cars are expected to jump as they go over bumps, and land with forces that would collapse a set of stock struts. Drummond supplies a custom spring and a custom extreme-duty rebuildable and adjustable shock body with this kit. They are designed to be used as a unit, and are not intended for use with other shock bodies or springs.

The Cusco Zero2R, Tein Mono-FLEX, and the DMS product line use an "inverted" design. In most coilovers, such as the Progress Auto kit, the shock rod is placed at the top of the assembly, and affixes to the top mount of the strut. This is a perfectly good design for almost all applications, but it can allow dirt and water to accumulate at the rod/shock body sealing surface. This problem is most apparent on rally cars and other off-pavement applications. Inverting the shock body and allowing dirt and water to drain out the bottom of the strut body extends the working life of these shocks.

Leading coil-over suspension kits on the market for the Subaru include:

Cusco Zero-1, Zero-2, Zero-2E, Zero-2R

Cusco suspension products are among the best on the market. The Zero-1 assembly is a lower-priced unit designed for a basic street upgrade with fully adjustable ride height. The shock insert in the Zero-1 is not adjustable. The Zero-2 is an upgrade from the Zero-1 and includes a 5-way adjustable shock insert. The shocks are the same size between the Zero-1 and Zero-2, so upgrades are possible. The Zero-2E allows electronic control of shock settings from the driver's seat, and the Zero-2R is an inverted 5-way adjustable shock design. Cusco also makes the entry-level Comp-S product, which does not include total height adjustment, and uses a non-adjustable

The Tein Mono-FLEX is one of the most popular aftermarket fully adjustable inverted shock coil-over setups on the market. This unit has total ride height adjustment, spring preload with two stacked springs, pillow ball camber-adjustable tops, and 16-level damping adjustment. This setup has it all. (Photo courtesy of Tein)

shock. These units come pre-assembled from Cusco—just install them and drive away.

Tein Coil-Overs

Another popular product among Subaru tuners is the Tein line of coil-overs. The Tein BASIC provides a good entry-level coil-over solution for all Imprezas since 2002, and the Legacy since 2005. Tein's Super Street kit provides 16-way adjustable rebound shocks for Imprezas back to 1993. Pillow ball tops are available for the Super Street kit. Tein's FLEX kit is a full total height-adjustable coil-over, with the 16-way adjustable shocks and adjustable tops. The FLEX kit is available for Legacies since 2005 and Imprezas back to 1993. The Mono-FLEX is Tein's inverted shock design, 16-way adjustable with pillow ball top, available for Imprezas since 2002. For Legacies back to 2000 and Imprezas since 2002, Tein offers the Comfort Sport line of inverted shock, 16-way-adjustable, with a hard rubber top mount. Tein offers EDFC (Electronic Damping Force Control)

Here's another option for a fully adjustable coil-over setup. Endura-tech offers a high-quality product that is well liked in the tuner community. These are available with a 4-way or 10-way adjustable damping shock. (Photo courtesy of Endura-tech)

on all of their adjustable shocks, allowing you to adjust damping from the driver's seat.

Endura-Tech Coil-Overs

Endura-Tech Coilovers feature 10-way adjustable shocks, pillow ball tops and a total height adjustable body. These struts are made to be comfortable and nimble. Endura-Tech says they recommend this product for the "in-between daily driver and weekend racer."

*Progress Auto
Coil-Overs*

Progress products are popular with autocrossers and drag racers. Progress uses a hard rubber top mount and a non-adjustable shock. These coil-overs fit Imprezas from 2002 to the present and Legacies since 2005. "Our shocks are handmade in our shop and you can request spring rates, or we have setups for each kind of racing. It's a twin-tube design, so it's compliant, but it handles really well on the track," says Joey Berry of the Progress Group.

Yet another option to consider for coil-overs are the Progress Auto struts. The Progress Auto products are not ride height adjustable, but do offer a strong design and polished look. Their success on the autocross circuit testifies to the value of these struts. (Photo courtesy of the Progress Group)

Alignment and Corner Weights

Just as all the great engine parts in the world won't help you much if they aren't properly tuned, your suspension needs to be tuned to give you the performance you've paid for. Suspension tuning is every bit as important as engine tuning, and in some respects it's harder to do. Tuning an engine, you can use a dyno and ECU readouts to measure torque, horsepower, timing, and air/fuel ratio. With suspension tuning, you have to rely more on feel and personal preference. You can (and you should) use accurate tools to set up your suspension, but it's harder to identify the optimum setup. One skill that professional racing drivers cultivate is the ability to describe a car's handling characteristics in precise terms, and to repeat a test lap the same way every time to get a valid test of new suspension settings. The rest of us just have to work at it.

Start by having your car aligned to the factory specifications. If you have substantial aftermarket modifications such as caster/camber plates, adjustable shock absorbers, or a coil-over suspension, you'll have more adjustability than with the stock components. Then from stock, make incremental changes and test your results until the car feels good to you. Don't be afraid to keep adjusting until the car no longer feels good, then work your way back to the optimum setting.

Alternately, find a credible source for good performance settings for your model and modification status. It goes without saying that what is a good suspension setup on a Legacy wagon is not necessarily good for an STI sedan. In all cases, however, let common sense and your personal comfort be your guide.

Setting Ride Height and Corner Weights

If you have changed over to a coil-over suspension, some new adjustments are available to you. Because you can change springs easily and set the total strut height and spring compression individually, you have more control over your ride height and the weight distribution to the four corners of your vehicle.

First, park on a flat, level surface. Set your basic ride height to appropriate (and legal) levels for your purposes. Measure your ride height from the ground to the same point on each side of the car. When you've got your ride height set, you can make adjustments to set your corner weights and correct your alignment. Then go back and check it all again, because each change you make affects the others.

You need a set of wheel scales to set weights. Sometimes scales can be rented from racing shops, but a better plan is to find a tuner or racing shop with a set of scales and take your car there for corner weighting. It takes a lot less time and effort, and probably yields better results. Be sure to bring your car in its usual configuration and sit in the driver's seat while the weights are taken. By adjusting each strut's total length and spring compression up or down a little, you can maintain a level ride (or the angle you want) and equalize weights side to side in the car. Most Subarus have a natural weight distribution of about 55 to 60% in the front to 40 to 45% in the back, and this can be adjusted slightly, but not much.

Some Basic Alignment Settings

In the table below, camber and caster are expressed as degrees, and toe is expressed in millimeters. The settings in **Table 7-1** should be a reasonable place to start your tuning process.

For each degree you change your front camber towards negative, you can expect to get about a half-degree of toe-out without separately adjusting your tie rods. So, changing both front wheels from -1.5 to -2.5 gives you about 1 degree additional toe-out.

Table 7-1: 2002 Impreza Sedan

Factory Settings:

F/R	Angle	Min	Max
Front	Caster	+2.1	+4.1
Front	Camber	-0.9	+0.1
Front	Toe	-0.3	+0.3
Rear	Camber	-1.9	-0.4
Rear	Toe	-0.3	+0.3

Sample Street Performance Setup:

F/R	Angle	Measurement
Front	Camber	-1.5 Degrees total
Front	Toe	-0.1 mm total
Rear	Camber	-2.0 Degrees total
Rear	Toe	-0.1 mm total

Sample Autocross Setup:

F/R	Angle	Measurement
Front	Camber	-3.0 Degrees total
Front	Toe	+1.0 mm total
Rear	Camber	-2.0 Degrees total
Rear	Toe	-0.1 mm total

BRAKES

Subaru gives you a good set of brakes with every car—and you can make them better with a little bit of effort. Every time you step on the brakes, you'll appreciate a good set of binders.

Most of the time, performance enthusiasts focus on how to make their cars go faster—we look for torque, top speed, and grip. But it's just as important that your car be able to stop as well as it goes—maybe more important if it's a car you drive on public roads. Beyond the considerations for safety, your car is more fun to drive with a really good brake system. Brakes don't cost much

compared to everything else you can buy, and the results are noticeable. If you are not confident in your ability to work on your brakes, take your car to a professional. This is one area where a screw-up can endanger others as well as yourself and your wallet.

All-Wheel Drive Won't Help You Stop

The AWD system in your Subaru is great for getting your car moving. Having all four wheels dig in and go can get you started on snow or even ice. AWD helps you corner better, too, as all four wheels help direct the car. But one thing AWD can't do for you is slow you down. Every car has brakes on all four wheels, so when it comes to braking, your Subaru is just another car. The efficiency of your brakes is based on the squeezing power and friction in your hydraulics, calipers, pads, rotors, and your wheels and tires.

Subaru Brake Description

Almost all Subarus discussed in this book use a 4-wheel disc brake system. Some early Legacies and Imprezas used rear drum brakes. Unless you have an STI sedan, your 4-wheel disc system came with single-piston (pistons are also known as "pots") calipers in the rear and two-piston calipers in front.

STI cars feature two-piston Subaru or Brembo calipers in the rear and four-piston calipers in front. Rotor (brake disc) sizes have varied over the years by model and year. Generally speaking, the higher-performance

models (2.5RS, WRX, STI, Legacy GT) have larger rotors than other cars. All front rotors delivered since 1990 have been vented, which is to say they have two abrasive surfaces with air spaces in between to keep them cool. Some rear rotors, in the 1991–1994 Legacy Turbo and the STI, are vented, but the vast majority are solid.

Subaru uses a vacuum-assisted brake master cylinder, an antilock braking system, and hard lines throughout the chassis. All Legacies and Imprezas use a dual-circuit brake system where one circuit actuates the left front and right rear brakes, and the other the right front and left rear. This allows the car to stop even if one circuit has failed. Additionally, there's a proportioning valve that assures that the rear brakes receive less pressure than the fronts, preventing rear brake lockup. The parking brake on 4-wheel disc models is a small set of drum brakes inside the "hat" of the rear discs.

The master cylinder in your car has plenty of pushing power to stop your car—you don't need to upgrade this item, though Perrin and Cusco do offer braces to support the brake master. Keep your brake master cylinder and vacuum assist canister in good shape and use brake fluid as recommended by Subaru and they'll last for years.

About Brake Fade

Brake fade refers to when your brakes get very hot and a couple of things happen. The most critical is

This is a stock front disc brake setup. It uses a 2-piston floating caliper and a basic vented brake disc. There's a lot of room for upgrades to this system.

The rear disc brake system shipped with most Subarus is good enough for most driving, but you can improve it with a bigger disc and better caliper than the single-piston free-floating unit that Subaru provides.

Many Subarus through the mid-1990s came with rear drum brakes. If you want to upgrade these, be ready to swap in a set of rear discs, hubs, and parking brake assemblies that go with the discs as well.

In this picture of a new set of Brembo rotors, you can see the difference between the front vented rotor (left) and the rear solid rotor. Also, notice the difference in the "hat" area—the rear solid rotor has a large deep hat to accommodate the parking brake shoes.

that your brake fluid can boil and become compressible. Since your brakes depend on pressure to work, the vaporized fluid compresses instead of your brakes squeezing the calipers. You feel this as a soft or springy brake pedal, and you don't slow down. In extreme cases, the brake pedal may go to the floor—not a good thing if you're on a race track headed into a corner!

Brake fluid is a mixture of oils and other ingredients, designed to have a very high boiling point. Most automakers use and recommend a Department of Transportation brake fluid standard called DOT3. Most brake fluids that you buy in auto parts stores are DOT3, and it's perfectly adequate for normal driving applications. Just change the fluid every year or so, because DOT3 fluid absorbs water, and that lowers its boiling point and can corrode your brake system. Repeated heat cycles also "cook" the fluid and reduce its effectiveness.

DOT5 standard brake fluid uses silicone in its mixture to further raise its boiling point and heat resistance. DOT5 fluids do not absorb water, but this is not necessarily a good thing—it means that any water that does make it into your brakes travels along as a "bubble," and may not be expelled when you bleed the system.

High-grade racing and performance brake fluids are commonly available in DOT3 or DOT4 blends, but you should need them only if you plan to go racing or stage rallying, or if you live in the mountains and drive on mountain roads every day. But it doesn't hurt to have great brake fluid, either.

Sacha Potter's 1994 Legacy 2.2 Turbo

Sacha Potter is a college student in Washington D.C., and he found this extra-clean Legacy Turbo and made it his ride. Only lightly modified, the car is just right for Sacha's taste right now, though it might get more goodies later on. Sacha played it smart and began his upgrades with a good set of brakes.

Here's how Sacha likes his ride:

- WRX front brake conversion with Hawk HPS pads
- Goodridge braided stainless steel brake lines
- Racingbrake front rotors

- K&N air filter
- WRX wheels
- Toyo Proxes tires
- Whiteline front sway bar w/ endlinks

Sacha's Legacy has relatively few modifications, but the ones he has selected are designed to improve drivability in what is already a very sporty package. (Photo courtesy of Sacha Potter)

things in the right order and in balance, and making sure that your brakes fit under your wheels. Then you can move on to the fun part—thinking about braided stainless steel lines, slotted or cross-drilled rotors, solid or vented rear rotors, 2, 4, or 6 piston calipers, and a good pad compound. We look at each of these areas in turn.

Brake Hydraulics

The stock flexible brake lines run from the ends of the hard lines in your wheel wells to the brake calipers. These lines need to be flexible in order to move with your wheels as you drive. The stock lines are made from a layered reinforced rubber, and they're pretty good, but they do inflate slightly when you press on the brakes—the older they get, the more they balloon, and eventually crack. This expansion steals some of your braking pressure and contributes to a spongy pedal feel. You can fix this with a set of stainless steel braided brake lines. Using ordinary hand tools, you can install these lines yourself in a couple of hours. You need to bleed your brakes when you're done, so be sure you've got a friend to help, some fluid, rubber hose, and the small wrenches to fit the bleed nipples—while you're at it, go ahead and install speed bleeders at this time.

Some good hydraulic system products are:

Perrin Master Cylinder Stiffi

The Perrin brake master cylinder support "stiffi" easily solves a common

Upgrading Your Brakes

The places where you can improve your car's braking system are at the four corners, by upgrading your flexible brake lines, calipers, pads, and rotors. Subaru has made the brake system easy to work on, and most people with reasonable mechanical aptitude can get good results in a home garage.

A few practical factors should be considered when you think about upgrading your brakes, and those include making sure that you upgrade

This brace mounts to the very strong shock tower, and holds the master cylinder in place against the firewall, eliminating flex.

Subaru braking issue: the master cylinder mount on the firewall flexes under with hard braking. This adjustable support bolts to the driver-side shock tower to fix the problem.

Goodridge Brake Lines

Goodridge makes high-quality kits for many cars, including Subarus. These kits come with upgraded banjo bolts and fresh sealing washers, and you should use the hardware in the kit instead of your stock banjos when performing the installation. You can use the WRX kit on any Impreza with 4-wheel disc brakes.

Super Brake Fluid

Several good brands of high-temp racing brake fluid are available. Motul, ATE, Wilwood, and Castrol all make fluids with boiling points well over 400 degrees F. You can get enough to replace your stock fluid for $20 to $30, but be sure to carry some extra, as you will not be able to mix other fluids into your system once you select a high-performance mixture.

This photo shows three good bottles of brake fluid. The ones on the left and right are DOT3/DOT4 fluid for daily driving use. In the center is a can of ATE super blue racing brake fluid. This is the stuff you want when you're dealing with enough heat to glow your rotors during track racing or rally racing.

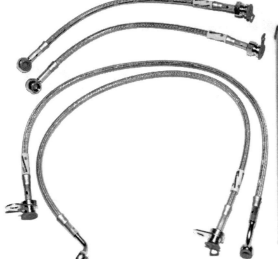
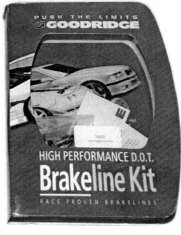

A set of steel braided brake lines, like these from Goodridge, really improve your pedal feel. Many drivers are surprised by how much firmer the brake pedal becomes.

Speed Bleeders

You can purchase speed bleeder nipples at any good automotive supply shop for about $10 each. These are standard metric bleed nipples with a one-way valve built in. They prevent your system from sucking air back in during the bleed process. They are made to fit all Subarus back to 1990, and there's no work required—just take out your old parts and screw in the speed bleeders the next time you bleed your brakes. These are the only things I've found in over 25 years that really work to improve the bleeding process.

Brake Pads

Brake pads are another easy upgrade for your system. By choosing a better set of brake pads, you can get more stopping power and resistance to brake fade. Besides boiling brake fluid, some low-cost brake pads contribute to fade because they don't work as well when they get very hot. Conversely, racing brake pads tend not to work well when cold, and need to be warmed up before they grip. You probably won't ever reach the optimum heat range for a racing pad like the Hawk Blue or Black compound in normal driving. But Hawk, like most other high-performance brake manufactur-

ers, also makes a line of high-performance street pads designed for your car. This is one area where "racing parts" aren't necessarily better for your purposes.

New pads frequently "outgas" and may feel greasy as you "cook out" some of the remaining volatile solvents from the pad material. This is called green fade, and it's why you should always bed in a new set of brakes very well before you rely on them for high performance. Racers sometimes use a retired kitchen toaster oven to bake their pads before use. Do this outside or in your workshop because it smells terrible and may produce some smoke. You can also find a nice long empty stretch of road and lightly ride the brake until you feel your new pads start to fade. Then drive some more without using the brakes and let them cool. Then repeat the process until the green fade is over.

You can improve your overall brake performance with a set of upgraded brake pads without worrying about cold pads, because there are so many different types and grades of pad to choose from. You can buy pads that are ceramic-based, organic, or metal-infused. AEM, Brembo, EBC, Ferodo, Axxis, Hawk, Wilwood, Carbotech,

Performance Friction—all of these manufacturers and others make high-quality brake pads. Each brand has a following, usually very dedicated. In my experience, Axxis Metal Masters are a good choice for street applications, and Hawk Black pads are an excellent racing and track-day pad.

To choose a pad, talk to performance experts in your area—people who drive on the same roads in the same weather in the same kind of car as you—and find out what's working for them. Be prepared to try a few different brands and you'll find one that works well for you.

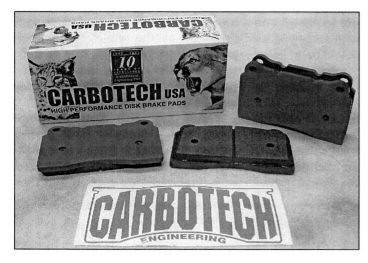

contact. It is simple to manufacture, but not as good as a fixed caliper for high-performance braking.

A fixed caliper has pistons on both sides of the caliper, and each side pushes the pad against the rotor. Because the caliper does not move, the system gives you a firmer pedal feel and better control of the rotor under braking. Virtually all aftermarket caliper upgrades are a fixed design. Most aftermarket front calipers use four (or six) pistons, with two (or three) on either side. Most aftermarket rear caliper upgrades offer two pistons with one on either side of the rotor.

These Carbotech brake pads are sold by fastwrx.com, where they're a popular choice. Carbotech pads are used widely for street and track applications. (Photo courtesy of Mach V Motorsports)

By increasing the number of pistons and changing the pad format, you are improving your braking efficiency by increasing your ability to squeeze the rotor, but you are also increasing the area of the rotor that is squeezed at any given time. Increasing the friction area gives you better brakes. Some good brake caliper products on the market are:

Brembo 2-Piston Rear Caliper Kit

This is the Brembo 2-piston rear caliper delivered on the STI. Because the STI uses a different hub and bolt pattern from every other Subaru, this upgrade is not a no-brainer, but you can perform a swap to install these on your WRX or other Impreza using a kit sold through fastwrx.com. This kit also requires that you change to a larger rear rotor, which is also available from fastwrx.com. These rotors are made to fit the stock WRX parking brake assembly, which is different from the STI assembly.

Calipers

The stock calipers on your Subaru are pretty good, for OEM brakes. But manufacturers tend to prefer solutions that are less expensive to manufacture, and so the calipers shipped with your Subaru (unless you get an STI, Spec.B, or other special performance edition) are designed as "floating" calipers. This means the brake pistons are on one side of the caliper, and the caliper body floats back and forth on a pair of posts.

The stock Subaru front caliper has two pistons on the inner side of the rotor while a stock Subaru rear caliper uses one piston on the inner side of the rotor. As you step on the brakes, the pistons extend and push the caliper body away from the rotor. This pulls the outer pad into contact with the rotor, and pushes the inner pad to

When buying calipers, be sure you get both a left and a right-side unit. Calipers are directional because they mount in the same position, but opposite orientation on your left and right wheels. In all cases, the bleed nipple must be on top of the caliper for it to work. If you mount a left-side caliper on the right, it will be upside-down and the bleed nipple will be on the bottom!

If you upgrade to a different set of calipers on your stock rotors, you shouldn't be in danger of interfering with your stock wheels. But be aware that you will likely have to change your pad format (shape and size) as well. Most aftermarket calipers use standard pad formats that are manufactured by many pad makers, but these are not necessarily compatible with the stock format.

The Brembo rear caliper used on the STI is a very popular upgrade. You need a replacement rear rotor to fit this caliper to the WRX, but these are readily available in a kit from fastwrx.com.

Wilwood Calipers

Wilwood makes a popular range of affordable high-performance calipers. Wilwood uses stainless steel pistons in all custom show and sport performance applications for their low heat transfer properties and resistance to corrosion. Road race kits feature SL6/ST calipers with Wilwood's proprietary Thermlock pistons for maximum heat protection in extreme heat environments.

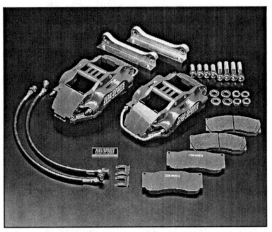

ZeroSports offers an excellent kit with everything you need to fit 4 or 6-piston calipers over your stock size front brake discs. Larger wheels are needed to clear these calipers, however. (Photo courtesy of ZeroSports)

ZeroSports 4 and 6-Piston Front Caliper Kits

Zero/Sports is a JDM aftermarket company just getting into the North American market with some really hot products. These brakes are designed for high-performance track-day and racing applications. The caliper kits include high-durability pads and attachment hardware. One very attractive feature is that these calipers can be used with the stock front brake discs.

2006–2007 Impreza WRX Front and Rear Calipers

You can install the 4-piston front and 2-piston rear caliper from the 2006–2007 Impreza WRX on older Imprezas with the use of alternate caliper brackets. This upgrade also includes the 1-inch larger rear rotors that come with the 2006–2007 WRX for a general upgrade that still uses factory parts.

Rotors

Upgrading your rotors generally goes along with changing your calipers, and that means a full brake kit, but upgrading your stock rotors has benefits, even if you can't afford the whole megillah of a big brake kit.

There are two ways you can get more out of your brake rotors. One is to use larger rotors. Larger rotors have more friction surface (also known as swept area), more mass to absorb and disperse heat, and you're getting better leverage on the wheel with a larger rotor. But a larger rotor generally requires an aftermarket caliper, so what's left?

You can still get a rotor upgrade by using the same diameter rotor with improved features. Usually this means a drilled, slotted, or better-vented rotor. A drilled or slotted rotor improves your braking performance by keeping itself clean and cool. It's also lighter, but not by much. The slots or holes pass under the pads as you brake, providing a place for the abraded material to go, and more surface area in contact with air for heat dissipation.

You can also buy a rotor with better venting. Most stock vented rotors can go on either side of the car because the vanes in between the two friction surfaces are radial—they travel straight out from the center. An upgraded rotor has curved vanes, which act like a centrifugal pump, flinging air from the center of the rotor out through the perimeter continuously as the wheel turns. Such rotors are marked as left side or right side. Brembo makes an excellent curved-vane front replacement rotor in solid or drilled configuration.

You can also buy two-piece rotors, which typically have a steel friction ring that is bolted to a separate (usually aluminum) center. The advantage of these designs is that they

This Rotora two-piece rotor offers both slots and drilled holes and is directionally vented. Rotora offers rotors in a variety of sizes—the 295mm rotors fit under 16-inch wheels, while their 330mm rotors require 17-inch wheels, and the extra-large 355mm rotors need 18-inch wheels.

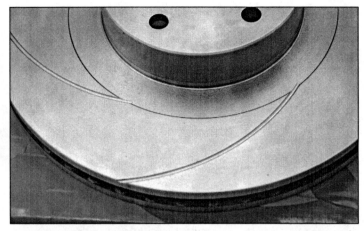

This picture shows the venting and the grooving on this Brembo rotor. Grooves help keep the pad and rotor clean and cool, while the directional venting vanes built into the rotor pump cooling air through as the rotor turns.

Directional grooves in the solid rear rotor help keep the pad and rotor clean and cool as well. Less force is applied to the rear brakes, so these rotors are not typically vented.

are lighter, the friction surface can be easily replaced, and they are more resistant to warping. They are also expensive.

Some good upgrade options for rotors are:

Legacy Turbo Vented Rear Rotor

The 1991–1994 Legacy Turbo used a vented rear rotor of the same 266mm diameter as most Imprezas except the STI. To switch to the Legacy Turbo rotors, you must also swap in the Legacy calipers and caliper mounting brackets. Note that this caliper uses a different brake pad from the Impreza caliper, so you need a new set of pads as well.

Legacy H6 Rear Rotor

The 2001 and later Legacy Outback H6 uses a rotor that is 11.3 inches in diameter, which is 1 inch larger than the stock Impreza rotors through 2005. A simple mounting bracket suffices to install this larger rear brake on your Impreza.

Brembo Slotted Rotors

These front and rear rotors are an excellent first upgrade choice because they are made in the stock diameters for most Imprezas and Legacies. They use directional curved vanes, and have slots engraved in the friction surfaces for cleaning and heat dissipation.

Big Brake Kits

When you're ready to go all the way, it's time for a big brake kit. Depending on the kit you choose, you might even need to buy new wheels and tires at the same time to clear your new binders.

The advantages of a big brake kit are numerous—you have better leverage, more pressure on the pads, bigger pads, more swept area, vented and drilled rotors, and your choice of high-performance pads. Plus they look great, especially if you have some open wheels to show off your kit. There aren't too many downsides to a big

brake kit—a little extra weight, and of course the expense, especially if you have to modify your parking brake setup to work with a set of performance rear discs.

The main consideration when you're thinking about a brake kit is much the same as for all the individual components—will this kit work with the kind of driving you're going to do? Even if you plan on street driving only, chances are you'll love a big brake kit provided you choose a good all-around pad and not a racing pad.

Here are some leading brake kits on the market:

StopTech WRX Big Brake Kits

StopTech offers both front and rear brake kits for the WRX and Impreza. The kit includes four-piston calipers for the front and two-piston for the rear. Front two-piece rotors are almost 13 inches in diameter, and feature directional cooling vanes, optional drilled friction surfaces, and an aluminum hub. The two-piece rear rotors are slotted and also have directional vanes and aluminum hubs. The kit from fastwrx.com comes with

This is the four-piston front caliper from the StopTech big brake kit. You need 17-inch wheels at least to clear this caliper, but you get great stopping power.

braided stainless brake lines and high-performance brake pads as well as a complete supply of required fasteners. The StopTech big brake kit requires 17-inch wheels, but not all 17s fit over the brakes, so some research is required.

Brembo Big Brake Kit

This Brembo kit brings your WRX, Impreza, or Legacy up to STI performance standards. Each kit includes four Brembo "gold" calipers as delivered with the STI. The front rotors are 326mm x 30mm (12.8 x 1.2 inch). The rear rotors are made to fit the WRX parking brake setup while using the Brembo STI rear caliper. This kit does not fit on an STI, as the brake discs are made to fit the standard non-STI bolt pattern. The kit from fast-wrx.com includes Goodridge braided stainless steel brake lines and Ferodo brake pads.

Wilwood Brake Kit

Wilwood makes a complete two-piece rotor kit that covers the front and back ends of your car. The front kit includes billet Superlite 6-piston calipers in red or black finish, your choice of 13 or 14-inch GT Racing or SRP performance rotors with GT Series aluminum centers, and a set of pads. The rear kit is in Wilwood's Pro Series, and includes 4-piston calipers finished in red or black, two-piece 12.2 or 13-inch GT Racing or

This is the Brembo big brake kit with 326mm vented front rotors. It is made to fit the stock non-STI Subaru hub bolt pattern.

SRP performance rotors, steel center hat for the parking brake, and a set of pads. This kit supports the original equipment parking brake.

Rotora Big Brake Kit

Rotora offers a 6-piston front brake kit with two-piece cross-drilled and slotted rotors in 355 mm or 330 mm diameters. The kit also includes anodized black caliper mounting brackets, Rotora race pads, and stainless-steel braided brake lines. Optional upgrades to the kit include Rotora's ceramic or HH formulated race pads.

This is the Rotora 6-piston kit with drilled and grooved two-piece rotors. This is a lot of brake, and requires an 18-inch wheel like this Volk.

WHEELS AND TIRES

Your wheels are one of the most visible features on your car, and so most people naturally select them carefully for style. Everyone knows that good tires are critical to good performance, but your wheels are also an important performance component. It's easy to make a wheel choice that is both stylish and a performance enhancement.

Your wheels and tires are the final component in the power delivery chain—the parts that physically connect your car to the ground. Thus, they have a great impact on your car's acceleration, handling, and braking. The consequences of tire selection are well known, but remember also that the weight and offset of your wheels affects the way your springs and shocks work, and the weight and diameter of your wheels affects your car's braking ability.

If you plan to compete using special tires, you should buy an extra set of wheels and keep your competition rubber on them. Autocrossers, rallycrossers, racers, and winter sports enthusiasts should all have a dedicated set of doughnuts kept in good condition for playtime.

This chapter looks at some considerations to keep in mind when selecting wheels and tires.

The Physics Of Wheels

Moment of Inertia has nothing to do with the amount of time it takes you to get off the couch—but it has a lot to do with accelerating your car. Moment

For a serious time attack car, the sticky tires that you need for great lap times won't last 5,000 miles on the street. A spare set of wheels is a good investment for competition rubber.

Beauty must be in the eye of the beholder, because the orange wheels on this Legacy Turbo don't appeal to many people.

This OZ Racing wheel is made to be both light and strong to handle the rigors of racing.

These 17-inch Advan TC II wheels easily clear this nice AP brake kit.

of inertia is a measurement of how much torque it takes to accelerate an object in angular rotation around an axis—to spin a wheel, for example. People sometimes call this "polar moment of inertia," but that's not strictly accurate. Polar moment of inertia is a measurement of an object's inertial resistance to twisting as torsion is applied to it.

Without breaking out the physics textbooks, a small wheel takes less energy to spin up than a large wheel of the same mass because the mass is concentrated close to the axis of rotation. This is why pure racing clutches are made so small—to help your engine spin up faster. It's also why 20-inch and larger wheels (almost never seen on Subarus) are bad for both acceleration and braking performance. It takes more effort to get that wheel rolling, and it also takes more effort to stop it once it's going!

To use an extreme example, monster trucks need huge torquey engines in large part to get those giant tires moving, but the vast majority of Subarus are rolling on wheels of 18 inches or smaller. The differences in moment of inertia are tiny between 16 and 18 inches. So don't worry about going to 17 or 18 inches to clear your big brake kit—it's no big deal.

Next, your wheels and tires are usually among the biggest contributors to your car's unsprung weight. Remember from Chapter 7 that unsprung weight stresses your suspension and shocks. You don't have to buy the absolute lightest wheels and tires on the market, but be aware of weight when you're making your selections. It's surprising how heavy some wheels are.

Finally, the wheel/tire combo affects acceleration not just by maintaining grip, but also because the total diameter of your tire affects your final drive ratio—a taller tire is just like a taller gear. There's a tradeoff between acceleration performance and top speed inherent in the diameter of the wheel and tire combination you choose.

Selecting Wheels

Selecting wheels should be fun—and the following information should help you get started. Most Subaru-specific retailers know the fitment issues on wheels that they sell. A general-purpose wheel and tire shop may not. Another good source for this information is the Internet—the Subaru forums have archived information or current experience with the fitment of a wide variety of wheels.

There are a few factors to keep in mind when selecting wheels:

- Will the inner diameter of this wheel clear my brakes, struts, tie rod ends, and any aftermarket parts I plan to put on in the future?

- Will the outer diameter of this wheel, plus the tire I plan to run, clear my fender wells? Even if I lower the car?

- Is the width of this wheel suitable for the tires I plan to buy?

- Is the width of this wheel suitable for my car's suspension and wheel wells?

- Does this wheel have an offset within the workable range for my car?

- Is this wheel strong enough for my purposes?

Terms to Understand

Wheel Diameter: Wheel diameter is the distance across the center of the wheel

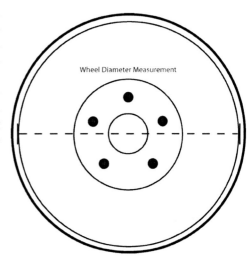

Measure the diameter of your wheel from the bead sealing surfaces, not the edge of the rim. If you measure incorrectly, it usually adds 1 inch to your measurement.

from bead sealing surface to bead sealing surface—not from the edges of the rim. Measuring from the edges of the rim can add an inch or more to your measurement.

Wheel Width: Wheel width is the distance across the width of the wheel from bead sealing surface to bead sealing surface—again not from the edges of the rim. Measuring from the edges of the rim can add half an inch or more to this measurement.

inboard of the centerline, and zero offset is where the torque circle is on the centerline.

Bolt Pattern: For a 5-bolt wheel as used on Subarus, measure from the far edge of one bolt hole to the center of the second bolt hole over. This measurement is also known as the Pitch Circle Diameter (PCD).

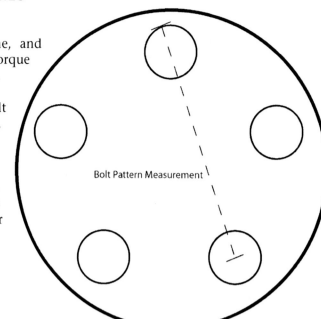

Bolt Pattern Measurement

This cutaway drawing shows the wheel width measurement and location of the bead sealing surfaces. If you measure to the outside of the rim, you'll think your wheels are wider than they are.

The dotted line indicates the measurement to make to find the PCD (Pitch Circle Diameter) or bolt pattern of a 5-lug wheel. Measure from the far end of any hole to the middle of one of the opposite holes.

Wheel Offset: Wheel offset is the distance between the back of the torque circle (the surface where you bolt the wheel to the hub) and the measured center of the wheel width. A wheel with positive offset is where the torque circle is outboard of the centerline of the wheel width. Negative offset is where the torque circle is

Wheel Diameter

Selecting a wheel diameter is probably the first thing you need to decide. Most modern Subarus come with 16-inch wheels, though many early Imprezas came with 13 and 14-inch wheels and early Legacies came with 14 or 15-inch wheels. The performance cars of the late 1990s (2.5RS

and Legacy GT) came with 16-inch wheels, and by the time of the introduction of the WRX in 2002, all Subarus except base-model Foresters came with 16-inch wheels. The basic Forester went to 16-inch wheels in 2003. 17-inch wheels have always been a dealer option for the WRX.

From its introduction in 2004, the STI came with 17-inch wheels, and in 2005 the Legacy GT went to 17 inches as well. Following the trend, in

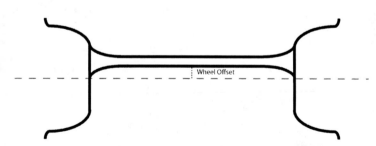

To measure the wheel offset, find the centerline of the wheel as shown in this cutaway drawing, then measure from that plane to the face of the torque circle. Many wheels now have this measurement embossed on the rim along with the width and diameter.

Older 15-inch Legacy wheels fit well and look good on this Impreza rally car.

Wheel Strength

The variety of wheel styles available on the market has never been greater than today, but be aware that not all wheels are equally strong. If you plan on doing some hard cornering, be aware that you can put a great deal of stress on your wheels. You want your wheels to be strong enough not to flex or break under cornering, and you want them to be light as well. To achieve that end, look for wheels with many spokes, preferably designed in a web pattern. These are popular with racers for their lightweight and strong design. Wheels with a very open face and very few spokes are more likely to flex and eventually break.

This Konig wheel is nice, light, and stylish for street use, but is not a racer's choice.

The wheels on this racecar (note that only three of them are touching the ground) use many conjoined spokes for strength.

2006 the WRX and 2.5i went to 17-inch wheels. The 2006–2007 Legacy Spec.B has raised the bar again with 18-inch wheels from the factory.

Within the 16 to 18-inch range and a modern car, your minimum wheel size is usually dictated by your brake plans, and sometimes by the tires you want to run. Most brake kits state the minimum specs for wheel diameter, but bear in mind that this is no guarantee that a particular wheel of the specified diameter will fit over a particular brake. Offset and wheel structure comes into play as well. There's no test better than fitting the actual wheel/tire over the brake in your fender and checking for interference throughout your suspension travel range.

Wheel Width

The next factor to consider is wheel width. You can generally find any given style of wheel in a range of diameters and widths, but generally speaking as the diameter increases, the available range of widths also moves upward. You won't find 18X5 wheels outside of a specialty shop.

The old 13 and 14-inch wheels were 5 to 6.5 inches wide, and some of the 15-inch wheels were 7 inches wide. The Subaru standard 16-inch wheels delivered with modern cars are 6.5 to 7.5 inches wide. The stock 17-inch wheels are 7 to 8 inches wide, and the 18-inch wheels on the Legacy GT

This 2005 Legacy GT has the new-style 17-inch wheels.

This 2004 STI has the stock silver-tone BBS 17-inch wheels with the 5 x 100 bolt pattern.

This 2006 STI has gold-tone BBS wheels with the 5 x 114.3 bolt pattern.

This WRX wagon shows off the 2006 and later stock 17-inch wheels nicely.

The wide fenders on 2002 and later Impreza sedans will accommodate a slightly wider tire than on previous Imprezas or the wagons. These wheels are Rota Tarmac II, 17x7.5 in Cadmium Pearl, and the tires are Pirelli PZero Nero M&S 215/45-17.

Even by 2006, the wagon version of the Impreza has not changed its fender lines.

Spec.B are 7 inches wide. Aftermarket 16 to 18-inch wheels marketed to Subaru owners for street use generally range from 7 to 8.5 inches wide, with the majority at 7 inches.

Wheel width is also a critical consideration in conjunction with the tires you're selecting. A tire uses air pressure to keep its lips sealed against the wheel (called the bead seal), and if your tires are too narrow and your wheels too wide, the lips will be stretched to meet the beads. This can lead to tires coming off of the bead at high speed or during cornering, which can be disastrous. Conversely, if your tires are too wide and your rims are too narrow, the tire will be forced to balloon out from the rim and you'll get bad handling and a bad bead seal. In general, plan for your wheel width to roughly match the tread width of your tires.

Your tire retailer should be able to tell you if you have a width problem. But again, there's no test for wheel width as good as putting one on your car and moving the steering and suspension through its full range of motion while checking for rubbing. In general, you can fit slightly wider wheels on the 2002+ Impreza sedans due to their flared fenders. Wagons and pre-2002 Imprezas and Legacies have a little less space.

This 17-inch 5zigen ProRacer has a +48 offset and is made to fit all Legacy, Imprezas, and Foresters.

Wheel Offset

Wheel offset is the last critical dimension to look at when selecting your wheels. Correct offset is important to ensure that your wheels clear your brakes and to avoid fender rubbing. All stock Subaru wheels are designed with positive offset of about +50 to +55mm. 15-inch stock wheels use a +55mm offset, while stock 16 and 17-inch wheels use +53 or +55mm.

Aftermarket wheels have a slightly broader range of offsets, from as low as +38mm up to +55mm. In general, the greater the diameter of the wheel, the more the offset tends to be lower, but realize that they still use a minimum of about +38mm of offset. That's only 1.7 centimeters (about 3/4 an inch) of difference between the high and low limits.

In general, if you keep your wheel offset pretty close to stock for the diameter of wheel you're using, it shouldn't cause wheel clearance problems. If you get too far out of tolerance range, under about +48mm, you are likely to have rubbing problems. As always, test fit the actual wheel if you're not sure.

Wheel Weight

As you know, wheels are unsprung weight, and you want to keep that under control. Stock 16-inch Subaru alloy wheels weigh about 16 to 18 pounds apiece. Not bad for stock wheels from an automaker who doesn't want to have to replace broken wheels under warranty. Aftermarket wheels from 15 to 17 inches in diameter generally range from about 12 to 22 pounds, and most average about 16 to 18 pounds. 18-inch wheels are somewhat heavier on average, usually weighing about 18 to 25 pounds.

Bolt Pattern

Subaru bolt patterns are easy—almost all Subarus since 1990 use a 5 on 100mm bolt pattern. This means that from the far edge of one bolt hole to the center of the second bolt hole over is 100mm. 2005 and later STI Imprezas and Legacy Spec.B cars use a 5 x 114.3mm bolt pattern because of a different and larger wheel bearing assembly. Both 5x100 and 5x114.3 are common import bolt patterns, which helps to offer you a great variety of wheels that are likely to fit your car.

Lug Nuts and Studs

When you're buying wheels, be sure to ask if your stock lug nuts will work with your new wheels. Lug nuts and wheels have mating surfaces that should be machined to the same angles; otherwise they only touch in a small ring, which stresses both the wheel and the nut. Lug nuts are cheap—make sure you have the right ones—but if you change them, carry enough spare stock ones in your glove box to mount your spare tire, and make sure your lug wrench fits both sets of nuts.

If you are planning for serious competition, you may also want to upgrade your wheel lug studs. Racers typically choose longer, thicker lug studs with a smaller, smooth end to aid in getting the nut started onto the threads. They use steel lug nuts without caps or chrome because strength overrides all considerations of style when it comes to keeping the wheels on a race-car. Racing suppliers make a wide variety of wheel studs that can be installed on your car, but it usually requires a hydraulic press and occasionally some machining, so you'll want to have that work done at a good machine shop.

Selecting Tires

Selecting a brand and a particular model of tire is almost a religious question. Each brand has its following, and people swear by their favorite tires as the best. In truth, any high-quality well-known name-brand tire rated for

This Volk 18-inch racing wheel has +50 positive offset. Also, note how much space it has around that StopTech brake caliper, and the unusual Allen-head lug nuts.

Table 9-1: Stock Tire Size Chart	
WRX	205/55-16, 215/45-17
2.5RS	205/55-16
2.5i	225/45-17
STI	225/45-17
Impreza	165/80-13, 175/70-14, 185/70-14, 195/60-14, 195/60-15, 205/60-15, 205/55-15, 205/55-16
Forester	205/70-15, 215/60-16
Forester XT	215/55-17
Legacy	185/70-14, 195/60-15, 205/60-15
Outback	195/60-15, 205/75-15, 225/60-16, 225/55-17
Legacy GT	205/55-16, 205/65-16
Spec.B	215/45-18

Yokohama designed this tire specifically for the kind of stresses that a sports sedan generates. It's primarily a dry tire, but also offers good wet-weather performance. Note the large blocks of rubber for good dry traction. (Photo courtesy of Yokohama Tires)

the kind of driving you're planning to do is likely to be a good choice. Street tires today have tremendous grip, and most perform well in both wet and dry environments.

Table 9-1 shows most of the various tire sizes delivered with different models of Legacies and Imprezas since 1990.

Selecting a replacement tire requires some tradeoffs. The very best dry traction tires tend to be very scary on wet pavement, and completely useless on gravel, snow, or ice. For most street cars, you want to get a tire with good all-around performance, since you don't want to choose between swapping shoes or going surfing every time it rains.

Dedicated autocrossers, track day competitors, and rallycrossers usually have a set of competition tires that they install on race day, and another set of good street tires for general use.

Here are some example tires to illustrate the variety available to you.

Racing Tires

The Yokohama ADVAN A048 is a DOT-approved racing tire. Some time back, racing organizations decided to limit costs by requiring drivers to run tires approved for street use. Shortly, the drivers demanded a tire that was approved, but was really a racing tire. The A048 is the latest of that kind of tire. As you can see, this is not a rain tire, but an all-out sticky tire for smooth dry pavement.

This is Yokohama's latest DOT-approved radial racing tire. It's got a lot of rubber on the ground, but you wouldn't want to run this tire in the rain. (Photo courtesy of Yokohama Tires)

High-Performance Tires

The Yokohama ADVAN Sport, S-Drive, Neova, and S.4 tires are good examples of street performance tires. The Sport, S-Drive, and Neova are designed for ultra-high-speed applications, primarily on dry pavement. Yokohama says that the S.4 is specifically designed for sports sedans, and its tread design is more compatible with general high performance street driving with increased tread patterning for better wet weather control. A few similar tires include Kumho Ecsta series, and the Bridgestone Potenza RE070 and RE050A are used as the stock tires on the STI and Legacy Spec.B, respectively.

Standard All-Weather Tires

Basic stock Subaru come with all-season tires, and they're good enough

On the ADVAN Sport tire, note that the tread is not symmetrical from side to side. This is a directional tire, and somewhere on the side is an arrow showing which way the tire wants to roll. If you buy a set of these, make sure you get two left-side and two right-side tires. (Photo courtesy of Yokohama Tires)

for most people who don't care about high performance. These tires are harder and less sticky than the high-performance rubber, but they last longer and do well in the winter. Take a look at the tread pattern on the Yokohama T4 or Touring and note that the tread is deeper and allows water to exit through the sides. Modern Legacies and Foresters carry the Bridgestone or a Yokohama tire

Here's a non-directional high-performance tire. This one is likely very good in the wet, as those large tread grooves expel water as you drive. On dry pavement, the large blocks of rubber give you excellent grip. (Photo courtesy of Yokohama Tires)

The Kumho Ecsta is another great all-around high-performance tire. Kumho makes a wide variety of motorsports and high-performance tires to fit Subarus. (Photo courtesy of Kumho Tires)

A T-rated tire is good up to 118 mph, which is a lot faster than most people will ever drive. This is not a performance tire, but tires like these are seen on a lot of older Subarus. (Photo courtesy of Yokohama Tires)

The S-Drive is another of the latest tires to come from Yokohama, featuring its latest compounds and tread designs. Manufacturers change their tire offerings annually, so your favorite tire today is not likely to be available in a few years. (Photo courtesy of Yokohama Tires)

H-rated tires are specified for speeds up to 130 miles per hour. This tire still has a lot of rubber on the ground, but the designers are moving towards better rain and all-around driving with this tread. (Photo courtesy of Yokohama Tires)

This is a basic low-cost high-mileage street tire. This model has an 80,000-mile treadwear warranty from Yokohama, longer than most people own their cars. It offers that high mileage, but at the expense of grip. (Photo courtesy of Yokohama Tires)

from the factory, while Imprezas carry a variety of all-season tires.

Mud, Snow and Gravel Tires

For those who know they'll be driving in demanding winter conditions, mud and snow tires are an excellent choice. Many well-known brands are available, such as the Michelin X-Ice, Bridgestone Blizzak, and Pirelli Winter SnowSport. There are also imported brands such as the Nokian Hakkapeliitta line from Finland, where they know a few things about snow. For serious gravel work, such as performance rally, tires such as the Silverstone S-series are needed. These tires are made to grab the ground and hold it under any conditions. Other gravel (also known as "forest") rally tires include the Hankook Ventus, Pirelli T-series, and Yokohama AO35.

Silverstone Racing Tyres are used by many Subaru rallyists for their ability to withstand the punishment of performance driving on gravel roads. (Photo courtesy of Tabor Rally Team)

BODY AND INTERIOR

One of the most popular areas for modification on Subarus is the body-work. A great number of body kits are available on the market—some are good and some require a bit of work before they fit right. They range from very subtle and tasteful changes in the stock lines to garish stuff straight out of a comic book interpretation of a sports car.

Most bodywork changes you can find do not enhance your car's aerodynamics. They may accommodate larger wheels, bigger and better lights, or a front-mounted intercooler, but the vast majority of them are just made to look good. It's always amusing to find a car on which the owner has spent thousands of dollars on ultra-light carbon fiber parts, and then more thousands on 400 pounds of stereo speakers and amplifiers.

Aerodynamic Devices

There are a number of aerodynamic devices in use today, and it's helpful to review what they're called and what they're supposed to do. This section briefly reviews the major components in use today.

Wings

Wing is a term generally given to an aerodynamically shaped device that is mounted on braces at the rear of the car. Wings are also known as an airfoil. Purpose-built racecars such as Indy cars also have wings on the front end of the car, but sedans do not use those.

This car has a complete bodywork kit by Revolution Motorsports, featuring Kakumei carbon fiber body panels. Look and you'll see widened fender flares, a front-end kit, hood, wing, and side skirts on this 2002 WRX. (Photo courtesy of Revolution Motorsports)

Compare the heavily modified car to this stock WRX of the same vintage. It may be ordinary as dirt, but Subaru did a good job making this a handsome car.

Airfoils work because of their shape—convex on one side and slightly concave on the other. Air flows faster past the convex side than the concave. This creates lower pressure on the convex side, and higher pressure on the concave side, and the difference in pressure is felt as lift or downforce. The end plates keep air from spilling off the side of the wing, increasing the effect.

A wing on your car is fundamentally the same as a wing on an airplane, but where an airplane uses a wing to generate lift so it can fly, on a car we turn the airfoil upside down to generate downforce. Downforce is nice on a car because it adds effective weight, but not mass. If you were to put a scale under a moving Indy car, you'd find that at 220 mph, it's got something like 5,000 pounds of downforce on a 1,500-pound car.

In order for a wing to do you any good, it has to sit in the airflow over your car. The only Subaru to carry a real wing from the factory is the STI. The STI wing, especially in the 2006/2007 models with the roof spoiler, is high enough in the airflow to do some good.

Aftermarket wing makers generally don't have access to the kind of development and testing facilities that the automakers do. If you want to see the result of serious downforce requirements and the budget to figure out the best possible solution, take a look at the wings the Subaru World Rally Team

This wing on the back of the ESX Motorsports Pro Mod drag car offers some incredible downforce—and it is needed to keep traction under this car!

Subaru Rally Team USA cars use the stock STI aero package. In this shot you can see the roof spoiler (right at the top of the rear window) and the tall STI wing up in the airflow.

This is a sharp looking wing from APR Racing. Actual downforce is hard to prove outside of a wind tunnel.

Kakumei designed this wing to be similar to the ones used on Subaru World Rally Team cars. Nothing says import tuner hot rod like a big wing! (Photo courtesy of Revolution Motorsports)

uses on their WRC cars. These devices look like something taken off of a jet fighter, and they work even when the car is going sideways. That's the one to have if you need downforce.

But it's not practical for most of us to run a World Rally wing. And realistically, until you're going well in excess of reasonable street and highway speeds, no wing is going to do a whole lot more than gravity is already doing to pin down the rear end of a 3,000 pound sedan. So the bottom line is that you should regard your wing as an aesthetic decoration until you're

This tasteful spoiler on the back of an early turbo Legacy is a nice dress up and may just help the aerodynamics.

Rear spoilers improve a car's stability by creating turbulence in the airflow going over the back of the car, negating lift that your car is generating. If you stand back and look at a car from the side it looks a little like a wing, with the roofline as the convex side and the underside as the concave side. Moving that shape through the air can create lift. This effect is most pronounced on smoothly designed cars like Porsches. By disrupting the airflow over the top of the car, you eliminate the wing effect and reduce the amount of lift naturally generated by the shape of the car.

Spoilers can also be mounted on the roof of a car, as they are on the

While it's up in the airflow and shaped like a wing, it's doubtful that the device on the back of this WRX wagon is providing much downforce. But it does look nice and it may help to stir up the air and keep off some of the muck that accumulates on hatchback windows.

ready for serious racing—and then your wing will likely be specified for you in the racing rules.

Spoilers

Spoilers are often confused with wings because so many spoilers are mounted on the trunk lids of cars in the same place as a wing. The aerodynamic devices on the back of a WRX or 2.5RS/2.5i Impreza are not up in the airflow. They're down in the turbulent low-pressure area behind the cabin of a Subaru, and if you look closely, they are not designed to produce downforce. They are spoilers, not wings.

In the late 1990s, Subaru still gave the Legacy GT a small spoiler as an upgrade from the more basic models.

This is the "basket handle" spoiler used on the Impreza 2.5RS from 1998 to 2001.

The newer Legacy GT cars also offer a nice spoiler to remind everyone that this is a sports sedan.

This chin spoiler looks good and probably stirs up the air very nicely. (Photo courtesy of Revolution Motorsports)

This air dam is an absolute necessity on the ESX pro-mod class drag car.

2006–2007 STI, to direct air down to a wing. Some cars also use "chin" or "lip" spoilers on the front of a car to disrupt the air trying to pass underneath the car.

An air dam is a specific kind of spoiler. You see these frequently on track racing cars. They are flexible walls at the front of the car that brush the ground (or come close to it). As the car moves forward, the air dam prevents air from flowing under the car and generates low pressure under the body, sucking the car down to the ground. At various times, racers have put skirts along the sides of a car in addition to the air dam to enhance the vacuum—these are called "ground effects" and they are usually not allowed in formal racing. The most famous case was the Chapparal 2J "sucker car" which used skirts, and then added a large fan that sucked the air out from under the car. It was so effective at sticking the car to the ground that it was banned from Can-Am racing.

Splitters

A splitter is another implementation of the wing idea. With a splitter, you place a flat surface parallel to the ground at the bottom of the front bodywork. By sticking this plane out in

This APR Racing carbon fiber splitter doesn't weigh much at all, and offers some very tangible handling benefits for cars at speed. You can also see the APR canards on the lower fender in this shot.

front of your car, you create a high-pressure area on top of the plane because the air is running into your car's nose and "piling up" there—it cannot deflect downwards and under the car. With lower-pressure air flowing below the splitter, the nose of the car gains some downforce.

Canards

Canard is the French word for a duck. It also means to tell a lie, so how it came to describe little winglets on the front of a car is a mystery. But for our purposes, canards are small airfoils installed in front of the front wheels on the lower fenders. They are designed to add a little bit of downforce, like the diving planes on a submarine.

Diffusers

A diffuser is a special kind of spoiler—in this case, it's designed as an anti-spoiler. A diffuser sits underneath the rear bumper area of a car and directs airflow out from beneath the car smoothly into the low-pressure area that the car leaves behind as it moves forward. This helps stabilize the car in the airflow and allows the other aerodynamic devices to work to their best effect.

Body Kit Basics

It's great to go look at show cars with their amazing body kits—but the shots you see in the catalogs are quite different from what you get when you order the parts. Body kits are generally made of fiberglass, and they arrive unpainted, and they don't just snap on to the car. You generally have to fit and drill and mount your kit on your own—or pay a body shop to do it. If you don't have a lot of talent or a lot of experience with bodywork, you'll be much happier with the results if you take this project to a good body and paint shop.

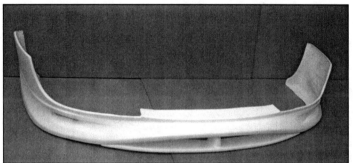

This is what your fancy chin spoiler looks like when it arrives. It needs sanding, priming, installation, and paint before your car looks cool. (Photo courtesy of Primitive Racing)

Here's a WRX sedan trunklid in fiberglass from Primitive Racing. It looks pretty good, but it's still a long way from the car show.

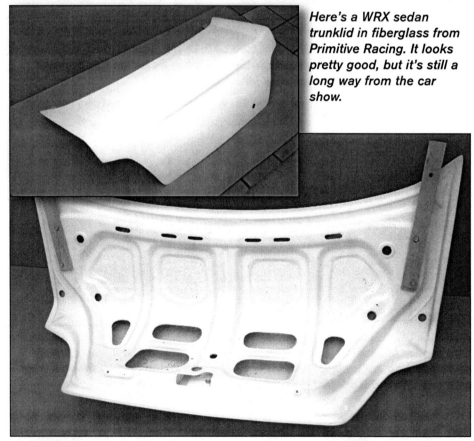

And here's the underside of the same trunk lid—great detail work, but you still need to install all your latching and locking hardware, and the hinges.

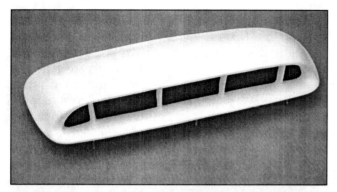

One of the easier body mods to make is a replacement hood scoop, since it's small and easily installed. Some people paint these a contrasting or neutral color like flat black to get a good result from a home-finished project.

Above: Here's a particularly fancy body kit—a Seibon Impreza fender made completely from carbon fiber. This is light, offers increased wheel well space, and it looks great, too. Notice that this car also uses a carbon front-end kit and a carbon

The normal wear and tear of road driving has taken its toll on this Impreza body kit, and on that front-mounted intercooler as well.

This car has a very modest kit that changes the valance around the radiator intake. Subtle, but it makes the car a little different from others on the road.

This Legacy body kit was freshly installed and painted when it was severely damaged by a car transport company on the way to a show. Repairing it may cost more than the original price of the kit!

Another danger with body kits is that they are fragile. In the regular world of street driving, lots of stuff gets thrown at the front of your car. Those little concrete parking blocks have destroyed thousands of chin spoilers and front end kits over the years. So if you get a nice kit, be ready to be very careful about curbs, driveways, speed bumps, and potholes. But no matter how careful you are, you might still take a rock (or worse) from under the car in front of you.

Most body kits alter the front or rear bumper and front air intake area. There are also "wide body" kits that increase the fender flare around your wheel wells. Some of these kits involve removing and replacing your fenders, while others "tack on" to the outside.

Some popular body kit manufacturers include:

Veilside

Veilside has been the alpha and omega of aftermarket body kit makers. Its products have appeared in *The Fast & The Furious* movie series, and It is widely recognized as a market leader. Based near the Tsukuba racing circuit in Japan, they have a healthy dealer network in North America.

Seibon

Seibon Carbon manufactures carbon fiber auto body parts such as hoods, trunk lids, mirror covers, radiator cooling plates, and fenders. It is among the leaders in the industry,

with very popular products. Seibon products are sold through an extensive dealer network.

APR Performance

APR Performance is based in California and makes aerodynamic products for the motorsports market. It specializes in carbon fiber and aluminum construction. You can buy direct from APR or they have resellers in several cities.

Kakumei

Kakumei body kits are imported and distributed in America by Revolution Motorsports. Its products are manufactured in Taiwan, and it offers everything from carbon fiber mirror covers to full body kits, hoods, and trunk lids.

This rear wide body kit from Kakumei installs on the door and rear fender to give a little more tire clearance.

This CWII Seibon hood looks great with this body kit. (Thanks to the Flat4 Club of Las Vegas)

This shot brings all the APR parts together at the front of the car—the air dam is integral to the body kit, the splitter is installed along with the canards. The hood is by Seibon.

The rear view shows the APR wing. You can just barely make out the diffuser underneath the rear end. Note that the wing is nice and high—up in the airflow where it can work to generate downforce.

This shot shows the Kakumei wide front fenders and front body kit, which retains the stock fog lights. Not all kits have space for those.

Another look at the Kakumei body kit with custom hood, front end, and wide front fenders. Note the carbon-fiber hood scoop and ventilation ducts. You can tell this is a show car because the body kit accommodates a front-mounted intercooler, so they don't really need that hood scoop at all.

vehicle body flex, and they fit with suspension brace products for 2002 and later Impreza chassis.

Roll Cages

A good roll cage is a necessity for a car that you plan on driving on a race track more than a couple times a year, and if you plan on driving to the limit of the car's potential. Besides holding

Chassis Stiffeners

Chassis stiffeners could be listed as suspension components, but they are really part of the bodywork of your car. All Subarus use a unibody design, which is to say, the chassis and body are made of stamped pieces of sheet steel, welded together. This is a very strong and rigid way to build a car, but all chassis flex to some degree under hard cornering. Chassis flex works against your suspension—slightly changing its geometry at the worst possible time. You can reduce chassis flex with stiffening braces that

install underneath your car, but for serious stiffening, there's nothing like a roll cage.

Chassis Braces

Several manufacturers make chassis braces. The strut tower bars we discussed in Chapter 7 are chassis braces, and the underbody braces serve the same kind of function—to hold the sheet metal portions of the chassis in position against torsion brought on by cornering.

As an example, both Perrin and Cusco offer lines of chassis braces to stiffen up your chassis and help reduce

This cage is a Cusco product, and is designed to fit around the dashboard where a custom cage tends to pass through the dashboard—with cutting and permanent holes. (Photo courtesy of Nukabe/Cusco)

A rear brace is a 4-point brace that works together with the central brace and the trunk brace to tie the rear suspension components together and help increase rear body rigidity. (Photo courtesy of Nukabe/Cusco)

Here's a look at a custom cage by Judd Weld of Grindesigns. Note the extensive cross bracing and the tight fit against the roof. This car will never again have a headliner or carpet or many other creature comforts, but you won't find a stiffer chassis anywhere. (Photo courtesy of All-WheelsDriven)

the driver's compartment open in a rollover, a roll cage helps stiffen the chassis.

Your choices with roll cages are essentially unlimited because a custom cage can include anything you want. You can also buy a premade "bolt-in" cage kit and install it yourself. Of the two, custom work costs a lot more, but it's worth it. A custom cage is generally (but not always) welded into the chassis of your car. It fits your car better and you can have the builder make the cage as complete or as unobtrusive as you like. A custom cage can also tie into your strut towers and potentially extend from bumper to bumper. Be sure you choose a good cage builder. Someone with experience in the local motorsports business is best, especially if you're building to a set of rules.

Bear in mind that if you choose a bolt-in cage, you'll be drilling some holes through your floor pan and various panels. If you choose a custom cage, you'll be welding plates and potentially penetrating bulkheads in your car. You can remove a bolt-in cage and fill the holes and walk that modification back, but a weld-in cage is forever and limits the resale market of your car to other racing enthusiasts.

Lights

Aftermarket lights are a great addition to any car. Check your local laws for limitations on the installation of things like High Intensity Discharge (Xenon) lights, extra fog lights, and rally/driving lights. Most Subarus come with fog lights installed—or at least a place to install them and the basic wiring, but you may have to string some wire or install a switch to make them work.

Many aftermarket light kits are on the market, available from dozens of different vendors. Each kit has its own installation issues. Some kits come with a bit of custom bodywork, such as those that substitute smaller lights for the stock headlight assemblies. Cutting into your car's wiring can lead to innumerable problems, so consider any of these upgrades carefully before you proceed.

For the serious enthusiast or rallyist, a light pod is a major custom piece. The advantage of a pod is that it can be removed when it's not needed. Of course, the installation hardware will still be there on your hood or front bumper. For night-time driving in areas without streetlights, you can't

beat a pod for lighting up the night. Several manufacturers, including Primitive Racing, make light pods designed to fit the hoods of a variety of Subaru models and years. Check your local laws, as some municipalities limit the number and intensity of lights that can be used.

Gauges and Indicators

Moving to the car's interior, one of the first areas you may want to consider for improvement is your selection

The stock WRX dash doesn't give you much information to work with—just the water temperature and a bunch of lights to tell you when things aren't right. You can get more information with a bank of gauges, and even more and better information with a digital dash display from your ECU.

This Impreza has an aftermarket two-light conversion with replacement bodywork around the lights. Such conversions may be easy or difficult to install based on the kit you select.

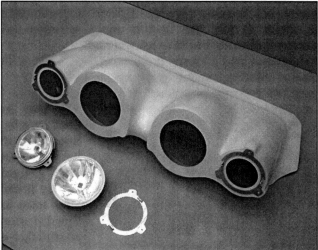

This Primitive Racing light pod fits 2002 and later Imprezas. It allows the installation of two large forward-facing lights, and two smaller lights that can be aimed outwards for peripheral lighting. The pod style keeps vibrations to a minimum, but it does require some installation hardware on your hood.

of gauges and indicators. In stock form, Subaru offers you few gauges: a water temperature gauge, a tach, and a bunch of "idiot lights" to tell you when things are outside of normal operating ranges.

Most performance enthusiasts want more information than that, plus

An aftermarket boost gauge is nice to have if you're wondering what your actual manifold pressure is doing. Defi also makes a digital "Defi-Link" in-dash display. (Photo courtesy of Defi)

the fact that a bunch of gauges looks pretty cool. You can upgrade as little or as much as you like in this area. Gauges and senders exist to tell you oil temperature and pressure, turbo boost, air-fuel mixture, exhaust gas temperature, and even tire pressures.

This little bracket holds a pair of gauges onto your steering column. This is a great place for boost, EGT, or air/fuel ratio gauges.

At the high end, you can purchase products like the Dash Display from EcuTek. This two-line display installs in your dashboard and works with any 1999 or later Subaru through the OBD II port. The Dash Display shows you specific error codes from your ECU (instead of the nearly useless "check engine" light.) You can display your current boost pressure, exhaust gas temperature, oil pressure, and various other statistics live at the push of a button.

You can buy gauge pods (some made of fancy carbon fiber) that fit on your dashboard, your steering column, or up on your A-pillar. These typically allow you to install up to three gauges of a standard size.

Hooking up aftermarket gauges can be tricky—you can take the input from your ECU, or you can install your own sensors and pull readings straight from those sensors. If you pull from the stock sensors, there's some risk that you won't get accurately calibrated readouts, or that you might cause the ECU to throw a Check Engine light through your standard dash instruments. In general, critical sensors such as exhaust gas temperature should be calibrated to the gauge being used. Consult an experienced shop for help with gauge selection and installation.

Steering Wheels & Shift Knobs

Your car's steering wheel is another safety component, because it houses the driver's air bag. Aftermarket wheels look and feel great, but you don't generally get to keep your car's airbag. It can also be difficult to get your horn and your automatic turn signal cancellers to work with an aftermarket wheel.

Among manufacturers of steering wheels, Momo is the leader in import fitments. Grant makes a wide variety of aftermarket wheels, and some are more appropriate than others for performance applications. In any case, the main advantage of an aftermarket

The stock steering wheel of a Subaru is typically a very good part. Most are leather wrapped and comfortable to hold.

This Grant wheel works well in a stage rally car. We put brightly colored tape at the 12 o'clock position so we know which way is up.

wheel is in the ability to custom-select the diameter, the configuration of the wheel, and the thickness of the ring. Select a wheel that is comfortable to hold. Remember that a larger wheel gives you more steering leverage, and even with power steering you may find turning a small wheel to be more of a chore than you expected.

You can also get a quick-release kit for your wheel. Many racers use these because they allow you to bring the wheel close to you, but then you can pop the wheel off the steering column for easy entry and exit from the driver's seat.

The other place you put your hand while you're driving is the shift knob. The stock knob Subaru gives you is good, but it's an item many folks like to replace. Carbon fiber and wooden knobs are popular and stylish, but for true high-performance applications, you can't beat a leather-covered knob for positive grip.

If you select an aftermarket knob, make sure it has the right threads to attach to your shift lever, and that the threaded part of the knob is well attached. You don't want the knob to come off in your hand!

Safety Equipment

As you modify your car for performance, one area where you don't want to cut corners is in your safety

This high-quality Momo steering wheel includes two button-switches that can be used to actuate the horn (some wiring is required) or any other device you may connect, such as intercooler spray or nitrous oxide.

This STI knob features the detent ring to prevent an accidental shift into reverse. The perforated leather makes a great gripping surface. This STI knob features the detent ring to prevent an accidental shift into reverse. The perforated leather makes a great gripping surface.

The stock seat on a 1997 Legacy GT is suitable for day-to-day driving, but not for racing of any kind.

The STI seat is comfortable, stylish, and you know it's strong enough to be included in a factory-produced car. This is a good choice for an interior dress-up.

If you look at the mounting, this racing seat has been mounted on brackets attached to the stock adjustable seat rails. This is a good mounting, and is suitable for street driving and light competition duty, while allowing the seat to be adjusted for different drivers.

gear. If you move out of street performance and into racing, many of these decisions are written into the preparation rules—you will have a certified racing seat, racing harness, fire extinguisher, and so on, or you won't be racing.

In all the modifications you make, ask yourself if what you're doing will compromise the basic safety margins built into your car from the factory. If it's going to put you in danger to make a mod, reconsider whether you really want to take that risk.

Apart from the expensive gear you put into a performance car, consider carrying a fire extinguisher and a good first-aid or winter-weather kit. It never hurts to be ready to help out others or yourself in an emergency. One great place to find all kinds of safety gear for your car is www.safedrives.com.

Seats

Your car's seats are a vital safety component. Together with the seat belts, air bags, and the body construction, the seats help keep you safe in an accident. Some aftermarket seats are very, very good, and some are not as good as the stock seats in a crash. Look for an FIA rating on a motorsports seat to indicate that it has passed stress testing.

But perhaps the biggest area where people compromise the safety of their seats is in the mounting. For street cars we like to be able to adjust the seat for different drivers, while in a race car people usually bolt the seat right to a welded-in brace for a fixed position. There are many aftermarket seat-mounting kits, and you should look carefully at any kit and choose one that is solid and well-made. Because your seats are so critical to your safety, you should have any aftermarket seats installed by a professional.

Grab the back of a seat and shake it back and forth. The stock seat will move some, and an old and worn seat may move quite a bit. An aftermarket performance seat, properly installed,

A good set of racing belts hold you in the car while you're driving as well as in an accident. 4-point driving belts are not nearly as good, and don't cost much less than a true 5 or 6-point racing harness.

should move very little. A hard-mounted FIA-rated racing seat should flex a little, but not move.

One more thing to note about seats is that most FIA-rated racing seats have a fixed position—you can't adjust the angle of the seatback. The hinges and stops that allow you to adjust the rake of the seat back are a weak point, and have been known to break or give way in an accident. Some racing seats are adjustable, but these are the exception rather than the rule. Also, because of the high side bolsters and shoulder supports, most racing seats do not work correctly with your stock seat belts and require a racing harness to properly hold you in the car.

Safety Belts

As you increase your performance level, think about increasing your safety gear as well. As mentioned before, a good racing seat helps hold you in place not just in an accident, but also as you drive. The second half of that equation is the racing harness. A good 5 or 6-point racing harness, well attached, keeps you planted in the seat, so you're not expending energy or mindshare on keeping your body under control while you drive. Leading manufacturers of quality harnesses include Simpson, G-Force, Willans, Sabelt, and others. Look for a harness that is SFI or FIA-rated. The 4-point "sport" belts on the market are less helpful than a real racing harness.

GETTING EXOTIC

Having a unique ride has always been part of the car hobby, and there's no shorter road to a unique car than by using custom or exotic, hard-to-find parts. The downside of exotics is that they almost always involve some heavy tradeoffs, mostly trading ease of availability and maintenance in favor of customization. This chapter looks at a few of the exotic pieces you can find for your car.

Some of these parts are easy to find, and some are harder to come by. The thing to remember is that exotic parts are limited by price and availability, but custom parts are limited only by your imagination.

JDM Parts

The grass is always greener on the other side of the fence, and that's the rule with JDM/USDM parts. Over in Japan, tuners are happy when they can get unusual (to them) USDM components to dress up their cars. Here, we admire the stuff that's just Plain Jane to Japanese or European owners.

"With JDM parts, you have to remember that these parts are made by Subaru for their home market, so you get this wonderful fit that you don't always get with aftermarket stuff," says Sean Sexton of Rallitek.

Whether you make the effort to find JDM parts, world market parts, or not is up to you, but here are some of the most popular JDM conversions used in the United States.

Jeff Perrin's personal ride has an H6 3.0-liter (EZ30) engine, rotated-mount turbocharger, front-mounted intercooler, Aquamist water injection, and it's mated to an STI 6-speed transmission. The car is a rolling showcase of exotic

JDM 2-Liter STI Engines

Gruppe-S sells imported JDM Version 7 and version 8 Subaru Impreza WRX STI EJ207 engines with a semi-closed deck and Subaru's Active Valve Control System (AVCS). As we mentioned in the Engine chapter, the EJ207 is and upgrade from the EJ205 because of its increased compression ratio, STI pistons, better cams, and the active valve control from the STI. The AVCS do not work with a USDM ECU, but Gruppe-S also sells a JDM ECU that allows you to run the AVCS.

Gruppe-S sells the parts, installs them, reflashes the ECU for you, and dyno-tunes your car, but just out of the box without the AVCS, you get about 20 additional horsepower out of the EJ207, and you'll impress your friends at the same time.

Cosworth High Performance JDM-Spec Camshafts

Cosworth offers JDM/Euro-profile high performance camshafts for the EJ257 engine. These cams feature 278 degrees of intake and 274 degrees of exhaust duration and lift heights of

---

This is the engine in Perrin's exotic test car. The H6 has never been turbocharged by Subaru, and it's never been fitted to a manual transmission from the factory, either. I've driven this car, and the low-end torque is like a rocket.

10.4mm on the intake and 10mm on the exhaust. USDM STI cams use 208 degrees duration and 9.75mm of lift for the exhaust and 9.55mm for intake.

JDM 5th and 6th Gear Close Ratio Conversion Kit

The USDM 6MT was compromised by the stringent U.S. regulations for fuel efficiency at freeway cruising speeds. The JDM transmission received close ratio 5th and 6th gears, which are available through Gruppe-S. You can convert your 6MT to be exactly like the JDM STI product with their kit. Gruppe-S can also rebuild your 6MT with the JDM parts if you prefer. Ratios provided in the JDM kit are:

5th Gear - 1.062:1 (0.971:1 stock)
6th Gear - 0.842:1 (0.756:1 stock)

JDM TGV Deletes for WRX

Rallitek imports the Subaru factory JDM intake housing, which has no TGV, replacing the stock USDM injector housing assembly. You may get a Check Engine light if you install these without some kind of ECU upgrade, but since this is a fairly exotic modification, chances are you've already done that.

JDM Body and Light Kits

Gruppe-S has imported a large variety of JDM body pieces, including front lip spoilers, rear skirts and aprons, rain guards, headlights and fog lights, and power mirrors. Additionally, it stocks a line of AeroSync replica JDM parts. If the JDM look is your thing, there's only one place to go.

Exotic Turbochargers

There was a time in the history of the automobile when a turbocharged

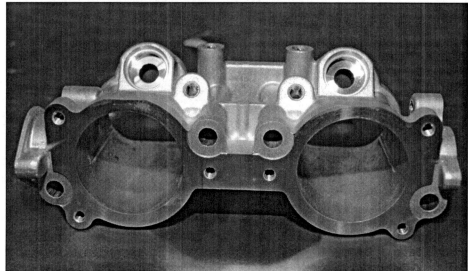

These TGV deletes take some ECU work to avoid throwing a check engine light, but can be worth it if you're building a high-power engine and you want clean flow in your intakes.

car was a pretty exotic thing. Many turbocharged cars are now on the market, and you have to look around some to find exotic turbo products. But they do exist—mostly they exist outside the United States.

Twin Turbos

If one turbo is good, then two turbos must be better. And indeed, that may be the case, because you can choose two smaller turbos that spool up faster and move the same amount (or more) of air. Any twin-turbo setup you find in the United States will be on an imported car from the world market or a custom piece of work, as shown in these photographs.

Subaru produced a twin-turbo Legacy GT with a 2-liter engine beginning in the 1993 and continuing until 2003. The turbos were sequential, and one was designed to produce great low-end power, and the other to take over

This Legacy GT was spotted with the JDM rain guards installed. Subtle, but worth a few points at the car show for sure.

Here's the left-hand turbo of a twin setup. Notice that this unit is being test-fit with an incomplete engine in the car, and it's mounted close to the exhaust port underneath the engine.

at higher RPMs. The system is reputed to be complex and installing and then governing the JDM sequential system on a USDM car would certainly be a difficult job.

Twin-Scroll Turbos

Twin-scroll turbos use dual turbine inputs to obtain a wider response range and quicker spool-up at low RPM. Twin scrolls are not widely used in the United States, but are popular overseas. To better understand the workings of a twin-scroll, we asked Robert Young at Forced Performance to explain them.

▶ *JZ: How is a twin-scroll turbo different from any other kind of turbo?*
RY: You don't generally see twin-scroll turbochargers in Subaru applications in the United States. There are no race applications or performance applications that use twin-scroll designs, as far as what's popular

This is the right-hand turbo on the same engine. A front-mount intercooler is an obvious choice for this setup, since both turbos are right there behind the bumper.

This cutaway shows the twinned inlets and turbine passages of this Garrett twin scroll turbo. The passages are shaped slightly differently to widen the operating range of the turbo.

in the United States. But people talk about them because, thanks to the Internet, people know what happens everywhere in the world. In Asia, and in other parts of the world, Subaru does create a twin-inlet, also called twin-entry or divided entry, turbine housing.

The purpose of doing that is to increase spool-up. By having two volutes in the housing instead of one volute, you take two cylinders' worth of air and run it through one size volute and the other two cylinders, and run it through a different size volute. For example, both volutes are going to be 4 square centimeters each, but they'll be at different radiuses. One's an outer scroll and one's an inner scroll. They might

start off right next to each other and look like a pair of sunglasses or something, but one is going to swing out wide and one will be in close to the turbine wheel. They're both going to enter at the same point on the turbine wheel, but the fact that they have different radiuses affects the angle at which the air enters into the turbine wheel. This accentuates one specific mass flow rate as far as how much efficiency and power it can use to drive the wheel. So by running two volutes at different radiuses in the housing, you can widen the operating range of any particular turbine housing.

JZ: On most headers and exhaust systems you can get, all 4 cylinders

feed out their exhaust into a single coupling, and the up-pipe comes from that coupling. So with a twin scroll, would you have twin up-pipes?

RY: You can have twin up pipes, or one up pipe with two internal passages. I'm not sure what the European version of the car uses because we don't really run into it in the States. But the split passages mix together as they enter the turbine wheel, then discharge out of the turbine wheel into one outlet. ■

Twin-Scroll Turbo Products

Paul Eklund of Primitive Racing is considering a twin-scroll setup for his open-class rally STI. "We're going to reconfigure our engine to gain some power with new heads and intakes, as well as adding a larger twin-scroll turbo and water injection. We hope to get more torque down low and faster spool-up with a twin scroll, since we are limited at the top end by the restrictor," he says.

If you want to obtain a twin-scroll turbo setup for your car, the following products are available:

JDM or AVO Twin-Scroll Turbo

Crawford Performance and Rallitek Performance both offer new imported JDM twin-scroll units. "The Garrett GT32 we use for our Legacy GT twin-scroll turbo kit is a factory twin-scroll turbo," says Quirt Crawford.

Rallitek offers an AVO twin scroll kit as well. "We sell the JDM twin-scroll turbos from the Legacy," says Sean Sexton. "In Japan, that's a 2-liter engine, and the twin scroll is capable of maybe 400 horsepower, but the AVO turbos designed for the US cars are quite a bit bigger than that and you can get quite a bit more power out of them."

The JDM turbo kit sold by Rallitek requires the use of the AVO twin-scroll exhaust header and up pipe kit. The stainless steel exhaust headers in the AVO kit merge into the twin turbo up pipe for the twin-scroll

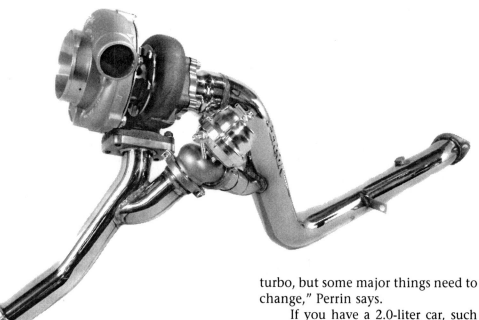

The Perrin Performance rotated mount turbo kit is the leading rotated-mount product on the market today. Improvements in the flow, wastegate performance, and boost control make it a compelling choice for the EJ257. (Photo courtesy of Perrin Performance)

turbo. This kit also includes a replacement oil pan and oil strainer. The pan and strainer are required because the twin-scroll exhaust manifold does not clear the stock units on a standard North American market car.

Rotated Mount Turbos

A rotated mount turbocharger kit is simply a different set of up and down pipes that reorient the turbo. Jeff Perrin of Perrin Performance believes in the rotated mount design, and offers a kit with all the necessary pieces. "The advantage of a rotated mount turbo kit is boost control, spool, and durability, but it depends on the car. Our kit fits 2002—and later Impreza WRX and STI— and the 2004–2005 Forester XT. You can't use the kit on an older Impreza or a stock Legacy turbo. It can be made to work on a Legacy

turbo, but some major things need to change," Perrin says.

If you have a 2.0-liter car, such as a WRX, a rotated-mount turbo does not offer much of an advantage because the turbos used with Perrin's kit are generally too large for an otherwise unmodified system. Beyond this, you can easily get to the maximum safe wheel horsepower for the stock WRX engine using a standard mount turbo that is cheaper to buy, cheaper to install, and that uses factory parts. "The 2.0-liter customers who buy the rotated kits are people who have a built engine, or who just want something different," Perrin says.

It's a different story for the 2.5-liter STI engine. The bolt-on turbos that make big power on the 2.5 tend to compromise top-end power, intake path, or maximum power. Because a rotated mount kit turns the intake off to the side, you can use a better-flowing path to the turbo intake.

Another advantage of the rotated mount design on the 2.5-liter engine is boost control. As we discussed in the chapter on turbos, the OEM turbo and many aftermarket turbos have trouble holding high boost pressures at high RPM. The Perrin rotated mount kit uses a 44mm Tial external wastegate that allows for high-rev boost control on all types and sizes of turbos. "We use off-the-shelf Garrett turbos because they are much more efficient, and we can get much more power from them with less backpressure to cause high exhaust temperatures and low power output," Perrin says.

Rotated turbo products on the market include:

Perrin Rotated Mount Turbo Kit for STI

The Perrin rotated mount kit includes a modified stainless steel up pipe and down pipe built to accept a Garrett turbocharger and a Tial 44mm wastegate. The turbo and wastegate are not part of the kit, but oil and water lines for Garrett products are part of the package. The Perrin rotated mount down pipe bolts to

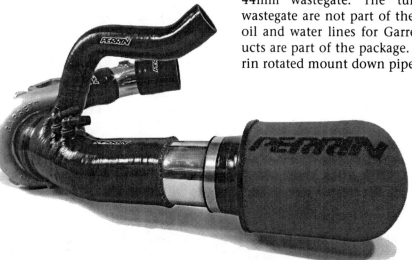

This is the intake system for the Perrin rotated mount turbo kit. It's a straight shot from that filter into the compressor wheel on that big Garrett. (Photo courtesy of Perrin Performance)

This is the Cusco aftermarket intercooler sprayer nozzle. This kit uses a controller box that mounts on the steering column to control the spray. You can also control the spray with a piggyback or standalone ECU. (Photo courtesy of Nukabe USA)

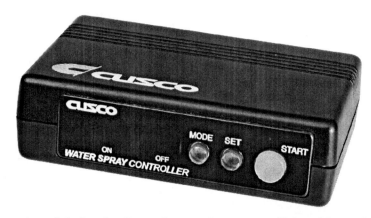

The control module for the Cusco intercooler sprayer. Using this module, you can set the system up to spray automatically or when you press the button. (Photo courtesy of Nukabe USA)

that owners can install the kit in three to five hours. The company has a tremendous amount of information on its website about this product.

Intercooler Sprayers

Since its introduction in 2004, the Impreza STI has been built with a button-actuated device that sprays water onto the intercooler to improve its function. This kind of device is also used on the Mitsubishi Lancer Evolution series, and numerous aftermarket versions are available for virtually all intercooled cars. Spraying the intercooler works just like spraying any hot object—the evaporation of the water helps cool it down and that temperature drop is passed on to your air charge.

Some aftermarket coolers spray evaporating nitrous oxide or carbon dioxide onto the intercooler in place of water. A few of those products are listed here:

Cusco Intercooler Sprayer
This dash-controlled Cusco intercooler sprayer can be set up to work automatically with a piggyback or standalone ECU, or you can actuate it with a button like the stock STI unit. This system requires that you install a reservoir for the water, typically in the trunk of your car.

Nitrous Express "N-tercooler" Intercooler Spray Kit
Nitrous Express offers this kit for supercharged or turbo applications where nitrous is not an option. By spraying liquid nitrous oxide or carbon dioxide onto the intercooler, this unit can reduce air inlet temperatures dramatically.

CryO2 Carbon Dioxide System and Intercooler Sprayer
Design Engineering Inc. makes several fuel and air-cooling products under the CryO2 brand name. This system is designed to deliver liquid carbon dioxide to a variety of devices

the stock exhaust or any aftermarket 3-inch exhaust system. "We offer the Garrett 2860RS, 3071R, 3076R, 3582R, 4088R turbos to fit the rotated mount kit," Perrin says.

GReddy Rotated Mount Turbo for STI
GReddy offers a rotated mount kit for the EJ257 STI engine, featuring their massive T67 turbo and some, but not all, of the hardware necessary

to mount and use it. GReddy state that the turbo generates 22-23 PSI and up to 380 to 410 wheel horsepower with their kit.

APS D/R Series Rotated Mount Turbo Kit
APS from Australia has a rotated kit for the EJ257 and the EJ205, too. It does suggest that only racing EJ205s should use the kit, but it is offering a complete kit, and estimates

This is the Perrin version of the Aquamist water injection system. This system can be programmed to come on at a certain boost or RPM level. (Photo courtesy of Perrin Performance)

to cool your liquid fuel, pre-turbo intake air, or intercooler charge. The basic kit includes a 5 or 10 pound carbon dioxide tank and all necessary pieces to actuate the system. The CryO2 Intercooler Sprayer is a separately purchased component that mounts directly to the top or front of the intercooler, and vents liquid Carbon Dioxide directly onto the cooling fins. The evaporation of the CO2 provides the cooling effect.

CryO2 Intercooler Water Sprayer Kit

The Cry02 Intercooler Water Sprayer Kit is designed to be used by itself or in conjunction with DEI's other CryO2 Intercooler Sprayers as a way to supercool intercoolers. By misting an intercooler's surface with water and then optionally venting CO2 onto the intercooler's cooling fins, the intercooler is further chilled.

Water/Alcohol Injection

Water injection is a technique that comes down to street use from the more exotic and expensive echelons of the racing world. This system involves injecting a very small amount of water into the intake stream to reduce combustion chamber intake charge temperatures to avoid detonation and burn the air/fuel mixture more efficiently.

Intake charge temperatures sufficient to cause auto-ignition happen when compression or boost is very high. Cars with small intercoolers or large powerful turbochargers are prone to detonation due to high air temperatures. But any time you're getting detonation not caused by gross errors in tuning, a water or methanol injection system may help.

For the 2-liter engine, you should consider water injection at

250 wheel horsepower, and the 2.5-liter can benefit from water at 300 wheel horsepower. If you've gone to a larger turbocharger, the safety margin you get from water injection is even more important.

Most water or methanol injection systems are triggered through a boost pressure sensor, and they deliver a fixed amount of water at all RPM levels. You want about a 10 to 20% water-to-fuel ratio at all times, and with a simple fixed-rate system you get too much water at low RPM and not enough at high RPM. More expensive systems can deliver a progressive rate of fuel as your RPM increases.

Here are a couple of representative water injection systems:

Aquamist Water Injection System

The Aquamist line of water injection products uses an electromagnetic high-pressure pump to inject water into your post-turbo intake stream. Its simpler systems are those like described above, triggered by boost, and they inject a fixed amount of water at all times. Other, more comprehensive systems, tap into fuel injector signals and increase water flow as the fuel flow increases. Perrin Performance has an advanced kit (call the PWI-1) that supplies everything you need to install water/methanol injection in your Subaru. This includes the computer, pump, hoses, and a digital readout to show you when it's working, if you're low on fluid, and if the flow isn't what it should be.

SMC Water/Alcohol Injection System

The SMC custom water/alcohol system for the WRX uses the Subaru 1 gallon washer fluid tank as a reservoir for a 50/50 mixture— commonly available denatured or isopropyl alcohol and distilled water. The kit includes a small auxiliary washer tank/pump that mounts in front of the battery. The prepared injection fluid can also be used to wash your windshield. The system uses an adjustable controller that automatically increases spray pressure as your boost rises.

Nitrous Oxide

The old nickname for nitrous oxide is Laughing Gas, and that's just as appropriate when you inject it into your motor—you'll laugh out loud at the improvement in power. Of course, you may also end up crying if you blow up your expensive engine—they don't generally show that part in movies.

Nitrous oxide is simply two nitrogen molecules bonded to an oxygen molecule. It helps your engine produce more power by putting more oxygen into the combustion chamber than ordinary air. That's why rockets use pure liquid oxygen—it's the best way to put the most oxygen into the combustion process.

Nitrous oxide is most often used in drag racing applications, with motors built to handle the power spikes you can get when you radically change your working mixture. As you might expect, nitrous oxide can explode and must be handled with extreme care. Numerous accounts exist (generally with impressive photos) of cars and garages blown to pieces when a Nitrous tank exploded.

The leading producer of nitrous oxide systems in North America is Nitrous Oxide Systems (NOS). You can get a NOS system for your car from its website at www.holley.com. Other manufacturers of nitrous oxide systems for Subaru include Edelbrock, Nitrous Express, and AEM.

As we noted before, nitrous oxide is not risk-free. Many racers who have used nitrous believe that it's best to choose a "wet" nitrous system, in which gasoline is injected along with the nitrous oxide at the nozzle of the nitrous injector. A 50 horsepower boost from nitrous (called a "shot") in a wet nitrous system is generally considered safe to use. But because nitrous becomes part of your whole engine system, it isn't "free" power. You have to consider the effect of the nitrous oxide on your overall air/fuel mixture and current boost levels at the moment you hit the button. If you exceed the amount of pressure your pistons and rods can take, you will break your engine—probably in a very spectacular and expensive way.

Exotic Engine: H6 Turbo/6MT

Subaru has been producing Legacies with the EZ30 (H6) 6-cylinder engine since 2001. There's nothing exotic about this engine when it's in an Outback. Subaru sells the H6 with automatic transmissions only, and the engine is tuned to produce just 243 horsepower.

But take one of these and give it a big turbo, then mate it up to a 6-speed STI transmission, and now you're up in the Subaru stratosphere. There's no kit (yet) to do this, but many people have now successfully made the swap, and the information on the procedure is filtering out.

For SEMA of 2005, Jeff Perrin of Perrin Performance took one of these EZ30R engines and dropped it into his 2006 STI. Before installing the engine, he installed Supertech custom low-compression forged pistons and added a Garrett GT3582R rotated mount turbo kit, Aquamist water injection, and the entire Perrin parts catalog. The result at 16psi of boost is about 450 horsepower at the wheels, with about the same lag as a stock STI, and a car that comes as close to a rocket sled as anything I've ever driven.

If you think this sounds like a swap you'd like to perform, some issues to consider are:

- You need to find a computer that can run this engine, which means splicing an H6 ECU into your car, or choosing a standalone ECU such as the HYDRA that is adaptable to 6 cylinders.

- You need to put an appropriate STI flywheel and clutch onto the H6. The engine will bolt up to the Impreza 5MT or 6MT; however don't forget to upgrade the clutch, because that OEM clutch will not hold the torque!

- You need to make an entirely custom header, uppipe, and downpipe, so get your TIG welder ready.

- You need to make an entirely custom boost tube system and intake for your turbo and Front Mount Intercooler.

- If you want a reasonably reliable engine, you need to put in low-compression forged pistons suitable for the turbo. If you want more than 450 wheel horsepower, you'd better think about the bottom end while you're at it.

At the beginning of 2007, Perrin was already replacing the bottom end to this project engine. By adding more custom parts by Pauter, Darton, and Supertech, and a Garrett GT4088R turbo for airflow, Perrin plans to have a solid engine capable of 1,000 horsepower. All things considered, there are probably easier ways to get crazy wheel horsepower, but none more exotic and cooler sounding than the plain old soccer mom engine from the L.L. Bean Edition Outback and the Tribeca SUV.

Exotic Transmissions

Exotic transmission options on your Subaru really come down to two available options: Dog boxes and sequential shift mechanisms.

Dog Box Transmission

The "dogs" in a dog box perform much the same function as the synchros in a normal transmission: they help the gears engage as you shift. But dog rings are bigger, stronger, and made to shift quickly. The way to shift a dog box is to grab the gear lever and start to pull (or push, as in the 2-3 or 4-5 upshift) the transmission out of gear towards the gear you want, then lift and reapply the gas as fast as you can. The gearshift lever quickly releases and snaps up to the next gear. This shifting style minimizes wear on the dog rings because they're designed to wear only as the gear selector moves. The longer you take to shift, the more wear you put on them. Of course, there is also an assumption implicit with a dog box that it will be serviced and replaced on a racing schedule—every race or two, at a minimum. Don't buy a dog box expecting it to last 100,000 miles without maintenance.

The advantage you gain with a dog box is the ability to shift gears in a fraction of a second. Smooth downshifts are accomplished by matching revs with a touch of throttle, or with a touch of the clutch.

Kaps Transmissions in the Czech Republic offers 5 and 6-speed dog box transmissions for the Subaru, and it offers the 5-speed version in your choice of the 5-speed or the 6-speed transmission case. The 6-speed is offered only in the 6-speed case. The 6MT case is obviously the better choice with its built-in oil pump, but some racing organizations insist that competitors use the original style of transmission case that was delivered with the car. KAPS dog box transmissions are offered in both 3.9:1 and 4.44:1 final drive ratios.

Dog boxes are available through Vermont Sports Car, the folks behind Subaru Rally Team USA. All SRTUSA cars use the standard 6-speed transmission case, but on the Open class cars, they install the Kaps 5-speed dog box gears instead of the stock or even RA gears. Lance Smith of Vermont Sports Car refers to the dog box transmission as his "secret weapon"—and it works.

Quaife America also sells a complete 5-speed dog ring gear set, with straight cut gears, two different ratio sets, and options to fit the 1999 and later transmissions or the 1993–1999 Impreza 5MT cases. Quaife has a synchro-based 5-speed gear set as well. And the well-known company MRT Performance in Australia sells a rally-tested dog ring gear set for the Subaru 5MT.

Sequential Transmissions

Kaps also produces a sequential shift manual transmission for Subarus. These are popular at the World Rally level. A sequential transmission works like the transmission on a motorcycle. When you move the shift lever in one direction, you select the next higher gear. To select a lower gear, you move the lever in the opposite direction.

Within the transmission, using the lever rotates a cylinder that engages a different gear depending on its rotational position. In this way you can step up or down through the gears reliably and quickly.

Kaps manufactures these transmission gearsets using the 6MT transmission case and custom-made internal parts. It goes without saying that these transmissions are extremely expensive.

The Bottom Line on Exotics

Exotic parts tend to be items that help you squeeze the last little bit of performance out of your engine. They should never be your first stop on the road to performance because some of them, such as nitrous oxide, can severely impact your engine's longevity. Other exotics don't offer much benefit unless you've already invested a lot of money in a special engine.

But exotics can also be fun—just choose your parts carefully and make sure that they will work with all your other mods.

SUBARUS IN COMPETITION

Competition cars are fundamentally different from street cars, even if you still drive them on the public roads. They are different because if you've built them right, you have subordinated every other consideration to building the car as best you can within the limits of the rules for the kind of racing (or showing) that you're doing.

Before you head for the garage to tear the carpet out of your daily driver, you need to understand that racing is a harsh and unforgiving sport. There's an ironclad rule that is reinforced every weekend on racetracks and rally roads all over the world. The first rule of racing is: *If you can't walk away from a total loss, walk away from racing.*

Every weekend of the year, someone somewhere completely wrecks a racecar. It happens rarely at autocrosses, but it happens. If you race long enough it will happen to you, sometimes on your first day. That's why everyone wears a helmet, not just the fast guys. If you're not ready to walk away from a total loss of your investment, don't even take it to the races.

That being said, racing a Subaru is the most fun you can have in a car with your clothes on. And there are lots of opportunities to compete in your daily driver. We'll take a quick look at each of the most common race formats and the Subaru that are beating the competition.

Autocross

Autocross is probably the safest form of racing you can find outside of a video game. Autocrosses are generally set up in a large parking lot, where cars run through a tight course made up of orange traffic pylons. Cars run one at a time, trying to be the fastest through the course. Time penalties are assessed for hitting the cones, so the fast way around the track is tight and on the racing line.

Autocross is a great way to race if you have only one car. Some Autocrossers go on to compete in other forms of racing, but many find a permanent racing home in the sport. Experienced autocross drivers are both fast and smooth—masters of fine-tuned car placement and control. A good autocross driver can make a transition to any other form of racing with ease.

Autocross requires a helmet, and that's about all the special equipment you need. An autocross should cost

Autocross is one of the safest and least expensive motorsports you can enter, and you can do it in your street car with absolutely no aftermarket gear at all. Of course, that's not what this guy did.

about $20 to $30 to enter, and you should expect three to five runs through the course for your money. A typical Autocross is a half-day or full-day affair, and you typically work the course (picking up cones) when you're not driving.

Subaru-specific and general-purpose sports car clubs all over the world hold autocrosses. The Sports Car Club of America (SCCA) sanctions local, regional, and national championships with a consistent set of rules and classes anywhere you go.

Using a 2.5RS for Autocross

SCCA Solo2 competitor Andy Howe of Salem, Oregon talks about his experience with a 1999 2.5RS sedan:

"I've driven my car in G Stock and Street Touring S. In G Stock, we fully prepared our car for the class, but really, not much is allowed! We swapped the stock struts for KYB AGX adjustable units and replaced the front sway bar with a stiffer bar and built some custom solid front endlinks. Add an alignment and DOT-legal race rubber, and that's 'fully prepped' on a budget. We even used the 6-spoke wheels that came as original equipment on the car," Howe says.

Moving to Street Touring from Stock provided Howe a little more latitude for tuning:

"In STS, I added a couple more suspension modifications. I swapped the struts and stock springs out in favor of coilovers with 6 kg/mm front springs and 5kg/mm rear springs. I added front camber plates. While I had to go back to a real street tire in this class, I still used the factory wheels," Howe says.

In both classes, it was important for Howe to maximize front grip, but the result had to be achieved in different ways.

"We used the stiff front sway bar in G Stock to reduce body roll and dynamic camber loss. We also used the adjustable dampers to help the car stay flat. In STS, the front camber plates allowed us to add front traction. Also, the stiffer springs that we used really allowed the car to stay flat while on course. The stiffer rear sway bar helped the car to rotate, but it shouldn't be overdone. We used an 18mm-22mm adjustable rear bar and found that in the rain the softest setting was very good, and in the dry the stiffest setting was best. We could also use the adjustability of the shocks to modify the car's behavior in slaloms and transitions," Howe says.

Howe has won numerous G Stock and STS events in his 2.5RS. In 2005, he took 2nd place in STS in the Northwest Region SCCA Solo2 Regional Series. Another driver in a 2.5RS won most of the events to take the series title, and third place was also occupied by a 2.5RS. The three Subaru drivers swept the season, winning all eight events in the series. In 2004, Subaru drivers also combined to win all 10 events of the NWR series.

Howe offers this advice for the beginner:

"Stock is a great place to start. The driver is the most important part of the car and Stock classes really allow a driver to develop. Once the driver is well developed, Stock can become frustrating because of the limitations on car development. STS was good to me because the car was fun to drive, both on course and on the street. Significantly more modification was allowed, but I was ready to tackle those subjects. It was a great way to have fun with a car that could comfortably and legally take me to work and back. The car is very versatile from the factory. It is important to appreciate it for what it is and not fuss about what it's not. When you look at it that way, the 2.5RS is simply incredible," he says.

Andy Howe's 1999 four-door 2.5RS has carried him to a lot of regional wins, and it still carries him to work each day.

Autocross competition classes vary a bit depending on the club organizing the event, but there are usually categories for factory-stock cars, street prepared, or street touring vehicles, and all-out unlimited cars. Within a preparation category, there are different classes according to the performance potential of the car. Get a hold of the rules for the events you plan to enter, and you can see where your car fits in. Typically, a moderately prepared suspension means that you compete in the street prepared category, while adding an additional turbo or other exotic mods may well put you into unlimited territory.

Stock category means stock: the car is not modified from the factory performance level. With very few exceptions, the car must meet the specifications listed in the Factory Service Manual for the particular model year and trim level. Street Prepared or Touring allows more modifications, generally limited to bolt-on performance parts. For example, while Stock class cars may change the front sway bar and shocks (within limits), in Street Touring a driver may also change the rear sway bar, springs, and add camber plates. Other popular Street Touring modifications include custom wheels, a cold air intake, and a reflash of the ECU.

Track Day

If your goal is to go a little faster, but you still need to keep your car street-legal, consider entering a track day. These events go by a lot of different names: High Performance Driver Education (HPDE), Street School, Driver Training Day, or Open Track Day, but they all mean the same thing: a dedicated racetrack with no stoplights, no police radar, and no minivans in the way. You can run these events in a stock vehicle or in your modified car.

A track day isn't a competition. Because a track day is not competitive, no one cares much what you have or have not done to your car, or how fast you drive. A friend of mine likes to say:

Time attack allows you to focus on the track and on your car without having to worry about who's in your mirrors.

"You can't win a track day, but you sure can lose." Racetracks have walls and curbs and gravel traps. If you lose control, you can wreck your car, and the greater speeds you can achieve on a track mean you might also hurt yourself. Be careful and remember the first rule of racing.

Most track days have different groups that are organized by driver experience or level of car prep. Don't be insulted if you're placed in the "beginner" group your first few times on the track. Typically you get a chalk talk from the lead instructor, and you have an instructor assigned to you. Instructors are typically amateur race drivers or experienced track day drivers. You can learn a lot from these people, so pay attention. Track days are the cheapest training available in performance driving.

Track days run anywhere from $100 on up. You need a helmet and your car must generally pass a basic technical inspection that includes a check for fluid leaks. Many brand-specific sports car clubs put on track days, but most allow any brand of car to enter.

If you build a Subaru for track days, there are generally no limits on

what you're allowed to do, but what you should do is focus on handling and brakes as well as on your engine. Subaru's symmetric AWD helps you go fast and it helps you corner, but it doesn't help you stop, especially if you're spinning across the grass towards the wall.

Time Attack

Time attack (also called time trial) is similar to an autocross in that you race by yourself against the clock, but in this form of competition you're not dodging pylons, you're on the racetrack at full speed. Touge (pronounced "tow-gay") racing is similar to time attack except there's a lead car and a follow car, and the two do not race side by side through the corners, but rather the lead car attempts to run away from the follow car.

Luke Russell of Fort Myers, Florida has a special time-attack car. He competes in the One Lap of America time trials each year, driving from track to track over eight consecutive days, looking for the fastest lap at each track.

"The idea is to do racing time trials during the day at one, or sometimes two, motorsports facilities. After the day's activities, you pack up all your things and drive your racecar all night to the next day's event. No support vehicles are allowed. All tools, luggage, tents, spare tire, food, etc., must be loaded into, or onto, your race car," Russell says.

Russell competes in a 2004 Subaru Impreza WRX STI. "It was loaded with goodies and had about 460 horse-power in race tune. In 2005 I was a solid first in class and 5th overall, one spot behind the Hennessey Viper, and a couple spots ahead of the Lingenfel-ter Twin Turbo Corvette. Then I hit a

Luke Russell's 2004 WRX STI

To keep the car on the street, but fast enough to compete in the One Lap and tear up the asphalt on an open track day, here's what makes Luke Russell go:

Engine Modifications:

- Ceramic coated pistons, combustion chamber, valves, exhaust ports, exhaust manifolds and turbo.
- Forced Performance Green Turbo
- Custom up-pipe w/ 44mm Tial External Wastegate
- Greddy Profec Electronic Boost Control
- Turbo XS Front Mount Intercooler
- 3" Silicone Inlet Pipe
- 3" Intake Manifold
- 800 cc injectors
- Turbo XS UTEC engine management
- Turbo XS Turbo Back 3" Exhaust w/ no cats
- Reverse hood scoop
- 255 lph fuel pump
- PWR Radiator
- Oil Cooler w/pump
- Braille Lightweight Battery

Suspension/Wheels/Brakes:

- JIC Coilovers FLTA2-RS w/ camber plates, custom valved w/ 500F/575R lb. springs
- Hotchkis competition sway bar kit (including bars, mounts, & heavy duty links)
- Silicone steering dampers
- 17" x 8.5" Rota Slipstream wheels
- 275 width Michelin Pilot PS2 street tires
- Carbotech FP8/9 Brake Pads
- Stainless Steel Brake Lines
- Racing Brake Fluid

Safety and Interior:

- Autopower Roll Cage & SFI-legal padding
- 2.5-lb fire extinguisher
- Video camera mount
- Recaro Pole Position seats, w/ side mounts and custom made chassis mount
- G-Force Harnesses
- MOMO race spec steering wheel, hub and adapter
- Extra Gauges (boost, oil temperature, exhaust gas temperature)

The 2005 incarnation of Russell's WRX came in fifth in the One Lap of America, beating modified Corvettes and a host of other cars in eight days of hard driving. It also carried all the team's luggage and spares from track to track. (Photo courtesy of Luke Russell)

wall and the fun was over. For 2006 I'm running the same STI. It is being completely rebuilt and should be rock solid reliable, pumping out 500 horsepower. This car should be highly competitive. I'm aiming for the top spot," he says.

Hill Climb

Hill Climbing is a specialized form of time trials or tarmac rally. In a hill climb, the organizers shut down a length of public road and contestants make a series of individual timed runs up the road. The direction is almost always up, because it's safer and easier to drive fast up a hill than down.

Depending on the club organizing the event, cars may be classed according to autocross, rally, or amateur racing preparation rules. In addition to your helmet, most hill climbs require you to carry fire extinguishers, and may require a flame-retardant driver's suit. Some hill climbs require roll bars or cages depending on the kind of car you've got.

Subarus do very well in hill climbs, from local events up to the famous Pike's Peak International Hill Climb, which is sanctioned as a stage rally. Power is typically a greater concern in hill climb racing, but don't neglect handling and braking. The consequences for losing control and leaving the road in a hill climb can be a long trip down a hillside, or a short trip into a tree. Refer to the first rule of racing for more information.

Andy Howe describes the value differences between setting a car up for autocross and for hill climb: "For autocross, we set our cars up to run right on the ragged edge of control. Such a setup might be great for 55 mph surrounded by cones. But the penalties for leaving the course with hill climbing are significantly greater than autocrossing. Consequently, a car that I'm driving at a hill climb will be more stable than one that I am autocrossing. Basically, the car will be less prone to oversteer, or put another way, it will understeer more. It is much easier to

recover a car that is understeering, and if I go off the road while understeering, I can choose what I hit. The biggest change when hill climbing is the driver's mentality. A successful hill climber recognizes that it's not always prudent to drive 10/10ths—an error at 10/10ths is an off," Howe says.

Drag Racing

If you talk about Subarus in drag racing, chances are you're talking about Easy Street. Based in Valencia, California, Easy Street Motorsports is also known as ESX, and they are the acknowledged leader in straight-line Subaru performance. As the official factory drag racing team of Subaru of America, ESX owner Ali Afshar has created the world's quickest Subaru for the strip.

The original Easy Street WRX runs between 9 and 10 seconds with a best 1/4-mile time of 9.14 seconds, by ESX driver Julie Stepan. The car runs in NHRA's Sport RWD class, which accepts

Amateur racing isn't necessarily less expensive than pro racing, but you can make it more affordable by your approach.

One of the great things about hill climb is that you can do it in a street car or a fully prepared race or rally car.

This wing on the back of a Subaru World Rally Team tarmac rally car offers some incredible downforce, and this car needs downforce to stay on the road!

AWD cars with a weight penalty. The latest ESX creation is an NHRA Pro Modified class car. The Mod is driven by Afshar himself and boasts 1,300 horsepower and 1/4-mile times in the high 7-second range at 175 mph.

For the amateur enthusiast, drag racing a Subaru is simple. In stock trim, a WRX runs the 1/4-mile in a little under 15 seconds. With street-level tuning and some practice, you can shave that down to the 13-second range. Most drag strips offer street-legal racing on a regular basis, and it's a popular sport for all ages.

Amateur/Club Racing

Subaru entered amateur track racing only in the last few years, but moved rapidly to the front of the pack. The leading sanctioning bodies for amateur "club" racing in the United States are the Sports Car Club of America (www.scca.com) and the National Auto Sport Association (www.nasaproracing.com). Both accept Subaru into at least one class.

Track racing is a fundamentally different game from other forms of racing. In this environment, you're not racing the clock for a fast time; you're racing door-handle to door-handle against other people. Your track-racing car is almost never street-legal, which means you bring it to the track on a trailer you purchased or rented, pulled by a truck or van you purchased or rented. It's not uncommon to spend much more on your tow rig than on your racecar.

A track-racing car requires a roll cage, racing seat, racing harness, fire system, and typically runs on racing tires. Track-racing a Subaru is an expensive proposition, but where else can you battle side by side with your competition?

Most Subarus race in "Touring Car" classes. These classes are for late-model sports sedans with limited modifications. Factors such as engine management, brake pads and suspension are allowed limited improvement, but the core engine must stay stock. If you want to get really crazy, there are also "unlimited" classes where you can test your wildest ideas against the best others have to offer.

Costs to run a competitive amateur racing program in a Subaru can easily top $50,000 to build a car and $20,000 annually to campaign it. If this is within your budget, talk to your preferred sanctioning body about class rules and safety requirements.

Dave Rosenblum manages ICY Racing (www.icyracing.com) of Phoenixville, Pennsylvania. ICY driver Chuck Hemmingson won the 2005 and 2006 SCCA T2 class national championships in an Impreza WRX STI, and the team is likely to continue to dominate the class into the future.

"The only thing you're allowed to do to the motor is reflash the ECU and use a high performance air filter like the K&N. We use an EcuTek system. On the exhaust, what you're allowed to do is run a cat-back system replacing the stock system with a 3-inch diameter pipe. We can see as much as a 35 horsepower gain in wheel horsepower on a chassis dyno," Rosenblum says.

With no engine or drivetrain modifications, tuning the engine and getting the most out of the driver are the keys to winning races for ICY.

"We do a couple different tunes. We have a basic practice tune, and then a special qualifying tune where we do only 3-4 laps and bring it in. Then we have a race tune in the middle of the other two so you don't abuse the car. Our tuner is constantly changing the ECU based on track conditions, including the weather. You need to have a relationship with your tuner, and you need to have him at the track with you. We're not going to tell you all our hidden secrets, but we have done a lot of tuning on our cars," Rosenblum says.

Rosenblum's cars are allowed a little more latitude in suspension design, but not much by most motorsports standards. The ICY racing cars use JRZ remote double-adjustable shocks, but the SCCA rules specify that the cars must use the stock Subaru springs and the stock spring perch.

"We cut the perch off, weld an adjusting ring to the perch, and put that on the shock. We adjust everything to maintain all the stock dimensions, including the ride height. We adjust for maximum negative camber both in front and rear, but you're not allowed to elongate the holes or anything. We run about 1.5 degrees of negative all around. We run Performance Friction brake pads front and rear. We use wheel spacers on the front of the car to adjust our track within the allowed amount. And we replaced the wheel studs with longer ARP ones," Rosenblum says.

"We run Autometer oil pressure, oil temperature, and exhaust gas temperature gauges from Hoerr Racing Products. We use Sabelt seats and belts, and our drivers use HANS devices for personal safety. We build an extremely sturdy roll cage to bring as much strength to the car as we can. It's a lot of tuning and massaging to get the car where we want it. They're bulletproof cars," Rosenblum says.

Pro Racing

If Club Racing doesn't cost enough to make you blink, you can always go Pro. Opportunities for Pro Racing in a Subaru include the US Touring Car Championship, Grand American Road Racing, and SPEED World Challenge.

Brian Lock of Scotts Valley, California has raced in both the US Touring Car Championship and the Grand-Am series. The young racer started his Subaru racing career with a 2002 WRX already prepared for the US Touring Car series. "We're battling the reputation of the car somewhat. We were really successful with it right off the bat, so people were sensitive about the all wheel drive," Lock says.

In professional racing the show is everything, so a winning car is always

Easy Street's Drag Racing Cars

The first Easy Street WRX runs in the popular RWD Sport class, which also accepts AWD cars with a 400-pound weight penalty over a similar RWD car. The car is driven by Julie Stepan of Texas.

This is Julie Stepan's ESX Motorsports RWD Sport class STI. It makes 850 horsepower at the flywheel using 32 pounds of boost. With a shot of nitrous and 38 pounds of boost, the car makes 1,050 horsepower.

- 2006 Subaru WRX STI at 3,200 pounds
- 2.5-liter STI engine
- Custom billet crank
- ESX rods and pistons
- ESX ported heads
- Valves 1mm larger than stock
- ESX custom cams
- Upgraded 9/16 block and head studs
- Fluidyne radiator
- Modified stock intake manifold to accommodate a larger turbo body

- ESX custom stainless steel header
- Innovative 74mm turbo
- Innovative external "Indy" waste gate
- ESX custom front intercooler
- Walbro fuel pump & regulator
- Four 1600cc fuel injectors – converted from side feed to top feed
- MoTeC M800 ECU
- ESX custom ECU programming
- MoTeC CDI ignition
- Bosch Marine coils (4)
- 3.5" exhaust & muffler
- 4AT automatic transmission, modified by ESX
- 8.5" billet torque converter by ProTorque
- Billet transmission input & output shafts, with a modified Power-Glide yoke
- Custom aluminum driveshaft
- Stock Subaru R180 rear diff
- Custom front axles from The Driveshaft Shop
- ESX custom rear axles
- CV Joints from a Porsche 935
- Custom suspension by Progress Suspension
- Arceo Wheels 16x8.5 +48 offset
- BFG 255/50-16 "Cheater slick"
- Brake Man 4-piston aluminum front calipers, 2-piston aluminum rear calipers
- Brake Man full floating brake discs with aluminum centers – wave rotor style
- Full factory interior (it even has power windows)
- NHRA-spec roll cage

The ESX Sport RWD car made 850 flywheel horsepower on 32 pounds of boost with no nitrous oxide. At 38 pounds of boost, with nitrous, the car made 1,050 flywheel horsepower. Julie's best time to date is 9.14 seconds in the 1/4-mile at a top speed of 156 mph. Her 60-foot launch time is 1.36 seconds.

penalized with weight and performance restrictions. "We couldn't do anything to the engine except ECU. It's pretty much a stock WRX, with a Stoptech big brake kit, Cobb ECU, and a custom AeroTurbine muffler. Gruppe S has been tuning the ECU. That's pretty much the only thing we can to do to the engine. They've been able to get us 50 horsepower over stock with ECU work. It's a blast to drive," Lock says.

Most pro racing organizations hold costs down on the engine, but

Two-time national champion driver Chuck Hemmingson schools a Big Money Waster at the 2006 SCCA Runoffs at Heartland Park Topeka.

This is Ali Afshar's purpose-built Pro Mod class NHRA dragster. It does the 1/4 mile in under 8 seconds and hits175 mph.

The second ESX drag racer runs in NHRA's exciting Pro Modified class, where it is driven by ESX owner Ali Afshar. In this class, very little of the car cannot be changed. With the power levels in use at this level of drag racing, most stock components would snap like pretzel sticks, and the car's mod list reflects it:

- Chrome-Moly tube frame chassis by Racecraft Inc. at 2100 pounds
- 2.5-liter STI engine running Sunoco Supreme NOS gasoline or methanol
- Peterson dry sump system
- Custom billet crank
- ESX rods and pistons
- ESX ported heads
- Valves 1mm larger than stock
- ESX custom cams
- ESX custom front intercooler
- Modified stock intake manifold to accommodate a larger turbo body

- ESX custom 4-2-1 stainless steel header
- Innovative custom turbo
- Innovative external "Indy" waste gate
- 5" exhaust exiting in front of the front wheel
- Waterman mechanical fuel pump
- Eight 1600cc fuel injectors – converted from side feed to top feed
- MoTeC M800 ECU
- ESX custom ECU programming
- MoTeC CDI ignition
- MSD coils (4)
- 4AT automatic transmission, modified by ESX
- Billet torque converter by ProTorque
- Ford 9" rear differential
- Four link rear suspension
- Koni electronic rear shocks
- Cadillac front hubs
- Strange Engineering custom front struts
- Custom front axles from The Driveshaft Shop
- ESX custom rear axles
- CV Joints from a Porsche 935
- American Racing wheels – 15x9
- Mickey Thompson 28x10.5W drag slicks
- Mark Williams carbon fiber brake rotors
- Carbon fiber bodywork by Kirkman Composites

This racecar makes 900 ft-lbs of torque at 5,000 rpm, and currently produces about 1,300 flywheel horsepower. "But we're looking for a lot more than that," says lead mechanic Jamie Montesalvo. The car is currently running 50 pounds of boost, but Montesalvo expects that to be up to 60 pounds by 2007. Afshar's 60-foot launch time is 1.22 seconds. His best 1/4-mile run so far is 7.9 seconds at a top speed of 176 mph, but the team's goal is 7.3 seconds at 190 mph. "We want to take the record off of HKS with their Nissan Skyline," Montesalvo says.

With the suspension development limitations in SCCA racing, you have to be ready to drive the car on stock springs and still go fast.

nearly all allow major upgrades to suspension and steering gear. "We're running a DMS 50mm Rally Tarmac suspension. They're unbelievable. I can smack overruns in that car and keep my foot in it, and I don't even feel it. The wheels just suck it up and keep going. We got 4 seconds a lap out of tuning the shocks. I think it's a real testament to DMS that we're able to be competitive at our weight, because we're 500 pounds heavier than any other car out there, and we don't have power on them on the straightaways," Lock says.

Lock's record in USTCC speaks for itself: "We won at Buttonwillow, took third place at the season opener at Cal-ifornia Speedway, fourth place at the San Jose Grand Prix, and second place at Infineon Raceway," Brian says.

Both Lock and ICY Racing are now looking towards Grand American Road Racing with new Subaru Legacy GT cars. Grand Am is an offshoot of NASCAR and offers national pro racing opportunities for production cars in conjunction with its popular Rolex Cup prototype and exotic sports car series.

The Subaru Legacy GT competes in Grand Am's "Street Tuner" class, which features a variety of popular high-performance sport compact cars. The class is limited to cars with four and six-cylinder engines, making

between 170 and 240 horsepower. Cars are equalized within the class by adding weight. The only major performance modifications allowed in Street Tuner are in the area of safety.

Drifting

Drifting is the art of controlling a skid and steering a car with the throttle. Invented in Japan, this motorsport is quickly gaining popularity in North America. What is unique about drifting is that the winner is not determined by a stopwatch or finish line, but rather by a judge who evaluates technique and difficulty. Drifting is the figure skating competition of the automotive world.

Drifting in the United States is still coming together. At the top of the sport, mainly on the West Coast and Hawaii, top teams from around the world appear at well-attended shows. At the grass-roots level, local clubs drift in parking lots and anywhere they can arrange permission.

One attraction of the sport is that there are very few rules. Drift cars are generally not limited in engine preparation or in development of the suspension, brakes, or transmission. D1GP, the leading sanctioning body, requires only a 2-wheel-drive car, basic

Brian Lock's US Touring Car Championship WRX. USTCC is sanctioned by NASA Pro Racing. The young Subaru racer is no stranger to the podium in this car.

Professional Racing is a great way to make a small fortune— all you have to do is start with a big fortune.

safety gear, and a legal exhaust system. This free format allows tuners wide latitude to build the most exotic machines they can afford.

Drifters overwhelmingly prefer rear-wheel-drive models, which has limited the application of Subarus in the sport. However, dedicated drifters have seen the potential of the brand and have started building custom rear-wheel-drive Subaru drift cars. The most famous of these is Nobushige Kumakubo of Japan's Team Orange. Kumakubo has built a drift car using both US and Japanese market components.

The Team Orange car uses an EJ257 engine with all custom internal parts. The crankshaft, rods, pistons, and cams were all custom-made at JUN Auto Mechanic in Japan. The engine is turbocharged using a GReddy TD06 SH25G, dialed up to 21.75 psi of boost. Exhaust is handled by a custom system that promotes free flow by opening from 60mm to 120mm as the gases move through the pipe. Altogether, the engine in the Team Orange Subaru is expected to deliver over 500 horsepower to the rear wheels.

An aftermarket 6-speed sequential transmission built by U.S. manufacturer Hollinger changed the Impreza to a conventional front engine/rear drive configuration. The car uses a custom-fabricated driveshaft and Cusco limited slip differential to complete the package. Team Orange kept their brakes mostly stock, with braided stainless steel flex lines and brake pads by Endless.

The intercooling and radiators for this all-out drifting car are also custom-made. At the top levels of the sport, not much is left of the car that came from the Subaru factory!

Rallycross

A rallycross takes place on a large grass or dirt field, with a course set up using traffic cones. Cars are timed as they drive the course as fast as possible, as in an Autocross. In the limited traction environment, especially after the first few cars have torn up the dirt some, you can get a taste of performance rally in your street car.

Subarus are popular in rallycross because they can do well straight off the showroom floor, and also respond very well to upgrades. Paul Eklund of Primitive Racing supplies specialty parts to rallycross and stage rally competitors.

"The typical Subaru Rallycrosser should be looking at underbody protection first, suspension strengthening, safety harnesses, helmets and possibly tires for their first mods, depending on what class they plan to run in," Eklund says.

The first investment in Rallycross should be a skidplate. Most courses are not perfectly smooth and ruts can develop in tight corners, so something other than a flimsy bit of plastic is recommended under the oil pan and exhaust headers. Simple, effective, bolt-on solutions are available for each Subaru model and year.

Another good choice for an early modification is a front strut tower bar. This bolt-on piece adds rigidity to the

ESX Motorsports in SPEED World Challenge

Perhaps the best-known sport compact road racing series is the SPEED World Challenge. The 2005 WRX STI competes in the upper division "GT" class in what has become one of the best shows in racing. ESX Motorsports is fielding a car with USTCC veteran Gary Sheehan at the wheel.

Here's what goes into the ESX SPEED World Challenge STI:

- 2005 Subaru WRX STI chassis at 3050 lbs
- 2.5 liter STI engine with stock crank and ESX rods and pistons
- Valves 1mm larger diameter than stock
- "Endurance" valve springs – less seat pressure for increased longevity
- Stock STI cams
- Stock intake and throttle body
- Walbro fuel pump and regulator
- IMS Fuel rails
- Nismo 740cc injectors
- MoTeC M800 ECU
- CDI ignition with 4 external coils
- Perrin front mount intercooler
- Blow through MAF
- Forced Performance GT35R turbo
- Tilton triple-plate clutch
- STI 6 speed transmission with Cusco diffs front and rear
- ESX custom axles and driveshaft
- Öhlins Group N rally car coilover suspension
- Stoptech 6 piston front brake calipers, 4 piston rear calipers
- 360mm front and 328mm rear brake rotors
- Arceo custom 18" wheels
- Toyo WC spec tire (305/35-18)
- 12 point custom roll cage – similar to WRC specifications, but with NASCAR-style door bars
- APR 2006 wide body light glass body kit
- Racetech carbon fiber seat

The ESX World Challenge WRX makes about 510 wheel horsepower at 22 pounds of turbo boost on the World Challenge spec fuel, but the team expects more after a round of equalizing adjustments from the series. "We're going to 26 pounds of boost, and shooting for 650 wheel horsepower with the MoTeC ECU. Hopefully, outside of the Cusco JGTC car we'll have the wildest Subaru road racing car out there," says ESX lead mechanic Jamie Montesalvo.

ICY racing is also getting into the pro racing game—in Grand Am Cup racing with this Legacy GT wagon.

Drifting is the latest motor sport to come out of Japan, and it's taking the racing world to a whole new level. The Team Orange Subarus are technically amazing, and the driving is first class. (Photo courtesy of Yuji Otsuki)

front of the car and helps keep the front suspension in its place over rough terrain and jumps. Competitors may also choose to combine a set of upgraded braided stainless brake lines with a good brake fluid such as Motul or Wilwood 600+ and brake pads like the PBR Delux. Brake pads that heat quickly (organic and delux compounds) are considered better than full metallic or ceramic on short but intense Rallycross courses.

Quality gear oil helps extend the life of the Subaru AWD gearbox. "For

Team Orange driver Nobushige Kumakubo shows off his style in his WRX. (Photo courtesy of Yuji Otsuki)

Rallycross, changing to NEO synthetic gear oil or RHD gear oil once a year should go a long way to saving your expensive transmission," Eklund says.

"For serious competitors, I recommend changing struts to the KYB-AGX adjustable struts with some slightly taller/stiffer springs. This allows the car to be tuned for each rallycross course. I usually recommend setting full soft in the front, and then dialing up the rear adjustment until the desired oversteer is generated," Eklund says. "The Tokico

coil over strut kit is also an affordable option which gives ride height adjustment and tuned valving."

One of the surprising things about performance building for off-street applications is the high-performance part you don't want. "A bigger rear swaybar is the wrong way to approach suspension tuning in rallycross, because it limits the rear suspension travel and often overpowers the springs and strut coming out of a hard corner," Eklund says. "I retain the stock rear bar, and add aluminum or steel and urethane rear end links for quicker swaybar response."

Tires and wheels are as important in rallycross as in any other form of competition. "If you stay with your stock 16-inch wheels, then Cooper has a 205/55/16 WeatherMaster that fits well," Eklund says. "There is also a 215/65/16 skinnier/taller version that is perfect for Foresters, Bajas, and Outbacks, which make great Rallycross cars."

The attraction of rallycross is similar to autocross: You can start with your street stock car, and add performance as your budget and your desires dictate.

Stage Rally

Stage Rally, also known as Pro-Rally, ClubRally, and Performance Rally, is where Subaru first earned its fame, and whole books have been written about Subaru's rally history. At the international level, the Subaru World Rally Team is a constant leader in the WRC, with several world championships to its credit.

Subaru utterly dominates stage rally in North America. At many rallies, more than half the entries are in Subarus. Subaru of America supports local rally organizers and competitors far better than any other automaker. In fact, most other automakers are barely aware of the existence of rally.

This has led to an abundance of specialty parts for the rallying Subaru. While the performance modifications detailed throughout this book are applicable to a Subaru in rally (depending on class rules, of course), there is also a thriving aftermarket in parts specifically oriented towards rally. Upgrades such as entire suspension kits costing nearly $15,000, underbody skid plates custom-fit to the model and year, alternate transmissions, and roof-mounted air vents are available for the serious rallyist.

Subarus compete in several classes in North American Rally. Most interesting is the Open class, where modification is the name of the game. Subarus of all kinds have been built up in this permissive class. The basic engine must be appropriate to the car, but rules are few and expenses are high. The latest Subaru Rally Team USA cars have been built for this class.

A popular choice for amateurs is the Production GT class, where the WRX and 2.5RS dominate the boards. This is a "mostly stock" class for turbocharged and AWD vehicles, and many Open class cars start out here.

Another popular class is FIA Group N, which has been home to the past generations of Subaru Rally Team USA and other top-echelon competitors who have ambitions in World Rally. Group N is a good class for the aspiring professional because a Group N vehicle can also compete as a "Production" car in the World Rally Championship. WRC cars are divided into two groups: the Group A "WRC" class for modified cars, and Group N "P-WRC" cars. It's the Group A cars that most people associate with WRC—they're the really fast ones.

When you build a Production GT rally car, there's actually very little you can change. This helps keep competition tight and expenses down. The following list covers most allowable modifications in this class.

The Team Orange WRX. It features sequential transmission, rear wheel drive, and over 500 wheel horsepower. (Photo courtesy of Yuji Otsuki)

Rallycross is a great place to learn your dirt and gravel skills, or just to play around and pretend you're Petter Solberg or Colin McRae.

Any car can be competitive in Rallycross, and it's a favorite place for old-school Subaru enthusiasts.

Chassis:
- You can seam-weld the body, and strengthen the chassis with a good rally cage.

Drivetrain:
- You can change the programming on the stock ECU, or you can use a piggyback unit.

One of the great attractions of rallycross is that you can take passengers along for the ride.

- You can increase your boost if you've got a turbo.
- You can make up a custom exhaust, provided you use the stock manifold and the system is street-legal.
- You can install a limited slip differential. Other than that, the engine, transmission, and final drive(s) must stay stock.

Suspension and Brakes:
- You can use adjustable spring seats (coilovers), and springs are free, provided they're the same type of spring (coil, leaf, or torsion bar) as stock.
- Shock absorbers are free, as long as they're the same type (Strut, for example) as stock.
- You can change or remove the sway bars.
- Wheels and tires are free, but must be the same diameter and size as stock.
- Brake pads and brake lines are free, but the rest of the brakes must remain stock.

Interior and Coachwork:
- You must use approved racing seats and harnesses, and you're allowed to strip the interior out of the car from the B pillar back. Steering wheels are free.
- You can have all the headlights, gauges, radios and computers you want.

Above: Matt Iorio in his open-class Impreza knows how to build a great rally car and knows how to tear up a stage road. (Photo courtesy of Joe Cantrell)

Deb Blanchard drives this very clean and well-maintained open class 2.5RS in stage rally events in the Pacific Northwest.

Vermont SportsCar and Subaru Rally Team USA

Vermont SportsCar builds rally cars and manages Subaru Rally Team USA. The team has been competing in Group N, but in mid-2006, the team made a change to Open class. During the transition, owner and team manager Lance Smith had a few things to say about the differences between the old and the new team cars.

"Currently we're using a JDM-spec 2-liter engine with all original components, so it is a homologated Spec.C car. We started with that because we started with Group N cars, but now we're moving to Open class. Typically, we would upgrade the engine, using STI's best quality crank, pistons, and rods. For the Open class cars, depending on what power level we're after, we might use a different brand as well," Smith says.

In both the Group N and Open class cars, SRTUSA uses the 2.0-liter engine from the WRX. As configured for Open class rallying, the engine produces about 340 horsepower at 6,000 rpm and 410 ft-lbs of torque at 4,000 rpm. For the Group N car, Vermont installed an IHI 34mm twin scroll turbo with a mandated 32mm inlet restrictor. In Open class, the engine received a mandated 34mm restrictor. For engine management, SRTUSA Group N cars used the Autronic ECU, while the Open car shifts to the MoTeC MA80 unit.

One of the many advantages built into an SRTUSA car is the dash. The Group N cars use a stock dash, per the rally rules, but the Open class cars use the MoTeC ECU to communicate with a GEMS (General Engine Management Systems) display dash from England. "This is unique," Smith says. "I don't think anyone else is doing that. Between those two units, we get a lot more inputs, and we can monitor a lot more things, like fuel temperature, fuel pressure, brake pressure, power steering pump pressure. There are just so many more things we can keep track of than on a standard car."

All SRTUSA cars use the standard 6-speed transmission case, but on the Open class cars, a 5-speed dog box gearset from Kaps in the Czech Republic is installed instead of stock gears. On all of Vermont's cars, power is delivered to the wheels through Smith's secret weapon:

"The biggest performance advantage we have comes with the way the center diff works. We change the preload on both the front and rear STI differentials to our driver's personal preference. The control system for the driver-controlled center differential is then highly modified. We have six programmable maps that the driver can choose from. We do our own mapping in-house, and each driver can have his or her own personal preference. That's where most of the gain is made over a normal street car or rally car that has not been tuned to this level. The driver can select one of his six different maps or switch it to manual on the fly. It's instantly adjustable," Smith says.

Another remarkable feature on these cars is the interaction between the handbrake and the differentials. "We use a hydraulic hand brake, operating on the rear brakes, and the center diff goes open when the handbrake is pulled. So there are a lot of unique things that happen to the car, and it helps you get around the corner very quickly. There are a lot of different types of diff control, but this is the one we've found to be the best," Smith says.

Both the SRTUSA 5-speed dog box gearset and tuned center diff control are available through Vermont SportsCar exclusively.

Keeping the car off the ground, the new Open class cars rely on Öhlins coilovers all-around. The Öhlins units offer adjustable ride height, high and low speed damping, and rebound, with a hydraulic bump stop. The team's Group N cars use the less expensive RS&SP coilovers. All Vermont SportsCar rally cars use STI top strut mounts. "We'll use a solid top mount or a rubber top mount, depending on whether it's a smooth rally or a rough rally," Smith says.

Stopping a rally car is just as important as making it go. Vermont's Group N cars have the same brakes you find in a standard 2006 USDM WRX. The new Open class cars use an AP Racing big brake kit available from STI.

Finally, all Vermont SportsCar vehicles are designed for safety. Smith uses Recaro SPG Pro-Racer seats with the head restraint feature and Sabelt harnesses designed for use with the HANS device.

This Subaru Rally Team USA car was driven by Travis Pastrana to the Rally America national championship in 2006.

Matt Iorio's Open Class Rally Car: "DP"

Notice the glowing brake rotors on Matt Iorio's "DP" rally car—he's really working those brakes!

Matt Iorio has been the 2004 Rookie of the Year and the 2005 North American Rally Cup winner, and he gave the factory team some tough competition in 2006. His car "DP" is a representative privateer Open class car. Here's what he's done to put his car up front:

- 2.0-liter Version 7 STI engine
    - 315 ft-lbs of torque at 3,900 rpm
    - 230 hp at 6,000 rpm
- Stroke lengthened slightly
- Stock heads, lightly ported
- STI Version 8 cams
- STI Version 8 Spec C intake manifold

- Custom twin-scroll exhaust manifold
- Power Enterprise twin scroll turbo – rotated to provide additional clearance
- Stock WRX intercooler
- Autronic ECU with boost control
- 6-speed transmission with JDM 5th and 6th gears
- Front diff ramp angles and preloads increased
- Electronic center diff
- Öhlins Group N coilover suspension
- Paladin Rally custom underbody protection
- Custom 3" exhaust that rides over the rear subframe for additional ground clearance
- Random Technology catalytic converter
- Custom rear sway bar, modified to accommodate the custom exhaust
- AP Racing brake kit
- 4-piston calipers front and rear
- Enkei wheels
- AIM stratodash dashboard
- Custom radiator by Ron Davis Radiators
- Corbeau seats & Sabelt harness
- PIAA lights
- Coralba computer

"There are always hundreds of other things I could do. We're always looking for ways to lower the center of gravity," Iorio says.

Roger Dauffenbach's Production GT Class Rally Car

Roger Dauffenbach's Production GT rally car doesn't look that much different from his daily driver WRX (rear), but underneath the skin, there are many differences.

Roger Dauffenbach drives a 2002 WRX in the Production GT class. Here's how his car is built for the class:

- Stock WRX Engine & Drivetrain
- Perrin Performance turbo uppipe, downpipe, panel filter and silicone turbo inlet hose.
- Roll cage to Rally America specifications
- RS&SP gravel coilover suspension
- Subaru STI Group N top mount for coilovers
- Primitive Racing front skid plate, rear diff protector, and rally spill kit
- High Density Polyethylene underbody /LDPE gas tank
- FIA roll cage padding and rally first aid kit
- Stock Subaru Vehicle Recovery Point on front. Custom rear VRP
- Silverstone Gravel Rally Tires
- Terratrip 202+ Terracom intercom
- A/C, cruise, and the stereo all still work!

TSD Rally

There's a traditional form of rally where being in a Subaru doesn't help you at all, but where Subaru owners are becoming an increasingly large percentage of participants. Time-Speed-Distance rallying, also known as Road Rallying, is a sport that is best described as a "driving game" played at legal speeds on public roads.

TSD rally is a logic puzzle. The object is to drive exactly the right course in exactly the right time. The course is not obvious, and this kind of rally requires the ability to think fast and remember course-following rules. Many performance rally enthusiasts run these rallies—another way to enjoy your ride and maybe take home a trophy!

You can Road Rally in any street-legal car, and most Subaru owners who come to Road Rally hear about it at a Rallycross or Stage Rally. Many Subaru clubs are starting to sanction Road Rallies, and the sport is almost as popular now as it was in its heyday in the 1960s.

Steven Walker of Seattle, Washington, competes in his 2004 WRX Wagon. Walker has a couple of key observations: "My odo is off by about 0.1 every 4 miles, and the speedo reads fast by about 1 mph from about 30 to 50. Though the passenger seat has pretty good support, it still requires the passenger to brace themselves with their legs to keep from flopping around too much when I hold speed

What's in a WRC Car?

The FIA World Rally Championship is divided into two classes. WRC Group A are the fast cars that you can see on television. In a Group A car, here's what the teams can change:

• Modify all engine intake and exhaust systems
• Change the engine position and orientation
• Add a turbocharger, even if none of the production models use one
• Modify the transmission to sequential shift
• Make the car AWD even if the production version is not
• Change the track and wheelbase of the car
• Modify the entire suspension layout, including all the attachment points for components

In addition to the allowances above, Group A cars have to meet the general Group A standards—which aren't very standard:

• Engine internals including camshafts, crankshaft, and valves are unlimited. Other engine components can be machined. The stock engine block must be preserved.
• All other engine-related components are unlimited, such as intercoolers, alternators, and engine management systems.
• Transmissions are unlimited.
• All differentials and the car's final drive ratio are unlimited.
• The brakes are unlimited.

In the P-WRC Group N, the rules allow quite a bit of work, but not as much as Group A:

• All suspension components (shocks, struts and springs) may be replaced, but you must keep the stock suspension geometry.
• Modified engine management systems are allowed.

More interestingly, here's what you are not allowed to modify in a Group N car:

• The braking system must remain stock, although the brake pads and brake lines are free.
• All internal engine parts must remain stock.
• The entire exhaust system, including the catalytic converter, must remain stock.
• The transmission and gear ratios must remain stock, but the gears themselves can be replaced with more durable substitutes.
• Differentials and the final drive ratio must remain stock.

A Subaru World Rally Team car is a completely modified vehicle—optimized to rally under some of the most brutal conditions imaginable. How cool is that? (Photo courtesy of Yuji Otsuki)

though a corner. I would like to improve this by upgrading to a set of STI seats," Walker says.

Car Show Competition

Away on the other side of the universe from stage rally and pro racing, there's the car show circuit. Building up your car and then showing it can be fun—if you're proud of your work and you want to share it with others. A judged show can also be humiliating, so tough up your ego before you enter.

Building a car for show is more art than science, and while performance counts, it's not the whole game by a long mile. Aesthetics and style count just as much, if not more. But the flip side is that you're completely free to express your vision and put it out there for everyone to see.

But don't make the mistake of thinking that building a show car is easier or cheaper than building a race-car—it's neither. You have to please some of the toughest critics in the business, not just go faster than some other guy.

Car-show competition is about imagination, style, and execution. Unless the show has a live racing component, your car's real-world performance will be measured by what's on the little sign you put up in front of your display. That being said, judges like to see a balanced, well-planned car that is likely to be as good as your dyno sheet says it is.

"What wins the most points with judges, besides cleanliness, is uniqueness and completeness," says Armin Ausejo, Style Editor of *Subiesport Magazine*. "A car that simply has the most expensive parts that money can buy is not going to win by default."

Winning show cars have tasteful mods in all areas—engine, suspension, wheels, brakes, bodywork, and interior. And the touches that put a car out in front of the others are always in the details—when you've attended carefully to the back side of your wheels, the inside of your exhaust tip, and the

underside of your dashboard, you'll have a car that can compete.

"A car that may not have the most expensive parts, but that has a unique look and a complete package will easily win most if not all of the time," Ausejo says.

Approach a car show as a chance to display what you've done and get ideas for what to do next. If you leave your ego at home, you can have a good time no matter what the judges think. Some people who come to the show will like your car best, and they'll be thrilled to talk to you about your car just because it's there.

Experienced TSD rallyists sometimes choose to use a rally computer—this is a super-accurate odometer mated to a computer that calculates your average speed based on the time and distance you've traveled.

This Legacy Baja owned by R. Dale Kraushaar was driven all the way to the shore of the Arctic Sea on the 2004 Alcan Winter Rally. This event is a 10-day, 5,000-mile competitive journey through some of the toughest weather on earth.

Rally racer Jamie "Subiegal" Thomas owns this very sweet 2.5RS, and she entered it in the Subiefest car show outside Seattle in 2006. With its tasteful mods and perfect execution, this car shows very well.

APPENDIX A
WEBSITES, CLUBS, BOOKS, RESOURCES

The following websites should prove helpful if you want to learn more about the products and organizations mentioned in this book:

Clubs/Organizations/Forums

bbs.scoobynet.com • *Subaru discussion forums*
www.clubwrx.net • *Club WRX*
www.i-club.com • *Impreza Club*
www.iwoc.co.uk • *Another great British Subaru site*
www.legacycentral.org • *Another Legacy enthusiast site*
www.legacygt.com • *Legacy enthusiast site*
www.nasioc.com • *North American Subaru Impreza Owners Club*

www.scoobymods.com • *Subaru modification forums*
www.scoobypedia.co.uk • *A great British Subaru site*
www.subaruforester.org • *Forester enthusiast site*
www.subaru-impreza.org • *Subaru Impreza Club*
www.subdriven.com • *A Subaru community*
www.subiesport.com • *Subiesport Magazine*
www.ultimatesubaru.org • *Ultimate Subaru Club*

Builders and Vendors:

www.airpowersystems.com.au • *APS Engineering*
www.avoturbo.com • *AVO Turbos*
www.boxer4racing.com • *Subaru performance parts in North Carolina*
www.carrilloind.com • *Carrillo connecting rods*
www.cobbtuning.com • *Excellent engines and performance parts*
www.cosworth.com • *Legendary engine builder*
www.crawfordperformance.com • *Great engines and performance parts*
www.cusco.co.jp • *Japanese Cusco site (see www.napsusa.com)*
www.dhcars.co.uk • *Zero/Sports*
www.dmsshocks.com • *DMS Rally and Race suspension*
www.edoperformance.com • *Edo Performance*
www.endura-tech.com • *Endura-Tech suspension and valve springs*
www.fastwrx.com • *Mach V Motorsports*
www.forcedperformance.com • *Forced Performance Turbos*
www.greddy.com • *Greddy turbos and accessories*
www.gruppe-s.com • *Gruppe-S JDM parts and other goodies*
www.jscspeed.com • *Subaru parts dealer*
www.kaazusa.com • *Kaaz gears and transmissions*
www.kakumei-motorsports.com • *Kakumei exhaust and body parts*
www.kaps.cz • *Gears and transmissions from the Czech Republic*
www.get-primitive.com • *Primitive Racing parts and advice*
www.mahle.com • *Mahle Pistons*

www.manleyperformance.com • *Manley connecting rods*
www.mrtrally.com.au • *Rally racing parts and forums*
www.napsusa.com • *Cusco U.S. distributor*
www.ncrally.com • *North Coast Subaru*
www.paladinrally.com • *Paladin Rally parts and advice*
www.pdxtuning.com • *PDXTuning parts and service*
www.perrinperformance.com • *Perrin parts and advice*
www.progressauto.com • *Progress Technology Suspension*
www.rallispec.com • *Rally-specific parts and development*
www.rallitek.com • *Rallitek parts and advice*
www.renickmotorsports.com • *Renick performance parts*
www.safedrives.com • *Safety gear of all kinds*
www.seiboncarbon.com • *Seibon carbon fiber parts*
www.spdusa.com • *SPD Tuning Service*
www.stoptech.com • *Great brakes*
www.subydude.com • *Subaru parts in central California*
www.taborrallyteam.com • *Silverstone Rally Tyres US Distributor*
www.turboxs.com • *Turbocharger products*
www.vtcar.com • *Vermont Sports Car/Subaru Rally Team USA*
www.whiteline.com.au • *Whiteline suspension in Australia*
www.wilwood.com • *Wilwood brakes*
www.wiseco.com • *Wiseco pistons*

Racing Organization Sites

www.d1gp.com • *D1 Grand Prix drifting*
www.grandamerican.com • *Grand American Road Racing*
www.gtlivetour.com • *GT Live interactive motorsports festivals*
www.hillclimb.org • *New England Hill Climb Association*
www.nasaproracing.com • *NASA Racing*
www.nasarallysport.com • *NASA Rally*
www.nhra.com • *National Hot Rod Association drag racing*
www.onelapofamerica.com • *One Lap of America trials*
www.ppihc.com • *Pikes Peak International Hill Climb*
www.rally-america.com • *Rally America*
www.scca.com • *SCCA Autocross, Rallycross, and Racing*

www.subiefest.com • *All Subaru Time Attack, Rallycross & Show*
www.ustcc.com • *US Touring Car Championship*
www.world-challenge.com • *SPEED World Challenge*
www.wrc.com • *World Rally Championship*

Official Subaru Sites

www.rally.subaru.com • *Subaru World Rally Team*
www.subaru.com/microsites/spt • *Subaru Performance Tuning*
www.subaru-sti.co.jp • *Subaru Tecnica International in Japan*

APPENDIX B
ENGINE TABLES

The following tables show some of the standard engine and component part numbers for the USDM WRX, JDM STI, USDM STI, and USDM Legacy GT models since 2002.

EJ205

The following series of tables details many of the identifying codes and part numbers used on the USDM EJ205 from 2002 to 2006.

EJ205 Engine Codes and Part Numbers

MY	Model Description	Engine Code	Engine Part Number	Turbocharger Part Number	ECU Code
MY02	WRX (mt)	EJ205AW3B9/BB	10100BH570	14411AA382/383	22611AF421/422/423/424/425
MY02	WRX (at)	EJ205AX3B9/BB	10100BH590	14411AA382/383	22611AF411/412/413/414
MY03	WRX (mt)	EJ205BW4BB	10100BK340	14411AA383	22611AJ030/031/032
MY03	WRX (at)	EJ205BX4BB	10100BK350	14411AA383	22611AJ040/041
MY04	WRX (mt)	EJ205BW6BB	10100BL310	14411AA383	22611AH791/792/793
MY04	WRX (at)	EJ205BX5BB	10100BL320	14411AA383	22611AH801/802/803
MY05	WRX (mt)	EJ205BW7BB	10100BM050	14411AA383	22611AJ890
MY05	WRX (at)	EJ205BX7BB	10100BM060	14411AA383	22611AJ900
MY06	WRX (mt)	EJ255BE8JB	10100BN370	14411AA630	22611AL350
MY06	WRX (at)	EJ255BP8JB	10100BN390	14411AA630	22611AL360

EJ205 Engine Internal Part Numbers

MY	Model Description	Block Part Number	Piston Part Number	Crank Part Number	Rod Part Number
MY02	WRX (mt)	10103AB330	12006AC350	12200AA210/240	12100AA080/081
MY02	WRX (at)	10103AB330	12006AC350	12200AA210/240	12100AA080/081
MY03	WRX (mt)	10103AB330	12006AC350	12200AA240	12100AA081/190
MY03	WRX (at)	10103AB330	12006AC350	12200AA240	12100AA081/190
MY04	WRX (mt)	10103AB330	12006AC350	12200AA240	12100AA081/190
MY04	WRX (at)	10103AB330	12006AC350	12200AA240	12100AA081/190
MY05	WRX (mt)	10103AB330	12006AC350	12200AA240	12100AA190/240
MY05	WRX (at)	10103AB330	12006AC350	12200AA240	12100AA190/240

EJ205 Head and Cam Part Numbers

MY	Model Description	Intake Cam Part Number	Exhaust Cam Part Number	Head Part Number	Valve Spring Part Number
MY02	WRX (mt)	13037AA101	13052AA101	11039AB361	13217AA193
MY02	WRX (at)	13037AA101	13052AA101	11039AB361	13217AA193
MY03	WRX (mt)	13037AA390/391	13052AA390/391	11039AB361	13217AA193
MY03	WRX (at)	13037AA390/391	13052AA390/391	11039AB361	13217AA193
MY04	WRX (mt)	13037AA391/490	13052AA391/490	11039AB361	13217AA193
MY04	WRX (at)	13037AA391/490	13052AA391/490	11039AB361	13217AA193
MY05	WRX (mt)	13037AA490	13052AA490	11039AB361	13217AA193
MY05	WRX (at)	13037AA490	13052AA490	11039AB361	13217AA193

EJ207

Although the EJ207 has been produced for the JDM for many years, in the interests of saving space, information for the 2005 model year only is included in the following tables. Information is provided for both the standard STI sedan and the Spec.C sedan.

EJ207 Engine Codes and Part Numbers

MY	Model Description	Feature Code	Engine Code	Engine Part Number	Turbo Part Number	ECU
MY05	Sedan WRX STI	GDBD4EH	EJ207DW7CR	10100BL920	14411AA542	22611AJ810
MY05	Sedan WRX STI spec C	GDBD4FH	EJ207DW7CR	10100BL920	14411AA493	22611AJ820

EJ207 Engine Internal Part Numbers

MY	Model Description	Block Part Number	Piston Part Number	Crank Part Number	Rod Part Number
MY05	Sedan WRX STI	11008AA980	12006AC430	12200AA270	12100AA180
MY05	Sedan WRX STI spec C	11008AA980	12006AC430	12200AA270	12100AA180

EJ207 Head and Cam Part Numbers

MY	Model Description	Intake Cam Part Number	Exhaust Cam Part Number	Head Part Number	Valve Spring Part Number
MY05	Sedan WRX STI	13037AA480	13052AA480	11039AB660	13217AA202
MY05	Sedan WRX STI spec C	13037AA480	13052AA480	11039AB660	13217AA202

Legacy EJ255 Engine Codes and Part Numbers

The following tables show the codes and part numbers associated with the 2005 Legacy EJ255:

MY	Model Description	Engine Code	Engine Part Number	Turbocharger Part Number	ECU Code
MY05	Legacy GT (mt)	EJ255BTAUB	10100BM510	14411AA51A	22611AA17A/B/C
MY05	Legacy GT (at)	EJ255BLAUB	10100BM520	14411AA51A	22611AA18A/B/C

Legacy EJ255 Engine Internal Part Numbers

MY	Model Description	Block Part Number	Piston Part Number	Crank Part Number	Rod Part Number
MY05	Legacy GT (mt)	10103AB440	12006AC390	12200AA260	12100AA180
MY05	Legacy GT (at)	10103AB440	12006AC390	12200AA260	12100AA180

Legacy EJ255 Head and Cam Part Numbers

MY	Model Description	Intake Cam Part Number	Exhaust Cam Part Number	Valve Spring Part Number	Head Part Number
MY05	Legacy GT (mt)	13037AA350	13052AA350	13217AA251	11039AB640
MY05	Legacy GT (at)	13037AA350	13052AA350	13217AA251	11039AB640

For 2006, the EJ255 was continued in the Legacy 2.5GT and it replaced the EJ205 in the Impreza WRX. In the WRX configuration, the engine is rated to produce 230 horsepower at 5,600 RPM, and 235 foot-pounds of torque at 3600 RPM.

Impreza EJ255 Engine Codes and Part Numbers

MY	Model Description	Engine Code	Engine Part Number	Turbocharger Part Number	ECU Code
MY06	Sedan WRX (mt)	EJ255BE8JB	10100BN370	14411AA630	22611AL350
MY06	Sedan WRX (at)	EJ255BP8JB	10100BN390	14411AA630	22611AL360

Impreza EJ255 Engine Internal Part Numbers

MY	Model Description	Block Part Number	Piston Part Number	Crank Part Number	Rod Part Number
MY06	Sedan WRX (mt)	10103AB330	12006AD210	12200AA330	12100AA180
MY06	Sedan WRX (at)	10103AB330	12006AD210	12200AA330	12100AA180

Impreza EJ255 Head and Cam Part Numbers

MY	Model Description	Intake Cam Part Number	Exhaust Cam Part Number	Head Part Number	Valve Spring Part Number
MY06	Sedan WRX (mt)	13037AA350	13052AA350	11039AB820	13217AA251
MY06	Sedan WRX (at)	13037AA350	13052AA350	11039AB820	13217AA251

EJ257

The following tables list important codes and part numbers for the EJ257.

EJ257 Engine Codes and Part Numbers

MY	Model Description	Engine Code	Engine Part Number	Turbo Part Number	ECU Code
MY04	WRX STI	EJ257BW5CB	10100BK600	14411A572	22611AJ240/241/242/243
MY05	WRX STI	EJ257BW7CH	10100BM070	14411A572	22611AJ930
MY06	WRX STI	EJ257BW8CH	10100BN380	14411A572	22611AL370

EJ257 Engine Internal Part Numbers

MY	Model Description	Block Part Number	Piston Part Number	Crank Part Number	Rod Part Number
MY04	WRX STI	10103AB440	12006AC390	12200AA260	12100AA180
MY05	WRX STI	10103AB440	12006AC390	12200AA260	12100AA180
MY06	WRX STI	10103AB440	12006AC390	12200AA330	12100AA180

EJ257 Head and Cam Part Numbers

MY	Model Description	Intake Cam Part Number	Exhaust Cam Part Number	Head Part Number	Valve Spring Part Number
MY04	WRX STI	13037AA350	13052AA350	11039AB640	13217AA251
MY05	WRX STI	13037AA350	13052AA350	11039AB640/910	13217AA251
MY06	WRX STI	13037AA350	13052AA350	11039AB910	13217AA251

CPSIA information can be obtained at www.ICGtesting.com
Printed in the USA
BVOW02s1145251114

376662BV00025B/572/P